PLAYS BY ANTON CHEKHOV, SECOND SERIES

By

Anton Chekhov

Translated, with an Introduction, by Julius West

INTRODUCTION

The last few years have seen a large and generally unsystematic mass of translations from the Russian flung at the heads and hearts of English readers. The ready acceptance of Chekhov has been one of the few successful features of this irresponsible output. He has been welcomed by British critics with something like affection. Bernard Shaw has several times remarked: "Every time I see a play by Chekhov, I want to chuck all my own stuff into the fire." Others, having no such valuable property to sacrifice on the altar of Chekhov, have not hesitated to place him side by side with Ibsen, and the other established institutions of the new theatre. For these reasons it is pleasant to be able to chronicle the fact that, by way of contrast with the casual treatment normally handed out to Russian authors, the publishers are issuing the complete dramatic works of this author. In 1912 they brought out a volume containing four Chekhov plays, translated by Marian Fell. All the dramatic works not included in her volume are to be found in the present one. With the exception of Chekhov's masterpiece, "The Cherry Orchard" (translated by the late Mr. George Calderon in 1912), none of these plays have been previously published in book form in England or America.

It is not the business of a translator to attempt to outdo all others in singing the praises of his raw material. This is a dangerous process and may well lead, as it led Mr. Calderon, to drawing the reader's attention to points of beauty not to be found in the original. A few bibliographical details are equally necessary, and permissible, and the elementary principles of Chekhov criticism will also be found useful.

The very existence of "The High Road" (1884); probably the earliest of its author's plays, will be unsuspected by English readers. During Chekhov's lifetime it a sort of family legend, after his death it became a family mystery. A copy was finally discovered only last year in the Censor's office, yielded up, and published. It had been sent in 1885 under the nom-de-plume "A. Chekhonte," and it had failed to pass. The Censor, of the time being had scrawled his opinion on the manuscript, "a depressing and dirty piece,—cannot be licensed." The name of the gentleman who held this view—Kaiser von Kugelgen—gives another reason for the educated Russian's low opinion of German-sounding institutions. Baron von Tuzenbach, the satisfactory person in "The Three Sisters," it will be noted, finds it as well, while he is trying to secure the favours of Irina, to declare that his German ancestry is fairly remote. This is by way of parenthesis. "The High Road," found after thirty years, is a most interesting document to the lover of Chekhov. Every play he wrote in later years was either a one-act farce or a four-act drama. [Note: "The Swan Song" may occur as an exception. This, however, is more of a Shakespeare recitation than anything else, and so neither here nor there.]

In "The High Road" we see, in an embryonic form, the whole later method of the plays—the deliberate contrast between two strong characters (Bortsov and Merik in this case), the careful individualization of each person in a fairly large group by way of an introduction to the main theme, the concealment of the catastrophe, germ-wise, in the actual character of the characters, and the of a distinctive group-atmosphere. It need scarcely be stated that "The High Road" is not a "dirty" piece according to Russian or to German standards; Chekhov was incapable of writing a dirty play or story. For the rest, this piece differs from the others in its presentation, not of Chekhov's favourite middle-classes, but of the moujik, nourishing, in a particularly stuffy atmosphere, an intense mysticism and an equally intense thirst for vodka.

"The Proposal" (1889) and "The Bear" (1890) may be taken as good examples of the sort of humour admired by the average Russian. The latter play, in another translation, was put on as a curtain-raiser to a cinematograph entertainment at a London theatre in 1914; and had quite a pleasant reception from a thoroughly Philistine audience. The humour is very nearly of the variety most popular over here, the psychology is a shade subtler. The Russian novelist or dramatist takes to psychology as some of his fellow-countrymen take to drink; in doing this he achieves fame by showing us what we already know, and at the same time he kills his own creative power. Chekhov just escaped the tragedy of suicide by introspection, and was only enabled to do this by the possession of a sense of humour. That is why we should not regard "The Bear," "The Wedding," or "The Anniversary" as the work of a merely humorous young man, but as the saving graces which made perfect "The Cherry Orchard."

"The Three Sisters" (1901) is said to act better than any other of Chekhov's plays, and should surprise an English audience exceedingly. It and "The Cherry Orchard" are the tragedies of doing nothing. The three sisters have only one desire in the world, to go to Moscow and live there. There is no reason on earth, economic, sentimental, or other, why they should not pack their bags and take the next train to Moscow. But they will not do it. They cannot do it. And we know perfectly well that if they were transplanted thither miraculously, they would be extremely unhappy as soon as ever the excitement of the miracle had worn off. In the other play Mme. Ranevsky can be saved from ruin if she will only consent to a perfectly simple step—the sale of an estate. She cannot do this, is ruined, and thrown out into the unsympathetic world. Chekhov is the dramatist, not of action, but of inaction. The tragedy of inaction is as overwhelming, when we understand it, as the tragedy of an Othello, or a Lear, crushed by the wickedness of others. The former is being enacted daily, but we do not stage it, we do not know how. But who shall deny that the base of almost all human unhappiness is just this inaction, manifesting itself in slovenliness of thought and execution, education, and ideal?

The Russian, painfully conscious of his own weakness, has accepted this point of view, and regards "The Cherry Orchard" as its master-study in dramatic form. They speak of the palpitating hush which fell upon the audience of the Moscow Art Theatre after the first fall of the curtain at the first performance—a hush so intense as to make Chekhov's friends undergo the initial emotions of assisting at a vast theatrical failure. But the silence ryes almost a sob, to be followed, when overcome, by an epic applause. And, a few months later, Chekhov died.

This volume and that of Marian Fell—with which it is uniform—contain all the dramatic works of Chekhov. It considered not worth while to translate a few fragments published posthumously, or a monologue "On the Evils of Tobacco"—a half humorous lecture by "the husband of his wife;" which begins "Ladies, and in some respects, gentlemen," as this is hardly dramatic work. There is also a very short skit on the efficiency of provincial fire brigades, which was obviously not intended for the stage and has therefore been omitted.

Lastly, the scheme of transliteration employed has been that, generally speaking, recommended by the Liverpool School of Russian Studies. This is distinctly the best of those in the field, but as it would compel one, e.g., to write a popular female name, "Marya," I have not treated it absolute respect. For the sake of uniformity with Fell's volume, the author's name is spelt Tchekoff on the title-page and cover.

J. W.

RUSSIAN WEIGHTS AND MEASURES AND MONEY EMPLOYED IN THE PLAYS, WITH ENGLISH EQUIVALENTS

```
1 verst = 3600 feet = 2/3 mile (almost)
1 arshin = 28 inches
1 dessiatin = 2.7 acres
1 copeck = 1/4 d
1 rouble = 100 copecks = 2s. 1d.
```

ON THE HIGH ROAD

A DRAMATIC STUDY

CHARACTERS

TIHON EVSTIGNEYEV, the proprietor of a inn on the main road
SEMYON SERGEYEVITCH BORTSOV, a ruined landowner
MARIA EGOROVNA, his wife
SAVVA, an aged pilgrim
NAZAROVNA and EFIMOVNA, women pilgrims
FEDYA, a labourer
EGOR MERIK, a tramp
KUSMA, a driver
POSTMAN
BORTSOV'S WIFE'S COACHMAN
PILGRIMS, CATTLE-DEALERS, ETC.

The action takes place in one of the provinces of Southern Russia

[The scene is laid in TIHON'S bar. On the right is the bar-counter and shelves with bottles. At the back is a door leading out of the house. Over it, on the outside, hangs a dirty red lantern. The floor and the forms, which stand against the wall, are closely occupied by pilgrims and passers-by. Many of them, for lack of space, are sleeping as they sit. It is late at night. As the curtain rises thunder is heard, and lightning is seen through the door.]

[TIHON is behind the counter. FEDYA is half-lying in a heap on one of the forms, and is quietly playing on a concertina. Next to him is BORTSOV, wearing a shabby summer overcoat. SAVVA, NAZAROVNA, and EFIMOVNA are stretched out on the floor by the benches.]

EFIMOVNA. [To NAZAROVNA] Give the old man a nudge dear! Can't get any answer out of him.

NAZAROVNA. [Lifting the corner of a cloth covering of SAVVA'S face] Are you alive or are you dead, you holy man?

SAVVA. Why should I be dead? I'm alive, mother! [Raises himself on his elbow] Cover up my feet, there's a saint! That's it. A bit more on the right one. That's it, mother. God be good to us.

NAZAROVNA. [Wrapping up SAVVA'S feet] Sleep, little father.

SAVVA. What sleep can I have? If only I had the patience to endure this pain, mother; sleep's quite another matter. A sinner doesn't deserve to be given rest. What's that noise, pilgrim-woman?

NAZAROVNA. God is sending a storm. The wind is wailing, and the rain is pouring down, pouring down. All down the roof and into the windows like dried peas. Do you hear? The windows of heaven are opened... [Thunder] Holy, holy, holy...

FEDYA. And it roars and thunders, and rages, sad there's no end to it! Hoooo... it's like the noise of a forest.... Hoooo.... The wind is wailing like a dog.... [Shrinking back] It's cold! My clothes are wet, it's all coming in through the open door... you might put me through a wringer.... [Plays softly] My concertina's damp, and so there's no music for you, my Orthodox brethren, or else I'd give you such a concert, my word!—Something marvellous! You can have a quadrille, or a polka, if you like, or some Russian dance for two.... I can do them all. In the town, where I was an attendant at the Grand Hotel, I couldn't make any money, but I did wonders on my concertina. And, I can play the guitar.

A VOICE FROM THE CORNER. A silly speech from a silly fool.

FEDYA. I can hear another of them. [Pause.]

NAZAROVNA. [To SAVVA] If you'd only lie where it was warm now, old man, and warm your feet. [Pause.] Old man! Man of God! [Shakes SAVVA] Are you going to die?

FEDYA. You ought to drink a little vodka, grandfather. Drink, and it'll burn, burn in your stomach, and warm up your heart. Drink, do!

NAZAROVNA. Don't swank, young man! Perhaps the old man is giving back his soul to God, or repenting for his sins, and you talk like that, and play your concertina.... Put it down! You've no shame!

FEDYA. And what are you sticking to him for? He can't do anything and you... with your old women's talk... He can't say a word in reply, and you're glad, and happy because he's listening to your nonsense.... You go on sleeping, grandfather; never mind her! Let her talk, don't you take any notice of her. A woman's tongue is the devil's broom—it will sweep the good man and the clever man both out of the house. Don't you mind.... [Waves his hands] But it's thin you are, brother of mine! Terrible! Like a dead skeleton! No life in you! Are you really dying?

SAVVA. Why should I die? Save me, O Lord, from dying in vain.... I'll suffer a little, and then get up with God's help.... The Mother of God won't let me die in a strange land.... I'll die at home.

FEDYA. Are you from far off?

SAVVA. From Vologda. The town itself.... I live there.

FEDYA. And where is this Vologda?

TIHON. The other side of Moscow....

FEDYA. Well, well, well.... You have come a long way, old man! On foot?

SAVVA. On foot, young man. I've been to Tihon of the Don, and I'm going to the Holy Hills. [Note: On the Donetz, south-east of Kharkov; a monastery containing a miraculous ikon.]... From there, if God wills it, to Odessa.... They say you can get to Jerusalem cheap from there, for twenty-ones roubles, they say....

FEDYA. And have you been to Moscow?

SAVVA. Rather! Five times....

FEDYA. Is it a good town? [Smokes] Well-standing?

Sews. There are many holy places there, young man.... Where there are many holy places it's always a good town....

BORTSOV. [Goes up to the counter, to TIHON] Once more, please! For the sake of Christ, give it to me!

FEDYA. The chief thing about a town is that it should be clean. If it's dusty, it must be watered; if it's dirty, it must be cleaned. There ought to be big houses... a theatre... police... cabs, which... I've lived in a town myself, I understand.

BORTSOV. Just a little glass. I'll pay you for it later.

TIHON. That's enough now.

BORTSOV. I ask you! Do be kind to me!

TIHON. Get away!

BORTSOV. You don't understand me.... Understand me, you fool, if there's a drop of brain in your peasant's wooden head, that it isn't I who am asking you, but my inside, using the words you understand, that's what's asking! My illness is what's asking! Understand!

TIHON. We don't understand anything.... Get back!

BORTSOV. Because if I don't have a drink at once, just you understand this, if I don't satisfy my needs, I may commit some crime. God only knows what I might do! In the time you've kept this place, you rascal, haven't you seen a lot of drunkards, and haven't you yet got to understand what they're like? They're diseased! You can do anything you like to them, but you must give them vodka! Well, now, I implore you! Please! I humbly ask you! God only knows how humbly!

TIHON. You can have the vodka if you pay for it.

BORTSOV. Where am I to get the money? I've drunk it all! Down to the ground! What can I give you? I've only got this coat, but I can't give you that. I've nothing on underneath.... Would you like my cap? [Takes it off and gives it to TIHON]

TIHON. [Looks it over] Hm.... There are all sorts of caps.... It might be a sieve from the holes in it....

FEDYA. [Laughs] A gentleman's cap! You've got to take it off in front of the mam'selles. How do you do, good-bye! How are you?

TIHON. [Returns the cap to BORTSOV] I wouldn't give anything for it. It's muck.

BORTSOV. If you don't like it, then let me owe you for the drink! I'll bring in your five copecks on my way back from town. You can take it and choke yourself with it then! Choke yourself! I hope it sticks in your throat! [Coughs] I hate you!

TIHON. [Banging the bar-counter with his fist] Why do you keep on like that? What a man! What are you here for, you swindler?

BORTSOV. I want a drink! It's not I, it's my disease! Understand that!

TIHON. Don't you make me lose my temper, or you'll soon find yourself outside!

BORTSOV. What am I to do? [Retires from the bar-counter] What am I to do? [Is thoughtful.]

EFIMOVNA. It's the devil tormenting you. Don't you mind him, sir. The damned one keeps whispering, "Drink! Drink!" And you answer him, "I shan't drink! I shan't drink!" He'll go then.

FEDYA. It's drumming in his head.... His stomach's leading him on! [Laughs] Your houour's a happy man. Lie down and go to sleep! What's the use of standing like a scarecrow in the middle of the inn! This isn't an orchard!

BORTSOV. [Angrily] Shut up! Nobody spoke to you, you donkey.

FEDYA. Go on, go on! We've seen the like of you before! There's a lot like you tramping the high road! As to being a donkey, you wait till I've given you a clout on the ear and you'll howl worse than the wind. Donkey yourself! Fool! [Pause] Scum!

NAZAROVNA. The old man may be saying a prayer, or giving up his soul to God, and here are these unclean ones wrangling with one another and saying all sorts of... Have shame on yourselves!

FEDYA. Here, you cabbage-stalk, you keep quiet, even if you are in a public-house. Just you behave like everybody else.

BORTSOV. What am I to do? What will become of me? How can I make him understand? What else can I say to him? [To TIHON] The blood's boiling in my chest! Uncle Tihon! [Weeps] Uncle Tihon!

SAWA. [Groans] I've got shooting-pains in my leg, like bullets of fire.... Little mother, pilgrim.

EFIMOVNA. What is it, little father?

SAVVA. Who's that crying?

EFIMOVNA. The gentleman.

SAVVA. Ask him to shed a tear for me, that I might die in Vologda. Tearful prayers are heard.

BORTSOV. I'm not praying, grandfather! These aren't tears! Just juice! My soul is crushed; and the juice is running. [Sits by SAVVA] Juice! But you wouldn't understand! You, with your darkened brain, wouldn't understand. You people are all in the dark!

SAVVA. Where will you find those who live in the light?

BORTSOV. They do exist, grandfather.... They would understand!

SAVVA. Yes, yes, dear friend.... The saints lived in the light.... They understood all our griefs.... You needn't even tell them.... and they'll understand.... Just by looking at your eyes.... And then you'll have such peace, as if you were never in grief at all—it will all go!

FEDYA. And have you ever seen any saints?

SAVVA. It has happened, young man.... There are many of all sorts on this earth. Sinners, and servants of God.

BORTSOV. I don't understand all this.... [Gets up quickly] What's the use of talking when you don't understand, and what sort of a brain have I now? I've only an instinct, a thirst! [Goes quickly to the counter] Tihon, take my coat! Understand? [Tries to take it off] My coat...

TIHON. And what is there under your coat? [Looks under it] Your naked body? Don't take it off, I shan't have it.... I'm not going to burden my soul with a sin.

[Enter MERIK.]

BORTSOV. Very well, I'll take the sin on myself! Do you agree?

MERIK. [In silence takes of his outer cloak and remains in a sleeveless jacket. He carries an axe in his belt] A vagrant may sweat where a bear will freeze. I am hot. [Puts his axe on the floor and takes off his jacket] You get rid of a pailful of sweat while you drag one leg out of the mud. And while you are dragging it out, the other one goes farther in.

EFIMOVNA. Yes, that's true... is the rain stopping, dear?

MERIK. [Glancing at EFIMOVNA] I don't talk to old women. [A pause.]

BORTSOV. [To TIHON] I'll take the sin on myself. Do you hear me or don't you?

TIHON. I don't want to hear you, get away!

MERIK. It's as dark as if the sky was painted with pitch. You can't see your own nose. And the rain beats into your face like a snowstorm! [Picks up his clothes and axe.]

FEDYA. It's a good thing for the likes of us thieves. When the cat's away the mice will play.

MERIK. Who says that?

FEDYA. Look and see... before you forget.

MERIN. We'll make a note of it.... [Goes up to TIHON] How do you do, you with the large face! Don't you remember me.

TIHON. If I'm to remember every one of you drunkards that walks the high road, I reckon I'd need ten holes in my forehead.

MERIK. Just look at me.... [A pause.]

TIHON. Oh, yes; I remember. I knew you by your eyes! [Gives him his hand] Andrey Polikarpov?

MERIK. I used to be Andrey Polikarpov, but now I am Egor Merik.

TIHON. Why's that?

MERIK. I call myself after whatever passport God gives me. I've been Merik for two months. [Thunder] Rrrr.... Go on thundering, I'm not afraid! [Looks round] Any police here?

TIHON. What are you talking about, making mountains out of mole-hills?... The people here are all right... The police are fast asleep in their feather beds now.... [Loudly] Orthodox brothers, mind your pockets and your clothes, or you'll have to regret it. The man's a rascal! He'll rob you!

MERIK. They can look out for their money, but as to their clothes—I shan't touch them. I've nowhere to take them.

TIHON. Where's the devil taking you to?

MERIK. To Kuban.

TIHON. My word!

FEDYA. To Kuban? Really? [Sitting up] It's a fine place. You wouldn't see such a country, brother, if you were to fall asleep and dream for three years. They say the birds there, and the beasts are—my God! The grass grows all the year round, the people are good, and they've so much land they don't know what to do with it! The authorities, they say... a soldier was telling me the other day... give a hundred dessiatins ahead. There's happiness, God strike me!

MERIK. Happiness.... Happiness goes behind you.... You don't see it. It's as near as your elbow is, but you can't bite it. It's all silly.... [Looking round at the benches and the people] Like a lot of prisoners.... A poor lot.

EFIMOVNA. [To MERIK] What great, angry, eyes! There's an enemy in you, young man.... Don't you look at us!

MERIK. Yes, you're a poor lot here.

EFIMOVNA. Turn away! [Nudges SAVVA] Savva, darling, a wicked man is looking at us. He'll do us harm, dear. [To MERIK] Turn away, I tell you, you snake!

SAVVA. He won't touch us, mother, he won't touch us.... God won't let him.

MERIK. All right, Orthodox brothers! [Shrugs his shoulders] Be quiet! You aren't asleep, you bandy-legged fools! Why don't you say something?

EFIMOVNA. Take your great eyes away! Take away that devil's own pride!

MERIK. Be quiet, you crooked old woman! I didn't come with the devil's pride, but with kind words, wishing to honour your bitter lot! You're huddled together like flies because of the cold—I'd be sorry for you, speak kindly to you, pity your poverty, and here you go grumbling away! [Goes up to FEDYA] Where are you from?

FEDYA. I live in these parts. I work at the Khamonyevsky brickworks.

MERIK. Get up.

FEDYA. [Raising himself] Well?

MERIK. Get up, right up. I'm going to lie down here.

FEDYA. What's that.... It isn't your place, is it?

MERIK. Yes, mine. Go and lie on the ground!

FEDYA. You get out of this, you tramp. I'm not afraid of you.

MERIK. You're very quick with your tongue.... Get up, and don't talk about it! You'll be sorry for it, you silly.

TIHON. [To FEDYA] Don't contradict him, young man. Never mind.

FEDYA. What right have you? You stick out your fishy eyes and think I'm afraid! [Picks up his belongings and stretches himself out on the ground] You devil! [Lies down and covers himself all over.]

MERIK. [Stretching himself out on the bench] I don't expect you've ever seen a devil or you wouldn't call me one. Devils aren't like that. [Lies down, putting his axe next to him.] Lie down, little brother axe... let me cover you.

TIHON. Where did you get the axe from?

MERIK. Stole it.... Stole it, and now I've got to fuss over it like a child with a new toy; I don't like to throw it away, and I've nowhere to put it. Like a beastly wife.... Yes.... [Covering himself over] Devils aren't like that, brother.

FEDYA. [Uncovering his head] What are they like?

MERIK. Like steam, like air.... Just blow into the air. [Blows] They're like that, you can't see them.

A VOICE FROM THE CORNER. You can see them if you sit under a harrow.

MERIK. I've tried, but I didn't see any.... Old women's tales, and silly old men's, too.... You won't see a devil or a ghost or a corpse.... Our eyes weren't made so that we could see everything.... When I was a boy, I used to walk in the woods at night on purpose to see the demon of the woods.... I'd shout and shout, and there might be some spirit, I'd call for the demon of the woods and not blink my eyes: I'd see all sorts of little things moving about, but no demon. I used to go and walk about the churchyards at night, I wanted to see the ghosts—but the women lie. I saw all sorts of animals, but anything awful—not a sign. Our eyes weren't...

THE VOICE FROM THE CORNER. Never mind, it does happen that you do see.... In our village a man was gutting a wild boar... he was separating the tripe when... something jumped out at him!

SAVVA. [Raising himself] Little children, don't talk about these unclean things! It's a sin, dears!

MERIK. Aaa... greybeard! You skeleton! [Laughs] You needn't go to the churchyard to see ghosts, when they get up from under the floor to give advice to their relations.... A sin!... Don't you teach people your silly notions! You're an ignorant lot of people living in darkness.... [Lights his pipe] My father was peasant and used to be fond of teaching people. One night he stole a sack of apples from the village priest, and he brings them along and tells us, "Look, children, mind you don't eat any apples before Easter, it's a sin." You're like that.... You don't know what a devil is, but you go calling people devils.... Take this crooked old woman, for instance. [Points to EFIMOVNA] She sees an enemy in me, but is her time, for some woman's nonsense or other, she's given her soul to the devil five times.

EFIMOVNA. Hoo, hoo, hoo.... Gracious heavens! [Covers her face] Little Savva!

TIHON. What are you frightening them for? A great pleasure! [The door slams in the wind] Lord Jesus.... The wind, the wind!

MERIK. [Stretching himself] Eh, to show my strength! [The door slams again] If I could only measure myself against the wind! Shall I tear the door down, or suppose I tear up the inn by the roots! [Gets up and lies down again] How dull!

NAZAROVNA. You'd better pray, you heathen! Why are you so restless?

EFIMOVNA. Don't speak to him, leave him alone! He's looking at us again. [To MERIK] Don't look at us, evil man! Your eyes are like the eyes of a devil before cockcrow!

SAVVA. Let him look, pilgrims! You pray, and his eyes won't do you any harm.

BORTSOV. No, I can't. It's too much for my strength! [Goes up to the counter] Listen, Tihon, I ask you for the last time.... Just half a glass!

TIHON. [Shakes his head] The money!

BORTSOV. My God, haven't I told you! I've drunk it all! Where am I to get it? And you won't go broke even if you do let me have a drop of vodka on tick. A glass of it only costs you two copecks, and it will save me from suffering! I am suffering! Understand! I'm in misery, I'm suffering!

TIHON. Go and tell that to someone else, not to me.... Go and ask the Orthodox, perhaps they'll give you some for Christ's sake, if they feel like it, but I'll only give bread for Christ's sake.

BORTSOV. You can rob those wretches yourself, I shan't.... I won't do it! I won't! Understand? [Hits the bar-counter with his fist] I won't. [A pause.] Hm... just wait.... [Turns to the pilgrim women] It's an idea, all the same, Orthodox ones! Spare five copecks! My inside asks for it. I'm ill!

FEDYA. Oh, you swindler, with your "spare five copecks." Won't you have some water?

BORTSOV. How I am degrading myself! I don't want it! I don't want anything! I was joking!

MERIK. You won't get it out of him, sir.... He's a famous skinflint.... Wait, I've got a five-copeck piece somewhere.... We'll have a glass between us—half each [Searches in his pockets] The devil... it's lost somewhere.... Thought I heard it tinkling just now in my pocket.... No; no, it isn't there, brother, it's your luck! [A pause.]

BORTSOV. But if I can't drink, I'll commit a crime or I'll kill myself.... What shall I do, my God! [Looks through the door] Shall I go out, then? Out into this darkness, wherever my feet take me....

MERIK. Why don't you give him a sermon, you pilgrims? And you, Tihon, why don't you drive him out? He hasn't paid you for his night's accommodation. Chuck him out! Eh, the people are cruel nowadays. There's no gentleness or kindness in them.... A savage people! A man is drowning and they shout to him: "Hurry up and drown, we've got no time to look at you; we've got to go to work." As to throwing him a rope—there's no worry about that.... A rope would cost money.

SAVVA. Don't talk, kind man!

MERIK. Quiet, old wolf! You're a savage race! Herods! Sellers of your souls! [To TIHON] Come here, take off my boots! Look sharp now!

TIHON. Eh, he's let himself go I [Laughs] Awful, isn't it.

MERIK. Go on, do as you're told! Quick now! [Pause] Do you hear me, or don't you? Am I talking to you or the wall? [Stands up]

TIHON. Well... give over.

MERIK. I want you, you fleecer, to take the boots off me, a poor tramp.

TIHON. Well, well... don't get excited. Here have a glass.... Have a drink, now!

MERIK. People, what do I want? Do I want him to stand me vodka, or to take off my boots? Didn't I say it properly? [To TIHON] Didn't you hear me rightly? I'll wait a moment, perhaps you'll hear me then.

[There is excitement among the pilgrims and tramps, who half-raise themselves in order to look at TIHON and MERIK. They wait in silence.]

TIHON. The devil brought you here! [Comes out from behind the bar] What a gentleman! Come on now. [Takes off MERIK'S boots] You child of Cain...

MERIK. That's right. Put them side by side.... Like that... you can go now!

TIHON. [Returns to the bar-counter] You're too fond of being clever. You do it again and I'll turn you out of the inn! Yes! [To BORTSOV, who is approaching] You, again?

BORTSOV. Look here, suppose I give you something made of gold.... I will give it to you.

TIHON. What are you shaking for? Talk sense!

BORTSOV. It may be mean and wicked on my part, but what am I to do? I'm doing this wicked thing, not reckoning on what's to come.... If I was tried for it, they'd let me off. Take it, only on condition that you return it later, when I come back from town. I give it to you in front of these witnesses. You will be my witnesses! [Takes a gold medallion out from the breast of his coat] Here it is.... I ought to take the portrait out, but I've nowhere to put it; I'm wet all over.... Well, take the portrait, too! Only mind this... don't let your fingers touch that face.... Please... I was rude to you, my dear fellow, I was a fool, but forgive me and... don't touch it with your fingers.... Don't look at that face with your eyes. [Gives TIHON the medallion.]

TIHON. [Examining it] Stolen property.... All right, then, drink.... [Pours out vodka] Confound you.

BORTSOV. Only don't you touch it... with your fingers. [Drinks slowly, with feverish pauses.]

TIHON. [Opens the medallion] Hm... a lady!... Where did you get hold of this?

MERIK. Let's have a look. [Goes to the bar] Let's see.

TIHON. [Pushes his hand away] Where are you going to? You look somewhere else!

FEDYA. [Gets up and comes to TIHON] I want to look too!

[Several of the tramps, etc., approach the bar and form a group. MERIK grips TIHON's hand firmly with both his, looks at the portrait, in the medallion in silence. A pause.]

MERIK. A pretty she-devil. A real lady....

FEDYA. A real lady.... Look at her cheeks, her eyes.... Open your hand, I can't see. Hair coming down to her waist.... It is lifelike! She might be going to say something.... [Pause.]

MERIK. It's destruction for a weak man. A woman like that gets a hold on one and... [Waves his hand] you're done for!

[KUSMA'S voice is heard. "Trrr.... Stop, you brutes!" Enter KUSMA.]

KUSMA. There stands an inn upon my way. Shall I drive or walk past it, say? You can pass your own father and not notice him, but you can see an inn in the dark a hundred versts away. Make way, if you believe in God! Hullo, there! [Planks a five-copeck piece down on the counter] A glass of real Madeira! Quick!

FEDYA. Oh, you devil!

TIHON. Don't wave your arms about, or you'll hit somebody.

KUSMA. God gave us arms to wave about. Poor sugary things, you're half-melted. You're frightened of the rain, poor delicate things. [Drinks.]

EFIMOVNA. You may well get frightened, good man, if you're caught on your way in a night like this. Now, thank God, it's all right, there are many villages and houses where you can shelter from the weather, but before that there weren't any. Oh, Lord, it was bad! You walk a hundred versts, and not only isn't there a village; or a house, but you don't even see a dry stick. So you sleep on the ground....

KUSMA. Have you been long on this earth, old woman?

EFIMOVNA. Over seventy years, little father.

KUSMA. Over seventy years! You'll soon come to crow's years. [Looks at BORTSOV] And what sort of a raisin is this? [Staring at BORTSOV] Sir! [BORTSOV recognizes KUSMA and retires in confusion to a corner of the room, where he sits on a bench] Semyon Sergeyevitch! Is that you, or isn't it? Eh? What are you doing in this place? It's not the sort of place for you, is it?

BORTSOV. Be quiet!

MERIK. [To KUSMA] Who is it?

KUSMA. A miserable sufferer. [Paces irritably by the counter] Eh? In an inn, my goodness! Tattered! Drunk! I'm upset, brothers... upset.... [To MERIK, in an undertone] It's my master... our landlord. Semyon Sergeyevitch and Mr. Bortsov.... Have you ever seen such a state? What does he look like? Just... it's the drink that brought him to this.... Give me some more! [Drinks] I come from his village, Bortsovka; you may have heard of it, it's 200 versts from here, in the Ergovsky district. We used to be his father's serfs.... What a shame!

MERIK. Was he rich?

KUSMA. Very.

MERIK. Did he drink it all?

KUSMA. No, my friend, it was something else.... He used to be great and rich and sober.... [To TIHON] Why you yourself used to see him riding, as he used to, past this inn, on his way to the town. Such bold and noble horses! A carriage on springs, of the best quality! He used to own five troikas, brother.... Five years ago, I remember, he cam here driving two horses from Mikishinsky, and he paid with a five-rouble piece.... I haven't the time, he says, to wait for the change.... There!

MERIK. His brain's gone, I suppose.

KUSMA. His brain's all right.... It all happened because of his cowardice! From too much fat. First of all, children, because of a woman.... He fell in love with a woman of the town, and it seemed to him that there wasn't any more beautiful thing in the wide world. A fool may love as much as a wise man. The girl's people were all right.... But she wasn't exactly loose, but just... giddy... always changing her mind! Always winking at one! Always laughing and laughing.... No sense at all. The gentry like that, they think that's nice, but we moujiks would soon chuck her out.... Well, he fell in love, and his luck ran out. He began to keep company with her, one thing led to another... they used to go out in a boat all night, and play pianos....

BORTSOV. Don't tell them, Kusma! Why should you? What has my life got to do with them?

KUSMA. Forgive me, your honour, I'm only telling them a little... what does it matter, anyway.... I'm shaking all over. Pour out some more. [Drinks.]

MERIK. [In a semitone] And did she love him?

KUSMA. [In a semitone which gradually becomes his ordinary voice] How shouldn't she? He was a man of means.... Of course you'll fall in love when the man has a thousand dessiatins and money to burn.... He was a solid, dignified, sober gentleman... always the same, like this... give me your hand [Takes MERIK'S hand] "How do you do and good-bye, do me the favour." Well, I was going one evening past his garden—and what a garden, brother, versts of it—I was going along quietly, and I look and see the two of them sitting on a seat and kissing each other. [Imitates the sound] He kisses her once, and the snake gives him back two.... He was holding her white, little hand, and she was all fiery and kept on getting closer and closer, too.... "I love you," she says. And he, like one of the damned, walks about from one place to another and brags, the coward, about his happiness.... Gives one man a rouble, and two to another.... Gives me money for a horse. Let off everybody's debts....

BORTSOV. Oh, why tell them all about it? These people haven't any sympathy.... It hurts!

KUSMA. It's nothing, sir! They asked me! Why shouldn't I tell them? But if you are angry I won't... I won't.... What do I care for them.... [Post-bells are heard.]

FEDYA. Don't shout; tell us quietly....

KUSMA. I'll tell you quietly.... He doesn't want me to, but it can't be helped.... But there's nothing more to tell. They got married, that's all. There was nothing else. Pour out another drop for Kusma the stony! [Drinks] I don't like people getting drunk! Why the time the wedding took place, when the gentlefolk sat down to supper afterwards, she went off in a carriage... [Whispers] To the town, to her lover, a lawyer.... Eh? What do you think of her now? Just at the very moment! She would be let off lightly if she were killed for it!

MERIK. [Thoughtfully] Well... what happened then?

KUSMA. He went mad.... As you see, he started with a fly, as they say, and now it's grown to a bumble-bee. It was a fly then, and now—it's a bumble-bee.... And he still loves her. Look at him, he loves her! I expect he's walking now to the town to get a glimpse of her with one eye.... He'll get a glimpse of her, and go back....

[The post has driven up to the in.. The POSTMAN enters and has a drink.]

TIHON. The post's late to-day!

[The POSTMAN pays in silence and goes out. The post drives off, the bells ringing.]

A VOICE FROM THE CORNER. One could rob the post in weather like this—easy as spitting.

MERIK. I've been alive thirty-five years and I haven't robbed the post once.... [Pause] It's gone now... too late, too late....

KUSMA. Do you want to smell the inside of a prison?

MERIK. People rob and don't go to prison. And if I do go! [Suddenly] What else?

KUSMA. Do you mean that unfortunate?

MERIK. Who else?

KUSMA. The second reason, brothers, why he was ruined was because of his brother-in-law, his sister's husband.... He took it into his head to stand surety at the bank for 30,000 roubles for his brother-in-law. The brother-in-law's a thief.... The swindler knows which side his bread's buttered and won't budge an inch.... So he doesn't pay up.... So our man had to pay up the whole thirty thousand. [Sighs] The fool is suffering for his folly. His wife's got children now by the lawyer and the brother-in-law has bought an estate near Poltava, and our man goes round inns like a fool, and complains to the likes of us: "I've lost all faith, brothers! I can't believe in anybody now!" It's cowardly! Every man has his grief, a snake that sucks at his heart, and does that mean that he must drink? Take our village elder, for example. His wife plays about with the schoolmaster in broad daylight, and spends his money on drink, but the elder walks about smiling to himself. He's just a little thinner...

TIHON. [Sighs] When God gives a man strength....

KUSMA. There's all sorts of strength, that's true.... Well? How much does it come to? [Pays] Take your pound of flesh! Good-bye, children! Good-night and pleasant dreams! It's time I hurried off. I'm bringing my lady a midwife from the hospital.... She must be getting wet with waiting, poor thing.... [Runs out. A pause.]

TIHON. Oh, you! Unhappy man, come and drink this! [Pours out.]

BORTSOV. [Comes up to the bar hesitatingly and drinks] That means I now owe you for two glasses.

TIHON. You don't owe me anything? Just drink and drown your sorrows!

FEDYA. Drink mine, too, sir! Oh! [Throws down a five-copeck piece] If you drink, you die; if you don't drink, you die. It's good not to drink vodka, but by God you're easier when you've got some! Vodka takes grief away.... It is hot!

BORTSOV. Boo! The heat!

MERIK. Dive it here! [Takes the medallion from TIHON and examines her portrait] Hm. Ran off after the wedding. What a woman!

A VOICE FROM THE CORNER. Pour him out another glass, Tihon. Let him drink mine, too.

MERIK. [Dashes the medallion to the ground] Curse her! [Goes quickly to his place and lies down, face to the wall. General excitement.]

BORTSOV. Here, what's that? [Picks up the medallion] How dare you, you beast? What right have you? [Tearfully] Do you want me to kill you? You moujik! You boor!

TIHON. Don't be angry, sir.... It isn't glass, it isn't broken.... Have another drink and go to sleep. [Pours out] Here I've been listening to you all, and when I ought to have locked up long ago. [Goes and looks door leading out.]

BORTSOV. [Drinks] How dare he? The fool! [to MERIK] Do you understand? You're a fool, a donkey!

SAVVA. Children! If you please! Stop that talking! What's the good of making a noise? Let people go to sleep.

TIHON. Lie down, lie down... be quiet! [Goes behind the counter and locks the till] It's time to sleep.

FEDYA. It's time! [Lies down] Pleasant dreams, brothers!

MERIK. [Gets up and spreads his short fur and coat the bench] Come on, lie down, sir.

TIHON. And where will you sleep.

MERIK. Oh, anywhere.... The floor will do.... [Spreads a coat on the floor] It's all one to me [Puts the axe by him] It would be torture for him to sleep on the floor. He's used to silk and down....

TIHON. [To BORTSOV] Lie down, your honour! You've looked at that portrait long enough. [Puts out a candle] Throw it away!

BORTSOV. [Swaying about] Where can I lie down?

TIHON. In the tramp's place! Didn't you hear him giving it up to you?

BORTSOV. [Going up to the vacant place] I'm a bit... drunk... after all that.... Is this it?... Do I lie down here? Eh?

TIHON. Yes, yes, lie down, don't be afraid. [Stretches himself out on the counter.]

BORTSOV. [Lying down] I'm... drunk.... Everything's going round.... [Opens the medallion] Haven't you a little candle? [Pause] You're a queer little woman Masha.... Looking at me out of the frame and laughing.... [Laughs] I'm drunk! And should you laugh at a man because he's drunk? You look out, as Schastlivtsev says, and... love the drunkard.

FEDYA. How the wind howls. It's dreary!

BORTSOV. [Laughs] What a woman.... Why do you keep on going round? I can't catch you!

MERIK. He's wandering. Looked too long at the portrait. [Laughs] What a business! Educated people go and invent all sorts of machines and medicines, but there hasn't yet been a man wise enough to invent a medicine against the female sex.... They try to cure every sort of disease, and it never occurs to them that more people die of women than of disease.... Sly, stingy, cruel, brainless.... The mother-in-law torments the bride and the bride makes things square by swindling the husband... and there's no end to it....

TIHON. The women have ruffled his hair for him, and so he's bristly.

MERIK. It isn't only I.... From the beginning of the ages, since the world has been in existence, people have complained.... It's not for nothing that in the songs and stories, the devil and the woman are put side by side.... Not for nothing! It's half true, at any rate... [Pause] Here's the gentleman playing the fool, but I had more sense, didn't I, when I left my father and mother, and became a tramp?

FEDYA. Because of women?

MERIK. Just like the gentleman... I walked about like one of the damned, bewitched, blessing my stars... on fire day and night, until at last my eyes were opened... It wasn't love, but just a fraud....

FEDYA. What did you do to her?

MERIK. Never you mind.... [Pause] Do you think I killed her?... I wouldn't do it.... If you kill, you are sorry for it.... She can live and be happy! If only I'd never set eyes on you, or if I could only forget you, you viper's brood! [A knocking at the door.]

TIHON. Whom have the devils brought.... Who's there? [Knocking] Who knocks? [Gets up and goes to the door] Who knocks? Go away, we've locked up!

A VOICE. Please let me in, Tihon. The carriage-spring's broken! Be a father to me and help me! If I only had a little string to tie it round with, we'd get there somehow or other.

TIHON. Who are you?

THE VOICE. My lady is going to Varsonofyev from the town.... It's only five versts farther on.... Do be a good man and help!

TIHON. Go and tell the lady that if she pays ten roubles she can have her string and we'll mend the spring.

THE VOICE. Have you gone mad, or what? Ten roubles! You mad dog! Profiting by our misfortunes!

TIHON. Just as you like.... You needn't if you don't want to.

THE VOICE. Very well, wait a bit. [Pause] She says, all right.

TIHON. Pleased to hear it!

[Opens door. The COACHMAN enters.]

COACHMAN. Good evening, Orthodox people! Well, give me the string! Quick! Who'll go and help us, children? There'll be something left over for your trouble!

TIHON. There won't be anything left over.... Let them sleep, the two of us can manage.

COACHMAN. Foo, I am tired! It's cold, and there's not a dry spot in all the mud.... Another thing, dear.... Have you got a little room in here for the lady to warm herself in? The carriage is all on one side, she can't stay in it....

TIHON. What does she want a room for? She can warm herself in here, if she's cold.... We'll find a place [Clears a space next to BORTSOV] Get up, get up! Just lie on the floor for an hour, and let the lady get warm. [To BORTSOV] Get up, your honour! Sit up! [BORTSOV sits up] Here's a place for you. [Exit COACHMAN.]

FEDYA. Here's a visitor for you, the devil's brought her! Now there'll be no sleep before daylight.

TIHON. I'm sorry I didn't ask for fifteen.... She'd have given them.... [Stands expectantly before the door] You're a delicate sort of people, I must say. [Enter MARIA EGOROVNA, followed by the COACHMAN. TIHON bows.] Please, your highness! Our room is very humble, full of blackbeetles! But don't disdain it!

MARIA EGOROVNA. I can't see anything.... Which way do I go?

TIHON. This way, your highness! [Leads her to the place next to BORTSOV] This way, please. [Blows on the place] I haven't any separate rooms, excuse me, but don't you be afraid, madam, the people here are good and quiet....

MARIA EGOROVNA. [Sits next to BORTSOV] How awfully stuffy! Open the door, at any rate!

TIHON. Yes, madam. [Runs and opens the door wide.]

MARIA. We're freezing, and you open the door! [Gets up and slams it] Who are you to be giving orders? [Lies down]

TIHON. Excuse me, your highness, but we've a little fool here... a bit cracked.... But don't you be frightened, he won't do you any harm.... Only you must excuse me, madam, I can't do this for ten roubles.... Make it fifteen.

MARIA EGOROVNA. Very well, only be quick.

TIHON. This minute... this very instant. [Drags some string out from under the counter] This minute. [A pause.]

BORTSOV. [Looking at MARIA EGOROVNA] Marie... Masha...

MARIA EGOROVNA. [Looks at BORTSOV] What's this?

BORTSOV. Marie... is it you? Where do you come from? [MARIA EGOROVNA recognizes BORTSOV, screams and runs off into the centre of the floor. BORTSOV follows] Marie, it is I... I [Laughs loudly] My wife! Marie! Where am I? People, a light!

MARIA EGOROVNA. Get away from me! You lie, it isn't you! It can't be! [Covers her face with her hands] It's a lie, it's all nonsense!

BORTSOV. Her voice, her movements.... Marie, it is I! I'll stop in a moment.... I was drunk.... My head's going round.... My God! Stop, stop.... I can't understand anything. [Yells] My wife! [Falls at her feet and sobs. A group collects around the husband and wife.]

MARIA EGOROVNA. Stand back! [To the COACHMAN] Denis, let's go! I can't stop here any longer!

MERIK. [Jumps up and looks her steadily in the face] The portrait! [Grasps her hand] It is she! Eh, people, she's the gentleman's wife!

MARIA EGOROVNA. Get away, fellow! [Tries to tear her hand away from him] Denis, why do you stand there staring? [DENIS and TIHON run up to her and get hold of MERIK'S arms] This thieves' kitchen! Let go my hand! I'm not afraid!... Get away from me!

MERIK. [Note: Throughout this speech, in the original, Merik uses the familiar second person singular.] Wait a bit, and I'll let go.... Just let me say one word to you.... One word, so that you may understand.... Just wait.... [Turns to TIHON and DENIS] Get away, you rogues, let go! I shan't let you go till I've had my say! Stop... one moment. [Strikes his forehead with his fist] No, God hasn't given me the wisdom! I can't think of the word for you!

MARIA EGOROVNA. [Tears away her hand] Get away! Drunkards... let's go, Denis!

[She tries to go out, but MERIK blocks the door.]

MERIK. Just throw a glance at him, with only one eye if you like! Or say only just one kind little word to him! God's own sake!

MARIA EGOROVNA. Take away this... fool.

MERIK. Then the devil take you, you accursed woman!

[He swings his axe. General confusion. Everybody jumps up noisily and with cries of horror. SAVVA stands between MERIK and MARIA EGOROVNA.... DENIS forces MERIK to one side and carries out his mistress. After this all stand as if turned to stone. A prolonged pause. BORTSOV suddenly waves his hands in the air.]

BORTSOV. Marie... where are you, Marie!

NAZAROVNA. My God, my God! You've torn up my your murderers! What an accursed night!

MERIK. [Lowering his hand; he still holds the axe] Did I kill her or no?

HIGH ROAD

TIHON. Thank God, your head is safe....

MERIK. Then I didn't kill her.... [Totters to his bed] Fate hasn't sent me to my death because of a stolen axe.... [Falls down and sobs] Woe! Woe is me! Have pity on me, Orthodox people!

Curtain.

THE PROPOSAL

CHARACTERS

STEPAN STEPANOVITCH CHUBUKOV, a landowner
NATALYA STEPANOVNA, his daughter, twenty-five years old
IVAN VASSILEVITCH LOMOV, a neighbour of Chubukov, a large and hearty, but very suspicious landowner

The scene is laid at CHUBUKOV's country-house

A drawing-room in CHUBUKOV'S house.

[LOMOV enters, wearing a dress-jacket and white gloves. CHUBUKOV rises to meet him.]

CHUBUKOV. My dear fellow, whom do I see! Ivan Vassilevitch! I am extremely glad! [Squeezes his hand] Now this is a surprise, my darling... How are you?

LOMOV. Thank you. And how may you be getting on?

CHUBUKOV. We just get along somehow, my angel, to your prayers, and so on. Sit down, please do.... Now, you know, you shouldn't forget all about your neighbours, my darling. My dear fellow, why are you so formal in your get-up? Evening dress, gloves, and so on. Can you be going anywhere, my treasure?

LOMOV. No, I've come only to see you, honoured Stepan Stepanovitch.

CHUBUKOV. Then why are you in evening dress, my precious? As if you're paying a New Year's Eve visit!

LOMOV. Well, you see, it's like this. [Takes his arm] I've come to you, honoured Stepan Stepanovitch, to trouble you with a request. Not once or twice have I already had the privilege of applying to you for help, and you have always, so to speak... I must ask your pardon, I am getting excited. I shall drink some water, honoured Stepan Stepanovitch. [Drinks.]

CHUBUKOV. [Aside] He's come to borrow money! Shan't give him any! [Aloud] What is it, my beauty?

LOMOV. You see, Honour Stepanitch... I beg pardon, Stepan Honouritch... I mean, I'm awfully excited, as you will please notice.... In short, you alone can help me, though I don't deserve it, of course... and haven't any right to count on your assistance....

CHUBUKOV. Oh, don't go round and round it, darling! Spit it out! Well?

LOMOV. One moment... this very minute. The fact is, I've come to ask the hand of your daughter, Natalya Stepanovna, in marriage.

CHUBUKOV. [Joyfully] By Jove! Ivan Vassilevitch! Say it again—I didn't hear it all!

LOMOV. I have the honour to ask...

CHUBUKOV. [Interrupting] My dear fellow... I'm so glad, and so on.... Yes, indeed, and all that sort of thing. [Embraces and kisses LOMOV] I've been hoping for it for a long time. It's been my continual desire. [Sheds a tear] And I've always loved you, my angel, as if you were my own son. May God give you both His help and His love and so on, and I did so much hope... What am I behaving in this idiotic way for? I'm off my balance with joy, absolutely off my balance! Oh, with all my soul... I'll go and call Natasha, and all that.

LOMOV. [Greatly moved] Honoured Stepan Stepanovitch, do you think I may count on her consent?

CHUBUKOV. Why, of course, my darling, and... as if she won't consent! She's in love; egad, she's like a love-sick cat, and so on.... Shan't be long! [Exit.]

LOMOV. It's cold... I'm trembling all over, just as if I'd got an examination before me. The great thing is, I must have my mind made up. If I give myself time to think, to hesitate, to talk a lot, to look for an ideal, or for real love, then I'll never get married.... Brr!... It's cold! Natalya Stepanovna is an excellent housekeeper, not bad-looking, well-educated.... What more do I want? But I'm getting a noise in my ears from excitement. [Drinks] And it's impossible for me not to marry.... In the first place, I'm already 35—a critical age, so to speak. In the second place, I ought to lead a quiet and regular life.... I suffer from palpitations, I'm excitable and always getting awfully upset.... At this very moment my lips are trembling, and there's a twitch in my right eyebrow.... But the very worst of all is the way I sleep. I no sooner get into bed and begin to go off when suddenly something in my left side—gives a pull, and I can feel it in my shoulder and head.... I jump up like a lunatic, walk about a bit, and lie down again, but as soon as I begin to get off to sleep there's another pull! And this may happen twenty times....

[NATALYA STEPANOVNA comes in.]

NATALYA STEPANOVNA. Well, there! It's you, and papa said, "Go; there's a merchant come for his goods." How do you do, Ivan Vassilevitch!

LOMOV. How do you do, honoured Natalya Stepanovna?

NATALYA STEPANOVNA. You must excuse my apron and négligé... we're shelling peas for drying. Why haven't you been here for such a long time? Sit down. [They seat themselves] Won't you have some lunch?

LOMOV. No, thank you, I've had some already.

NATALYA STEPANOVNA. Then smoke.... Here are the matches.... The weather is splendid now, but yesterday it was so wet that the workmen didn't do anything all day. How much hay have you stacked? Just think, I felt greedy and had a whole field cut, and now I'm not at all pleased about it because I'm afraid my hay may rot. I ought to have waited a bit. But what's this? Why, you're in evening dress! Well, I never! Are you going to a ball, or what?—though I must say you look better. Tell me, why are you got up like that?

LOMOV. [Excited] You see, honoured Natalya Stepanovna... the fact is, I've made up my mind to ask you to hear me out.... Of course you'll be surprised and perhaps even angry, but a... [Aside] It's awfully cold!

NATALYA STEPANOVNA. What's the matter? [Pause] Well?

LOMOV. I shall try to be brief. You must know, honoured Natalya Stepanovna, that I have long, since my childhood, in fact, had the privilege of knowing your family. My late aunt and her husband, from whom, as you know, I inherited my land, always had the greatest respect for your father and your late mother. The Lomovs and the Chubukovs have always had the most friendly, and I might almost say the most affectionate, regard for each other. And, as you know, my land is a near neighbour of yours. You will remember that my Oxen Meadows touch your birchwoods.

NATALYA STEPANOVNA. Excuse my interrupting you. You say, "my Oxen Meadows...." But are they yours?

LOMOV. Yes, mine.

NATALYA STEPANOVNA. What are you talking about? Oxen Meadows are ours, not yours!

LOMOV. No, mine, honoured Natalya Stepanovna.

NATALYA STEPANOVNA. Well, I never knew that before. How do you make that out?

LOMOV. How? I'm speaking of those Oxen Meadows which are wedged in between your birchwoods and the Burnt Marsh.

NATALYA STEPANOVNA. Yes, yes.... They're ours.

LOMOV. No, you're mistaken, honoured Natalya Stepanovna, they're mine.

NATALYA STEPANOVNA. Just think, Ivan Vassilevitch! How long have they been yours?

LOMOV. How long? As long as I can remember.

NATALYA STEPANOVNA. Really, you won't get me to believe that!

LOMOV. But you can see from the documents, honoured Natalya Stepanovna. Oxen Meadows, it's true, were once the subject of dispute, but now everybody knows that they are mine. There's nothing to argue about. You see, my aunt's grandmother gave the free use of these Meadows in perpetuity to the peasants of your father's grandfather, in return for which they were to make bricks for her. The peasants belonging to your father's grandfather had the free use of the Meadows for forty years, and had got into the habit of regarding them as their own, when it happened that...

NATALYA STEPANOVNA. No, it isn't at all like that! Both my grandfather and great-grandfather reckoned that their land extended to Burnt Marsh—which means that Oxen Meadows were ours. I don't see what there is to argue about. It's simply silly!

LOMOV. I'll show you the documents, Natalya Stepanovna!

NATALYA STEPANOVNA. No, you're simply joking, or making fun of me.... What a surprise! We've had the land for nearly three hundred years, and then we're suddenly told that it isn't ours! Ivan Vassilevitch, I can hardly believe my own ears.... These Meadows aren't worth much to me. They only come to five dessiatins [Note: 13.5 acres], and are worth perhaps 300 roubles [Note: £30.], but I can't stand unfairness. Say what you will, but I can't stand unfairness.

LOMOV. Hear me out, I implore you! The peasants of your father's grandfather, as I have already had the honour of explaining to you, used to bake bricks for my aunt's grandmother. Now my aunt's grandmother, wishing to make them a pleasant...

NATALYA STEPANOVNA. I can't make head or tail of all this about aunts and grandfathers and grandmothers! The Meadows are ours, and that's all.

LOMOV. Mine.

NATALYA STEPANOVNA. Ours! You can go on proving it for two days on end, you can go and put on fifteen dress-jackets, but I tell you they're ours, ours, ours! I don't want anything of yours and I don't want to give up anything of mine. So there!

LOMOV. Natalya Ivanovna, I don't want the Meadows, but I am acting on principle. If you like, I'll make you a present of them.

NATALYA STEPANOVNA. I can make you a present of them myself, because they're mine! Your behaviour, Ivan Vassilevitch, is strange, to say the least! Up to this we have always thought of you as a good neighbour, a friend: last year we lent you our threshing-machine, although on that account we had to put off our own threshing till November, but you behave to us as if we were gipsies. Giving me my own land, indeed! No, really, that's not at all neighbourly! In my opinion, it's even impudent, if you want to know....

LOMOV. Then you make out that I'm a land-grabber? Madam, never in my life have I grabbed anybody else's land, and I shan't allow anybody to accuse me of having done so.... [Quickly steps to the carafe and drinks more water] Oxen Meadows are mine!

NATALYA STEPANOVNA. It's not true, they're ours!

LOMOV. Mine!

NATALYA STEPANOVNA. It's not true! I'll prove it! I'll send my mowers out to the Meadows this very day!

LOMOV. What?

NATALYA STEPANOVNA. My mowers will be there this very day!

LOMOV. I'll give it to them in the neck!

NATALYA STEPANOVNA. You dare!

LOMOV. [Clutches at his heart] Oxen Meadows are mine! You understand? Mine!

NATALYA STEPANOVNA. Please don't shout! You can shout yourself hoarse in your own house, but here I must ask you to restrain yourself!

LOMOV. If it wasn't, madam, for this awful, excruciating palpitation, if my whole inside wasn't upset, I'd talk to you in a different way! [Yells] Oxen Meadows are mine!

NATALYA STEPANOVNA. Ours!

LOMOV. Mine!

NATALYA STEPANOVNA. Ours!

LOMOV. Mine!

[Enter CHUBUKOV.]

CHUBUKOV. What's the matter? What are you shouting at?

NATALYA STEPANOVNA. Papa, please tell to this gentleman who owns Oxen Meadows, we or he?

CHUBUKOV. [To LOMOV] Darling, the Meadows are ours!

LOMOV. But, please, Stepan Stepanitch, how can they be yours? Do be a reasonable man! My aunt's grandmother gave the Meadows for the temporary and free use of your grandfather's peasants. The peasants used the land for forty years and got as accustomed to it as if it was their own, when it happened that...

CHUBUKOV. Excuse me, my precious.... You forget just this, that the peasants didn't pay your grandmother and all that, because the Meadows were in dispute, and so on. And now everybody knows that they're ours. It means that you haven't seen the plan.

LOMOV. I'll prove to you that they're mine!

CHUBUKOV. You won't prove it, my darling.

LOMOV. I shall!

CHUBUKOV. Dear one, why yell like that? You won't prove anything just by yelling. I don't want anything of yours, and don't intend to give up what I have. Why should I? And you know, my beloved, that if you propose to go on arguing about it, I'd much sooner give up the meadows to the peasants than to you. There!

LOMOV. I don't understand! How have you the right to give away somebody else's property?

CHUBUKOV. You may take it that I know whether I have the right or not. Because, young man, I'm not used to being spoken to in that tone of voice, and so on: I, young man, am twice your age, and ask you to speak to me without agitating yourself, and all that.

LOMOV. No, you just think I'm a fool and want to have me on! You call my land yours, and then you want me to talk to you calmly and politely! Good neighbours don't behave like that, Stepan Stepanitch! You're not a neighbour, you're a grabber!

CHUBUKOV. What's that? What did you say?

NATALYA STEPANOVNA. Papa, send the mowers out to the Meadows at once!

CHUBUKOV. What did you say, sir?

NATALYA STEPANOVNA. Oxen Meadows are ours, and I shan't give them up, shan't give them up, shan't give them up!

LOMOV. We'll see! I'll have the matter taken to court, and then I'll show you!

CHUBUKOV. To court? You can take it to court, and all that! You can! I know you; you're just on the look-out for a chance to go to court, and all that.... You pettifogger! All your people were like that! All of them!

LOMOV. Never mind about my people! The Lomovs have all been honourable people, and not one has ever been tried for embezzlement, like your grandfather!

CHUBUKOV. You Lomovs have had lunacy in your family, all of you!

NATALYA STEPANOVNA. All, all, all!

CHUBUKOV. Your grandfather was a drunkard, and your younger aunt, Nastasya Mihailovna, ran away with an architect, and so on.

LOMOV. And your mother was hump-backed. [Clutches at his heart] Something pulling in my side.... My head.... Help! Water!

CHUBUKOV. Your father was a guzzling gambler!

NATALYA STEPANOVNA. And there haven't been many backbiters to equal your aunt!

LOMOV. My left foot has gone to sleep.... You're an intriguer.... Oh, my heart!... And it's an open secret that before the last elections you bri... I can see stars.... Where's my hat?

NATALYA STEPANOVNA. It's low! It's dishonest! It's mean!

CHUBUKOV. And you're just a malicious, double-faced intriguer! Yes!

LOMOV. Here's my hat.... My heart!... Which way? Where's the door? Oh!... I think I'm dying.... My foot's quite numb.... [Goes to the door.]

CHUBUKOV. [Following him] And don't set foot in my house again!

NATALYA STEPANOVNA. Take it to court! We'll see!

[LOMOV staggers out.]

CHUBUKOV. Devil take him! [Walks about in excitement.]

NATALYA STEPANOVNA. What a rascal! What trust can one have in one's neighbours after that!

CHUBUKOV. The villain! The scarecrow!

NATALYA STEPANOVNA. The monster! First he takes our land and then he has the impudence to abuse us.

CHUBUKOV. And that blind hen, yes, that turnip-ghost has the confounded cheek to make a proposal, and so on! What? A proposal!

NATALYA STEPANOVNA. What proposal?

CHUBUKOV. Why, he came here so as to propose to you.

NATALYA STEPANOVNA. To propose? To me? Why didn't you tell me so before?

CHUBUKOV. So he dresses up in evening clothes. The stuffed sausage! The wizen-faced frump!

NATALYA STEPANOVNA. To propose to me? Ah! [Falls into an easy-chair and wails] Bring him back! Back! Ah! Bring him here.

CHUBUKOV. Bring whom here?

NATALYA STEPANOVNA. Quick, quick! I'm ill! Fetch him! [Hysterics.]

CHUBUKOV. What's that? What's the matter with you? [Clutches at his head] Oh, unhappy man that I am! I'll shoot myself! I'll hang myself! We've done for her!

NATALYA STEPANOVNA. I'm dying! Fetch him!

CHUBUKOV. Tfoo! At once. Don't yell!

[Runs out. A pause. NATALYA STEPANOVNA wails.]

NATALYA STEPANOVNA. What have they done to me! Fetch him back! Fetch him! [A pause.]

[CHUBUKOV runs in.]

CHUBUKOV. He's coming, and so on, devil take him! Ouf! Talk to him yourself; I don't want to....

NATALYA STEPANOVNA. [Wails] Fetch him!

CHUBUKOV. [Yells] He's coming, I tell you. Oh, what a burden, Lord, to be the father of a grown-up daughter! I'll cut my throat! I will, indeed! We cursed him, abused him, drove him out, and it's all you... you!

NATALYA STEPANOVNA. No, it was you!

CHUBUKOV. I tell you it's not my fault. [LOMOV appears at the door] Now you talk to him yourself [Exit.]

[LOMOV enters, exhausted.]

LOMOV. My heart's palpitating awfully.... My foot's gone to sleep.... There's something keeps pulling in my side.

NATALYA STEPANOVNA. Forgive us, Ivan Vassilevitch, we were all a little heated.... I remember now: Oxen Meadows really are yours.

LOMOV. My heart's beating awfully.... My Meadows.... My eyebrows are both twitching....

NATALYA STEPANOVNA. The Meadows are yours, yes, yours.... Do sit down.... [They sit] We were wrong....

LOMOV. I did it on principle.... My land is worth little to me, but the principle...

NATALYA STEPANOVNA. Yes, the principle, just so.... Now let's talk of something else.

LOMOV. The more so as I have evidence. My aunt's grandmother gave the land to your father's grandfather's peasants...

NATALYA STEPANOVNA. Yes, yes, let that pass.... [Aside] I wish I knew how to get him started.... [Aloud] Are you going to start shooting soon?

LOMOV. I'm thinking of having a go at the blackcock, honoured Natalya Stepanovna, after the harvest. Oh, have you heard? Just think, what a misfortune I've had! My dog Guess, whom you know, has gone lame.

NATALYA STEPANOVNA. What a pity! Why?

LOMOV. I don't know.... Must have got twisted, or bitten by some other dog.... [Sighs] My very best dog, to say nothing of the expense. I gave Mironov 125 roubles for him.

NATALYA STEPANOVNA. It was too much, Ivan Vassilevitch.

LOMOV. I think it was very cheap. He's a first-rate dog.

NATALYA STEPANOVNA. Papa gave 85 roubles for his Squeezer, and Squeezer is heaps better than Guess!

LOMOV. Squeezer better than. Guess? What an idea! [Laughs] Squeezer better than Guess!

NATALYA STEPANOVNA. Of course he's better! Of course, Squeezer is young, he may develop a bit, but on points and pedigree he's better than anything that even Volchanetsky has got.

LOMOV. Excuse me, Natalya Stepanovna, but you forget that he is overshot, and an overshot always means the dog is a bad hunter!

NATALYA STEPANOVNA. Overshot, is he? The first time I hear it!

LOMOV. I assure you that his lower jaw is shorter than the upper.

NATALYA STEPANOVNA. Have you measured?

LOMOV. Yes. He's all right at following, of course, but if you want him to get hold of anything...

NATALYA STEPANOVNA. In the first place, our Squeezer is a thoroughbred animal, the son of Harness and Chisels, while there's no getting at the pedigree of your dog at all.... He's old and as ugly as a worn-out cab-horse.

LOMOV. He is old, but I wouldn't take five Squeezers for him.... Why, how can you?... Guess is a dog; as for Squeezer, well, it's too funny to argue.... Anybody you like has a dog as good as Squeezer... you may find them under every bush almost. Twenty-five roubles would be a handsome price to pay for him.

NATALYA STEPANOVNA. There's some demon of contradiction in you to-day, Ivan Vassilevitch. First you pretend that the Meadows are yours; now, that Guess is better than Squeezer. I don't like people who don't say what they mean, because you know perfectly well that Squeezer is a hundred times better than your silly Guess. Why do you want to say it isn't?

LOMOV. I see, Natalya Stepanovna, that you consider me either blind or a fool. You must realize that Squeezer is overshot!

NATALYA STEPANOVNA. It's not true.

LOMOV. He is!

NATALYA STEPANOVNA. It's not true!

LOMOV. Why shout, madam?

NATALYA STEPANOVNA. Why talk rot? It's awful! It's time your Guess was shot, and you compare him with Squeezer!

LOMOV. Excuse me; I cannot continue this discussion: my heart is palpitating.

NATALYA STEPANOVNA. I've noticed that those hunters argue most who know least.

LOMOV. Madam, please be silent.... My heart is going to pieces.... [Shouts] Shut up!

NATALYA STEPANOVNA. I shan't shut up until you acknowledge that Squeezer is a hundred times better than your Guess!

LOMOV. A hundred times worse! Be hanged to your Squeezer! His head... eyes... shoulder...

NATALYA STEPANOVNA. There's no need to hang your silly Guess; he's half-dead already!

LOMOV. [Weeps] Shut up! My heart's bursting!

NATALYA STEPANOVNA. I shan't shut up.

[Enter CHUBUKOV.]

CHUBUKOV. What's the matter now?

NATALYA STEPANOVNA. Papa, tell us truly, which is the better dog, our Squeezer or his Guess.

LOMOV. Stepan Stepanovitch, I implore you to tell me just one thing: is your Squeezer overshot or not? Yes or no?

CHUBUKOV. And suppose he is? What does it matter? He's the best dog in the district for all that, and so on.

LOMOV. But isn't my Guess better? Really, now?

CHUBUKOV. Don't excite yourself, my precious one.... Allow me.... Your Guess certainly has his good points.... He's pure-bred, firm on his feet, has well-sprung ribs, and all that. But, my dear man, if you want to know the truth, that dog has two defects: he's old and he's short in the muzzle.

LOMOV. Excuse me, my heart.... Let's take the facts.... You will remember that on the Marusinsky hunt my Guess ran neck-and-neck with the Count's dog, while your Squeezer was left a whole verst behind.

CHUBUKOV. He got left behind because the Count's whipper-in hit him with his whip.

LOMOV. And with good reason. The dogs are running after a fox, when Squeezer goes and starts worrying a sheep!

CHUBUKOV. It's not true!... My dear fellow, I'm very liable to lose my temper, and so, just because of that, let's stop arguing. You started because everybody is always jealous of everybody else's dogs. Yes, we're all like that! You too, sir, aren't blameless! You no sooner notice that some dog is better than your Guess than you begin with this, that... and the other... and all that.... I remember everything!

LOMOV. I remember too!

CHUBUKOV. [Teasing him] I remember, too.... What do you remember?

LOMOV. My heart... my foot's gone to sleep.... I can't...

NATALYA STEPANOVNA. [Teasing] My heart.... What sort of a hunter are you? You ought to go and lie on the kitchen oven and catch blackbeetles, not go after foxes! My heart!

CHUBUKOV. Yes really, what sort of a hunter are you, anyway? You ought to sit at home with your palpitations, and not go tracking animals. You could go hunting, but you only go to argue with people and interfere with their dogs and so on. Let's change the subject in case I lose my temper. You're not a hunter at all, anyway!

LOMOV. And are you a hunter? You only go hunting to get in with the Count and to intrigue.... Oh, my heart!... You're an intriguer!

CHUBUKOV. What? I an intriguer? [Shouts] Shut up!

LOMOV. Intriguer!

CHUBUKOV. Boy! Pup!

LOMOV. Old rat! Jesuit!

CHUBUKOV. Shut up or I'll shoot you like a partridge! You fool!

LOMOV. Everybody knows that—oh my heart!—your late wife used to beat you.... My feet... temples... sparks.... I fall, I fall!

CHUBUKOV. And you're under the slipper of your housekeeper!

LOMOV. There, there, there... my heart's burst! My shoulder's come off.... Where is my shoulder? I die. [Falls into an armchair] A doctor! [Faints.]

CHUBUKOV. Boy! Milksop! Fool! I'm sick! [Drinks water] Sick!

NATALYA STEPANOVNA. What sort of a hunter are you? You can't even sit on a horse! [To her father] Papa, what's the matter with him? Papa! Look, papa! [Screams] Ivan Vassilevitch! He's dead!

CHUBUKOV. I'm sick!... I can't breathe!... Air!

NATALYA STEPANOVNA. He's dead. [Pulls LOMOV'S sleeve] Ivan Vassilevitch! Ivan Vassilevitch! What have you done to me? He's dead. [Falls into an armchair] A doctor, a doctor! [Hysterics.]

CHUBUKOV. Oh!... What is it? What's the matter?

NATALYA STEPANOVNA. [Wails] He's dead... dead!

CHUBUKOV. Who's dead? [Looks at LOMOV] So he is! My word! Water! A doctor! [Lifts a tumbler to LOMOV'S mouth] Drink this!... No, he doesn't drink.... It means he's dead, and all that.... I'm the most unhappy of men! Why don't I put a bullet into my brain? Why haven't I cut my throat yet? What am I waiting for? Give me a knife! Give me a pistol! [LOMOV moves] He seems to be coming round.... Drink some water! That's right....

LOMOV. I see stars... mist.... Where am I?

CHUBUKOV. Hurry up and get married and—well, to the devil with you! She's willing! [He puts LOMOV'S hand into his daughter's] She's willing and all that. I give you my blessing and so on. Only leave me in peace!

LOMOV. [Getting up] Eh? What? To whom?

CHUBUKOV. She's willing! Well? Kiss and be damned to you!

NATALYA STEPANOVNA. [Wails] He's alive... Yes, yes, I'm willing....

CHUBUKOV. Kiss each other!

LOMOV. Eh? Kiss whom? [They kiss] Very nice, too. Excuse me, what's it all about? Oh, now I understand... my heart... stars... I'm happy. Natalya Stepanovna.... [Kisses her hand] My foot's gone to sleep....

NATALYA STEPANOVNA. I... I'm happy too....

CHUBUKOV. What a weight off my shoulders.... Ouf!

NATALYA STEPANOVNA. But... still you will admit now that Guess is worse than Squeezer.

LOMOV. Better!

NATALYA STEPANOVNA. Worse!

CHUBUKOV. Well, that's a way to start your family bliss! Have some champagne!

LOMOV. He's better!

NATALYA STEPANOVNA. Worse! worse! worse!

CHUBUKOV. [Trying to shout her down] Champagne! Champagne!

Curtain.

THE WEDDING

CHARACTERS

EVDOKIM ZAHAROVITCH ZHIGALOV, *a retired Civil Servant.*
NASTASYA TIMOFEYEVNA, *his wife*
DASHENKA, *their daughter*
EPAMINOND MAXIMOVITCH APLOMBOV, *Dashenka's bridegroom*
FYODOR YAKOVLEVITCH REVUNOV-KARAULOV, *a retired captain*
ANDREY ANDREYEVITCH NUNIN, *an insurance agent*
ANNA MARTINOVNA ZMEYUKINA, *a midwife, aged 30, in a brilliantly red dress*
IVAN MIHAILOVITCH YATS, *a telegraphist*
HARLAMPI SPIRIDONOVITCH DIMBA, *a Greek confectioner*
DMITRI STEPANOVITCH MOZGOVOY, *a sailor of the Imperial Navy (Volunteer Fleet)*
GROOMSMEN, GENTLEMEN, WAITERS, ETC.

The scene is laid in one of the rooms of Andronov's Restaurant

[A brilliantly illuminated room. A large table, laid for supper. Waiters in dress-jackets are fussing round the table. An orchestra behind the scene is playing the music of the last figure of a quadrille.]

[ANNA MARTINOVNA ZMEYUKINA, YATS, and a GROOMSMAN cross the stage.]

ZMEYUKINA. No, no, no!

YATS. [Following her] Have pity on us! Have pity!

ZMEYUKINA. No, no, no!

GROOMSMAN. [Chasing them] You can't go on like this! Where are you off to? What about the *grand ronde? Grand ronde, s'il vous plait*! [They all go off.]

[Enter NASTASYA TIMOFEYEVNA and APLOMBOV.]

NASTASYA TIMOFEYEVNA. You had much better be dancing than upsetting me with your speeches.

APLOMBOV. I'm not a Spinosa or anybody of that sort, to go making figures-of-eight with my legs. I am a serious man, and I have a character, and I see no amusement in empty pleasures. But it isn't just a matter of dances. You must excuse me, maman, but there is a good deal in your behaviour which I am unable to understand. For instance, in addition to objects of domestic importance, you promised also to give me, with your daughter, two lottery tickets. Where are they?

NASTASYA TIMOFEYEVNA. My head's aching a little... I expect it's on account of the weather.... If only it thawed!

APLOMBOV. You won't get out of it like that. I only found out to-day that those tickets are in pawn. You must excuse me, *maman*, but it's only swindlers who behave like that. I'm not doing this out of egoisticism [Note: So in the original]—I don't want your tickets—but on principle; and I don't allow myself to be done by anybody. I have made your daughter happy, and if you don't give me the tickets to-day I'll make short work of her. I'm an honourable man!

NASTASYA TIMOFEYEVNA. [Looks round the table and counts up the covers] One, two, three, four, five...

A WAITER. The cook asks if you would like the ices served with rum, madeira, or by themselves?

APLOMBOV. With rum. And tell the manager that there's not enough wine. Tell him to prepare some more Haut Sauterne. [To NASTASYA TIMOFEYEVNA] You also promised and agreed that a general was to be here to supper. And where is he?

NASTASYA TIMOFEYEVNA. That isn't my fault, my dear.

APLOMBOV. Whose fault, then?

NASTASYA TIMOFEYEVNA. It's Andrey Andreyevitch's fault.... Yesterday he came to see us and promised to bring a perfectly real general. [Sighs] I suppose he couldn't find one anywhere, or he'd have brought him.... You think we don't mind? We'd begrudge our child nothing. A general, of course...

APLOMBOV. But there's more.... Everybody, including yourself, *maman*, is aware of the fact that Yats, that telegraphist, was after Dashenka before I proposed to her. Why did you invite him? Surely you knew it would be unpleasant for me?

NASTASYA TIMOFEYEVNA. Oh, how can you? Epaminond Maximovitch was married himself only the other day, and you've already tired me and Dashenka out with your talk. What will you be like in a year's time? You are horrid, really horrid.

APLOMBOV. Then you don't like to hear the truth? Aha! Oh, oh! Then behave honourably. I only want you to do one thing, be honourable!

[Couples dancing the *grand ronde* come in at one door and out at the other end. The first couple are DASHENKA with one of the GROOMSMEN. The last are YATS and ZMEYUKINA. These two remain behind. ZHIGALOV and DIMBA enter and go up to the table.]

GROOMSMAN. [Shouting] Promenade! Messieurs, promenade! [Behind] Promenade!

[The dancers have all left the scene.]

YATS. [To ZMEYUKINA] Have pity! Have pity, adorable Anna Martinovna.

ZMEYUKINA. Oh, what a man!... I've already told you that I've no voice to-day.

YATS. I implore you to sing! Just one note! Have pity! Just one note!

ZMEYUKINA. I'm tired of you.... [Sits and fans herself.]

YATS. No, you're simply heartless! To be so cruel—if I may express myself—and to have such a beautiful, beautiful voice! With such a voice, if you will forgive my using the word, you shouldn't be a midwife, but sing at concerts, at public gatherings! For example, how divinely you do that *fioritura*... that... [Sings] "I loved you; love was vain then...." Exquisite!

ZMEYUKINA. [Sings] "I loved you, and may love again." Is that it?

YATS. That's it! Beautiful!

ZMEYUKINA. No, I've no voice to-day.... There, wave this fan for me... it's hot! [To APLOMBOV] Epaminond Maximovitch, why are you so melancholy? A bridegroom shouldn't be! Aren't you ashamed of yourself, you wretch? Well, what are you so thoughtful about?

APLOMBOV. Marriage is a serious step! Everything must be considered from all sides, thoroughly.

ZMEYUKINA. What beastly sceptics you all are! I feel quite suffocated with you all around.... Give me atmosphere! Do you hear? Give me atmosphere! [Sings a few notes.]

YATS. Beautiful! Beautiful!

ZMEYUKINA. Fan me, fan me, or I feel I shall have a heart attack in a minute. Tell me, please, why do I feel so suffocated?

YATS. It's because you're sweating....

ZMEYUKINA. Foo, how vulgar you are! Don't dare to use such words!

YATS. Beg pardon! Of course, you're used, if I may say so, to aristocratic society and....

ZMEYUKINA. Oh, leave me alone! Give me poetry, delight! Fan me, fan me!

ZHIGALOV. [To DIMBA] Let's have another, what? [Pours out] One can always drink. So long only, Harlampi Spiridonovitch, as one doesn't forget one's business. Drink and be merry.... And if you can drink at somebody else's expense, then why not drink? You can drink.... Your health! [They drink] And do you have tigers in Greece?

DIMBA. Yes.

ZHIGALOV. And lions?

DIMBA. And lions too. In Russia zere's nussing, and in Greece zere's everysing—my fazer and uncle and brozeres—and here zere's nussing.

ZHIGALOV. H'm.... And are there whales in Greece?

DIMBA. Yes, everysing.

NASTASYA TIMOFEYEVNA. [To her husband] What are they all eating and drinking like that for? It's time for everybody to sit down to supper. Don't keep on shoving your fork into the lobsters.... They're for the general. He may come yet....

ZHIGALOV. And are there lobsters in Greece?

DIMBA. Yes... zere is everysing.

ZHIGALOV. Hm.... And Civil Servants.

ZMEYUKINA. I can imagine what the atmosphere is like in Greece!

ZHIGALOV. There must be a lot of swindling. The Greeks are just like the Armenians or gipsies. They sell you a sponge or a goldfish and all the time they are looking out for a chance of getting something extra out of you. Let's have another, what?

NASTASYA TIMOFEYEVNA. What do you want to go on having another for? It's time everybody sat down to supper. It's past eleven.

ZHIGALOV. If it's time, then it's time. Ladies and gentlemen, please! [Shouts] Supper! Young people!

NASTASYA TIMOFEYEVNA. Dear visitors, please be seated!

ZMEYUKINA. [Sitting down at the table] Give me poetry.

> "And he, the rebel, seeks the storm,
> As if the storm can give him peace."

Give me the storm!

YATS. [Aside] Wonderful woman! I'm in love! Up to my ears!

[Enter DASHENKA, MOZGOVOY, GROOMSMEN, various ladies and gentlemen, etc. They all noisily seat themselves at the table. There is a minute's pause, while the band plays a march.]

MOZGOVOY. [Rising] Ladies and gentlemen! I must tell you this.... We are going to have a great many toasts and speeches. Don't let's wait, but begin at once. Ladies and gentlemen, the newly married!

[The band plays a flourish. Cheers. Glasses are touched. APLOMBOV and DASHENKA kiss each other.]

YATS. Beautiful! Beautiful! I must say, ladies and gentlemen, giving honour where it is due, that this room and the accommodation generally are splendid! Excellent, wonderful! Only you know, there's one thing we haven't got—electric light, if I may say so! Into every country electric light has already been introduced, only Russia lags behind.

ZHIGALOV. [Meditatively] Electricity... h'm.... In my opinion electric lighting is just a swindle.... They put a live coal in and think you don't see them! No, if you want a light, then you don't take a coal, but something real, something special, that you can get hold of! You must have a fire, you understand, which is natural, not just an invention!

YATS. If you'd ever seen an electric battery, and how it's made up, you'd think differently.

ZHIGALOV. Don't want to see one. It's a swindle, a fraud on the public.... They want to squeeze our last breath out of us.... We know then, these... And, young man, instead of defending a swindle, you would be much better occupied if you had another yourself and poured out some for other people—yes!

APLOMBOV. I entirely agree with you, papa. Why start a learned discussion? I myself have no objection to talking about every possible scientific discovery, but this isn't the time for all that! [To DASHENKA] What do you think, *ma chère*?

DASHENKA. They want to show how educated they are, and so they always talk about things we can't understand.

NASTASYA TIMOFEYEVNA. Thank God, we've lived our time without being educated, and here we are marrying off our third daughter to an honest man. And if you think we're uneducated, then what do you want to come here for? Go to your educated friends!

YATS. I, Nastasya Timofeyevna, have always held your family in respect, and if I did start talking about electric lighting it doesn't mean that I'm proud. I'll drink, to show you. I have always sincerely wished Daria Evdokimovna a good husband. In these days, Nastasya Timofeyevna, it is difficult to find a good husband. Nowadays everybody is on the look-out for a marriage where there is profit, money....

APLOMBOV. That's a hint!

YATS. [His courage failing] I wasn't hinting at anything.... Present company is always excepted.... I was only in general.... Please! Everybody knows that you're marrying for love... the dowry is quite trifling.

NASTASYA TIMOFEYEVNA. No, it isn't trifling! You be careful what you say. Besides a thousand roubles of good money, we're giving three dresses, the bed, and all the furniture. You won't find another dowry like that in a hurry!

YATS. I didn't mean... The furniture's splendid, of course, and... and the dresses, but I never hinted at what they are getting offended at.

NASTASYA TIMOFEYEVNA. Don't you go making hints. We respect you on account of your parents, and we've invited you to the wedding, and here you go talking. If you knew that Epaminond Maximovitch was marrying for profit, why didn't you say so before? [Tearfully] I brought her up, I fed her, I nursed her.... I cared for her more than if she was an emerald jewel, my little girl....

APLOMBOV. And you go and believe him? Thank you so much! I'm very grateful to you! [To YATS] And as for you, Mr. Yats, although you are acquainted with me, I shan't allow you to behave like this in another's house. Please get out of this!

YATS. What do you mean?

APLOMBOV. I want you to be as straightforward as I am! In short, please get out! [Band plays a flourish]

THE GENTLEMEN. Leave him alone! Sit down! Is it worth it! Let him be! Stop it now!

YATS. I never... I... I don't understand.... Please, I'll go.... Only you first give me the five roubles which you borrowed from me last year on the strength of a *piqué* waistcoat, if I may say so. Then I'll just have another drink and... go, only give me the money first.

VARIOUS GENTLEMEN. Sit down! That's enough! Is it worth it, just for such trifles?

A GROOMSMAN. [Shouts] The health of the bride's parents, Evdokim Zaharitch and Nastasya Timofeyevna! [Band plays a flourish. Cheers.]

ZHIGALOV. [Bows in all directions, in great emotion] I thank you! Dear guests! I am very grateful to you for not having forgotten and for having conferred this honour upon us without being standoffish And you must not think that I'm a rascal, or that I'm trying to swindle anybody. I'm speaking from my heart—from the purity of my soul! I wouldn't deny anything to good people! We thank you very humbly! [Kisses.]

DASHENKA. [To her mother] Mama, why are you crying? I'm so happy!

APLOMBOV. *Maman* is disturbed at your coming separation. But I should advise her rather to remember the last talk we had.

YATS. Don't cry, Nastasya Timofeyevna! Just think what are human tears, anyway? Just petty psychiatry, and nothing more!

ZMEYUKINA. And are there any red-haired men in Greece?

DIMBA. Yes, everysing is zere.

ZHIGALOV. But you don't have our kinds of mushroom.

DIMBA. Yes, we've got zem and everysing.

MOZGOVOY. Harlampi Spiridonovitch, it's your turn to speak! Ladies and gentlemen, a speech!

ALL. [To DIMBA] Speech! speech! Your turn!

DIMBA. Why? I don't understand.... What is it!

ZMEYUKINA. No, no! You can't refuse! It's you turn! Get up!

DIMBA. [Gets up, confused] I can't say what... Zere's Russia and zere's Greece. Zere's people in Russia and people in Greece.... And zere's people swimming the sea in karavs, which mean sips, and people on the land in railway trains. I understand. We are Greeks and you are Russians, and I want nussing.... I can tell you... zere's Russia and zere's Greece...

[Enter NUNIN.]

NUNIN. Wait, ladies and gentlemen, don't eat now! Wait! Just one minute, Nastasya Timofeyevna! Just come here, if you don't mind! [Takes NASTASYA TIMOFEYEVNA aside, puffing] Listen... The General's coming... I found one at last.... I'm simply worn out.... A real General, a solid one—old, you know, aged perhaps eighty, or even ninety.

NASTASYA TIMOFEYEVNA. When is he coming?

NUNIN. This minute. You'll be grateful to me all your life. [Note: A few lines have been omitted: they refer to the "General's" rank and its civil equivalent in words for which the English language has no corresponding terms. The "General" is an ex-naval officer, a second-class captain.]

NASTASYA TIMOFEYEVNA. You're not deceiving me, Andrey darling?

NUNIN. Well, now, am I a swindler? You needn't worry!

NASTASYA TIMOFEYEVNA. [Sighs] One doesn't like to spend money for nothing, Andrey darling!

NUNIN. Don't you worry! He's not a general, he's a dream! [Raises his voice] I said to him: "You've quite forgotten us, your Excellency! It isn't kind of your Excellency to forget your old friends! Nastasya Timofeyevna," I said to him, "she's very annoyed with you about it!" [Goes and sits at the table] And he says to me: "But, my friend, how can I go when I don't know the bridegroom?" "Oh, nonsense, your excellency, why stand on ceremony? The bridegroom," I said to him, "he's a fine fellow, very free and easy. He's a valuer," I said, "at the Law courts, and don't you think, your excellency, that he's some rascal, some knave of hearts. Nowadays," I said to him, "even decent women are employed at the Law courts." He slapped me on the shoulder, we smoked a Havana cigar each, and now he's coming.... Wait a little, ladies and gentlemen, don't eat....

APLOMBOV. When's he coming?

NUNIN. This minute. When I left him he was already putting on his goloshes. Wait a little, ladies and gentlemen, don't eat yet.

APLOMBOV. The band should be told to play a march.

NUNIN. [Shouts] Musicians! A march! [The band plays a march for a minute.]

A WAITER. Mr. Revunov-Karaulov!

[ZHIGALOV, NASTASYA TIMOFEYEVNA, and NUNIN run to meet him. Enter REVUNOV-KARAULOV.]

NASTASYA TIMOFEYEVNA. [Bowing] Please come in, your excellency! So glad you've come!

REVUNOV. Awfully!

ZHIGALOV. We, your excellency, aren't celebrities, we aren't important, but quite ordinary, but don't think on that account that there's any fraud. We put good people into the best place, we begrudge nothing. Please!

REVUNOV. Awfully glad!

NUNIN. Let me introduce to you, your excellency, the bridegroom, Epaminond Maximovitch Aplombov, with his newly born... I mean his newly married wife! Ivan Mihailovitch Yats, employed on the telegraph! A foreigner of Greek nationality, a confectioner by trade, Harlampi Spiridonovitch Dimba! Osip Lukitch Babelmandebsky! And so on, and so on.... The rest are just trash. Sit down, your excellency!

REVUNOV. Awfully! Excuse me, ladies and gentlemen, I just want to say two words to Andrey. [Takes NUNIN aside] I say, old man, I'm a little put out.... Why do you call me your excellency? I'm not a general! I don't rank as the equivalent of a colonel, even.

NUNIN. [Whispers] I know, only, Fyodor Yakovlevitch, be a good man and let us call you your excellency! The family here, you see, is patriarchal; it respects the aged, it likes rank.

REVUNOV. Oh, if it's like that, very well.... [Goes to the table] Awfully!

NASTASYA TIMOFEYEVNA. Sit down, your excellency! Be so good as to have some of this, your excellency! Only forgive us for not being used to etiquette; we're plain people!

REVUNOV. [Not hearing] What? Hm... yes. [Pause] Yes.... In the old days everybody used to live simply and was happy. In spite of my rank, I am a man who lives plainly. To-day Andrey comes to me and asks me to come here to the wedding. "How shall I go," I said, "when I don't know them? It's not good manners!" But he says: "They are good, simple, patriarchal people, glad to see anybody." Well, if that's the case... why not? Very glad to come. It's very dull for me at home by myself, and if my presence at a wedding can make anybody happy, then I'm delighted to be here....

ZHIGALOV. Then that's sincere, is it, your excellency? I respect that! I'm a plain man myself, without any deception, and I respect others who are like that. Eat, your excellency!

APLOMBOV. Is it long since you retired, your excellency?

REVUNOV. Eh? Yes, yes.... Quite true.... Yes. But, excuse me, what is this? The fish is sour... and the bread is sour. I can't eat this! [APLOMBOV and DASHENKA kiss each other] He, he, he... Your health! [Pause] Yes.... In the old days everything was simple and everybody was glad.... I love simplicity.... I'm an old man. I retired in 1865. I'm 72. Yes, of course, in my younger days it was different, but—[Sees MOZGOVOY] You there... a sailor, are you?

MOZGOVOY. Yes, just so.

REVUNOV. Aha, so... yes. The navy means hard work. There's a lot to think about and get a headache over. Every insignificant word has, so to speak, its special meaning! For instance, "Hoist her top-sheets and mainsail!" What's it mean? A sailor can tell! He, he! —With almost mathematical precision!

NUNIN. The health of his excellency Fyodor Yakovlevitch Revunov-Karaulov! [Band plays a flourish. Cheers.]

YATS. You, your excellency, have just expressed yourself on the subject of the hard work involved in a naval career. But is telegraphy any easier? Nowadays, your excellency, nobody is appointed to the telegraphs if he cannot read and write French and German. But the transmission of telegrams is the most difficult thing of all. Awfully difficult! Just listen.

[Taps with his fork on the table, like a telegraphic transmitter.]

REVUNOV. What does that mean?

YATS. It means, "I honour you, your excellency, for your virtues." You think it's easy? Listen now. [Taps.]

REVUNOV. Louder; I can't hear....

YATS. That means, "Madam, how happy I am to hold you in my embraces!"

REVUNOV. What madam are you talking about? Yes.... [To MOZGOVOY] Yes, if there's a head-wind you must... let's see... you must hoist your foretop halyards and topsail halyards! The order is: "On the cross-trees to the foretop halyards and topsail halyards" and at the same time, as the sails get loose, you take hold underneath of the foresail and fore-topsail halyards, stays and braces.

A GROOMSMAN. [Rising] Ladies and gentlemen...

REVUNOV. [Cutting him short] Yes... there are a great many orders to give. "Furl the fore-topsail and the foretop-gallant sail!!" Well, what does that mean? It's very simple! It means that if the top and top-gallant sails are lifting the halyards, they must level the foretop and foretop-gallant halyards on the hoist and at the same time the top-gallants braces, as needed, are loosened according to the direction of the wind...

NUNIN. [To REVUNOV] Fyodor Yakovlevitch, Mme. Zhigalov asks you to talk about something else. It's very dull for the guests, who can't understand....

REVUNOV. What? Who's dull? [To MOZGOVOY] Young man! Now suppose the ship is lying by the wind, on the starboard tack, under full sail, and you've got to bring her before the wind. What's the order? Well, first you whistle up above! He, he!

NUNIN. Fyodor Yakovlevitch, that's enough. Eat something.

REVUNOV. As soon as the men are on deck you give the order, "To your places!" What a life! You give orders, and at the same time you've got to keep your eyes on the sailors, who run about like flashes of lightning and get the sails and braces right. And at last you can't restrain yourself, and you shout, "Good children!" [He chokes and coughs.]

A GROOMSMAN. [Making haste to use the ensuing pause to advantage] On this occasion, so to speak, on the day on which we have met together to honour our dear...

REVUNOV. [Interrupting] Yes, you've got to remember all that! For instance, "Hoist the topsail halyards. Lower the topsail gallants!"

THE GROOMSMAN. [Annoyed] Why does he keep on interrupting? We shan't get through a single speech like that!

NASTASYA TIMOFEYEVNA. We are dull people, your excellency, and don't understand a word of all that, but if you were to tell us something appropriate...

REVUNOV. [Not hearing] I've already had supper, thank you. Did you say there was goose? Thanks... yes. I've remembered the old days.... It's pleasant, young man! You sail on the sea, you have no worries, and [In an excited tone of voice] do you remember the joy of tacking? Is there a sailor who doesn't glow at the memory of that manoeuvre? As soon as the word is given and the whistle blown and the crew begins to go up—it's as if an electric spark has run through them all. From the captain to the cabin-boy, everybody's excited.

ZMEYUKINA. How dull! How dull! [General murmur.]

REVUNOV. [Who has not heard it properly] Thank you, I've had supper. [With enthusiasm] Everybody's ready, and looks to the senior officer. He gives the command: "Stand by, gallants and topsail braces on the starboard side, main and counter-braces to port!" Everything's done in a twinkling. Top-sheets and jib-sheets are pulled... taken to starboard. [Stands up] The ship takes the wind and at last the sails fill out. The senior officer orders, "To the braces," and himself keeps his eye on the mainsail, and when at last this sail is filling out and the ship begins to turn, he yells at the top of his voice, "Let go the braces! Loose the main halyards!" Everything flies about, there's a general confusion for a moment—and everything is done without an error. The ship has been tacked!

NASTASYA TIMOFEYEVNA. [Exploding] General, your manners.... You ought to be ashamed of yourself, at your age!

REVUNOV. Did you say sausage? No, I haven't had any... thank you.

NASTASYA TIMOFEYEVNA. [Loudly] I say you ought to be ashamed of yourself at your age! General, your manners are awful!

NUNIN. [Confused] Ladies and gentlemen, is it worth it? Really...

REVUNOV. In the first place, I'm not a general, but a second-class naval captain, which, according to the table of precedence, corresponds to a lieutenant-colonel.

NASTASYA TIMOFEYEVNA. If you're not a general, then what did you go and take our money for? We never paid you money to behave like that!

REVUNOV. [Upset] What money?

NASTASYA TIMOFEYEVNA. You know what money. You know that you got 25 roubles from Andrey Andreyevitch.... [To NUNIN] And you look out, Andrey! I never asked you to hire a man like that!

NUNIN. There now... let it drop. Is it worth it?

REVUNOV. Paid... hired.... What is it?

APLOMBOV. Just let me ask you this. Did you receive 25 roubles from Andrey Andreyevitch?

REVUNOV. What 25 roubles? [Suddenly realizing] That's what it is! Now I understand it all.... How mean! How mean!

APLOMBOV. Did you take the money?

REVUNOV. I haven't taken any money! Get away from me! [Leaves the table] How mean! How low! To insult an old man, a sailor, an officer who has served long and faithfully! If you were decent people I could call somebody out, but what can I do now? [Absently] Where's the door? Which way do I go? Waiter, show me the way out! Waiter! [Going] How mean! How low! [Exit.]

NASTASYA TIMOFEYEVNA. Andrey, where are those 25 roubles?

NUNIN. Is it worth while bothering about such trifles? What does it matter! Everybody's happy here, and here you go.... [Shouts] The health of the bride and bridegroom! A march! A march! [The band plays a march] The health of the bride and bridegroom!

ZMEYUKINA. I'm suffocating! Give me atmosphere! I'm suffocating with you all round me!

YATS. [In a transport of delight] My beauty! My beauty! [Uproar.]

A GROOMSMAN. [Trying to shout everybody else down] Ladies and gentlemen! On this occasion, if I may say so...

Curtain.

THE BEAR

CHARACTERS

ELENA IVANOVNA POPOVA, a landowning little widow, with dimples on her cheeks
GRIGORY STEPANOVITCH SMIRNOV, a middle-aged landowner
LUKA, Popova's aged footman

[A drawing-room in POPOVA'S house.]

[POPOVA is in deep mourning and has her eyes fixed on a photograph. LUKA is haranguing her.]

LUKA. It isn't right, madam.... You're just destroying yourself. The maid and the cook have gone off fruit picking, every living being is rejoicing, even the cat understands how to enjoy herself and walks about in the yard, catching midges; only you sit in this room all day, as if this was a convent, and don't take any pleasure. Yes, really! I reckon it's a whole year that you haven't left the house!

POPOVA. I shall never go out.... Why should I? My life is already at an end. He is in his grave, and I have buried myself between four walls.... We are both dead.

LUKA. Well, there you are! Nicolai Mihailovitch is dead, well, it's the will of God, and may his soul rest in peace.... You've mourned him—and quite right. But you can't go on weeping and wearing mourning for ever. My old woman died too, when her time came. Well? I grieved over her, I wept for a month, and that's enough for her, but if I've got to weep for a whole age, well, the old woman isn't worth it. [Sighs] You've forgotten all your neighbours. You don't go anywhere, and you see nobody. We live, so to speak, like spiders, and never see the light. The mice have eaten my livery. It isn't as if there were no good people around, for the district's full of them. There's a regiment quartered at Riblov, and the officers are such beauties—you can never gaze your fill at them. And, every Friday, there's a ball at the camp, and every day the soldier's band plays.... Eh, my lady! You're young and beautiful, with roses in your cheek—if you only took a little pleasure. Beauty won't last long, you know. In ten years' time you'll want to be a pea-hen yourself among the officers, but they won't look at you, it will be too late.

POPOVA. [With determination] I must ask you never to talk to me about it! You know that when Nicolai Mihailovitch died, life lost all its meaning for me. I vowed never to the end of my days to cease to wear mourning, or to see the light.... You hear? Let his ghost see how well I love him.... Yes, I know it's no secret to you that he was often unfair to me, cruel, and... and even unfaithful, but I shall be true till death, and show him how I can love. There, beyond the grave, he will see me as I was before his death....

LUKA. Instead of talking like that you ought to go and have a walk in the garden, or else order Toby or Giant to be harnessed, and then drive out to see some of the neighbours.

POPOVA. Oh! [Weeps.]

LUKA. Madam! Dear madam! What is it? Bless you!

POPOVA. He was so fond of Toby! He always used to ride on him to the Korchagins and Vlasovs. How well he could ride! What grace there was in his figure when he pulled at the reins with all his strength! Do you remember? Toby, Toby! Tell them to give him an extra feed of oats.

LUKA. Yes, madam. [A bell rings noisily.]

POPOVA. [Shaking] Who's that? Tell them that I receive nobody.

LUKA. Yes, madam. [Exit.]

POPOVA. [Looks at the photograph] You will see, Nicolas, how I can love and forgive.... My love will die out with me, only when this poor heart will cease to beat. [Laughs through her tears] And aren't you ashamed? I am a good and virtuous little wife. I've locked myself in, and will be true to you till the grave, and you... aren't you ashamed, you bad child? You deceived me, had rows with me, left me alone for weeks on end....

[LUKA enters in consternation.]

LUKA. Madam, somebody is asking for you. He wants to see you....

POPOVA. But didn't you tell him that since the death of my husband I've stopped receiving?

LUKA. I did, but he wouldn't even listen; says that it's a very pressing affair.

POPOVA. I do not re-ceive!

LUKA. I told him so, but the... the devil... curses and pushes himself right in.... He's in the dining-room now.

POPOVA. [Annoyed] Very well, ask him in.... What manners! [Exit LUKA] How these people annoy me! What does he want of me? Why should he disturb my peace? [Sighs] No, I see that I shall have to go into a convent after all. [Thoughtfully] Yes, into a convent.... [Enter LUKA with SMIRNOV.]

SMIRNOV. [To LUKA] You fool, you're too fond of talking.... Ass! [Sees POPOVA and speaks with respect] Madam, I have the honour to present myself, I am Grigory Stepanovitch Smirnov, landowner and retired lieutenant of artillery! I am compelled to disturb you on a very pressing affair.

POPOVA. [Not giving him her hand] What do you want?

SMIRNOV. Your late husband, with whom I had the honour of being acquainted, died in my debt for one thousand two hundred roubles, on two bills of exchange. As I've got to pay the interest on a mortgage to-morrow, I've come to ask you, madam, to pay me the money to-day.

POPOVA. One thousand two hundred.... And what was my husband in debt to you for?

SMIRNOV. He used to buy oats from me.

POPOVA. [Sighing, to LUKA] So don't you forget, Luka, to give Toby an extra feed of oats. [Exit LUKA] If Nicolai Mihailovitch died in debt to you, then I shall certainly pay you, but you must excuse me to-day, as I haven't any spare cash. The day after to-morrow my steward will be back from town, and I'll give him instructions to settle your account, but at the moment I cannot do as you wish.... Moreover, it's exactly seven months to-day since the death of my husband, and I'm in a state of mind which absolutely prevents me from giving money matters my attention.

SMIRNOV. And I'm in a state of mind which, if I don't pay the interest due to-morrow, will force me to make a graceful exit from this life feet first. They'll take my estate!

POPOVA. You'll have your money the day after to-morrow.

SMIRNOV. I don't want the money the day after tomorrow, I want it to-day.

POPOVA. You must excuse me, I can't pay you.

SMIRNOV. And I can't wait till after to-morrow.

POPOVA. Well, what can I do, if I haven't the money now!

SMIRNOV. You mean to say, you can't pay me?

POPOVA. I can't.

SMIRNOV. Hm! Is that the last word you've got to say?

POPOVA. Yes, the last word.

SMIRNOV. The last word? Absolutely your last?

POPOVA. Absolutely.

SMIRNOV. Thank you so much. I'll make a note of it. [Shrugs his shoulders] And then people want me to keep calm! I meet a man on the road, and he asks me "Why are you always so angry, Grigory Stepanovitch?" But how on earth am I not to get angry? I want the money desperately. I rode out yesterday, early in the morning, and called on all my debtors, and not a single one of them paid up! I was just about dead-beat after it all, slept, goodness knows where, in some inn, kept by a Jew, with a vodka-barrel by my head. At last I get here, seventy versts from home, and hope to get something, and I am received by you with a "state of mind"! How shouldn't I get angry.

POPOVA. I thought I distinctly said my steward will pay you when he returns from town.

SMIRNOV. I didn't come to your steward, but to you! What the devil, excuse my saying so, have I to do with your steward!

POPOVA. Excuse me, sir, I am not accustomed to listen to such expressions or to such a tone of voice. I want to hear no more. [Makes a rapid exit.]

SMIRNOV. Well, there! "A state of mind."... "Husband died seven months ago!" Must I pay the interest, or mustn't I? I ask you: Must I pay, or must I not? Suppose your husband is dead, and you've got a state of mind, and nonsense of that sort.... And your steward's gone away somewhere, devil take him, what do you want me to do? Do you think I can fly away from my creditors in a balloon, or what? Or do you expect me to go and run my head into a brick wall? I go to Grusdev and he isn't at home, Yaroshevitch has hidden himself, I had a violent row with Kuritsin and nearly threw him out of the window, Mazugo has something the matter with his bowels, and this woman has "a state of mind." Not one of the swine wants to pay me! Just because I'm too gentle with them, because I'm a rag, just weak wax in their hands! I'm much too gentle with them! Well, just you wait! You'll find out what I'm like! I shan't let you play about with me, confound it! I shall jolly well stay here until she pays! Brr!... How angry I am to-day, how angry I am! All my inside is quivering with anger, and I can't even breathe.... Foo, my word, I even feel sick! [Yells] Waiter!

[Enter LUKA.]

LUKA. What is it?

SMIRNOV. Get me some kvass or water! [Exit LUKA] What a way to reason! A man is in desperate need of his money, and she won't pay it because, you see, she is not disposed to attend to money matters!... That's real silly feminine logic. That's why I never did like, and don't like now, to have to talk to women. I'd rather sit on a barrel of gunpowder than talk to a woman. Brr!... I feel quite chilly—and it's all on account of that little bit of fluff! I can't even see one of these poetic creatures from a distance without breaking out into a cold sweat out of sheer anger. I can't look at them. [Enter LUKA with water.]

LUKA. Madam is ill and will see nobody.

SMIRNOV. Get out! [Exit LUKA] Ill and will see nobody! No, it's all right, you don't see me.... I'm going to stay and will sit here till you give me the money. You can be ill for a week, if you like, and I'll stay here for a week.... If you're ill for a year—I'll stay for a year. I'm going to get my own, my dear! You don't get at me with your widow's weeds and your dimpled cheeks! I know those dimples! [Shouts through the window] Simeon, take them out! We aren't going away at once! I'm staying here! Tell them in the stable to give the horses some oats! You fool, you've let the near horse's leg get tied up in the reins again! [Teasingly] "Never mind...." I'll give it you. "Never mind." [Goes away from the window] Oh, it's bad.... The heat's frightful, nobody pays up. I slept badly, and on top of everything else here's a bit of fluff in mourning with "a state of mind."... My head's aching.... Shall I have some vodka, what? Yes, I think I will. [Yells] Waiter!

[Enter LUKA.]

LUKA. What is it?

SMIRNOV. A glass of vodka! [Exit LUKA] Ouf! [Sits and inspects himself] I must say I look well! Dust all over, boots dirty, unwashed, unkempt, straw on my waistcoat.... The dear lady may well have taken me for a brigand. [Yawns] It's rather impolite to come into a drawing-room in this state, but it can't be helped.... I am not here as a visitor, but as a creditor, and there's no dress specially prescribed for creditors....

[Enter LUKA with the vodka.]

LUKA. You allow yourself to go very far, sir....

SMIRNOV [Angrily] What?

LUKA. I... er... nothing... I really...

SMIRNOV. Whom are you talking to? Shut up!

LUKA. [Aside] The devil's come to stay.... Bad luck that brought him.... [Exit.]

SMIRNOV. Oh, how angry I am! So angry that I think I could grind the whole world to dust.... I even feel sick.... [Yells] Waiter!

[Enter POPOVA.]

POPOVA. [Her eyes downcast] Sir, in my solitude I have grown unaccustomed to the masculine voice, and I can't stand shouting. I must ask you not to disturb my peace.

SMIRNOV. Pay me the money, and I'll go.

POPOVA. I told you perfectly plainly; I haven't any money to spare; wait until the day after to-morrow.

SMIRNOV. And I told you perfectly plainly I don't want the money the day after to-morrow, but to-day. If you don't pay me to-day, I'll have to hang myself to-morrow.

POPOVA. But what can I do if I haven't got the money? You're so strange!

SMIRNOV. Then you won't pay me now? Eh?

POPOVA. I can't.

SMIRNOV. In that case I stay here and shall wait until I get it. [Sits down] You're going to pay me the day after to-morrow? Very well! I'll stay here until the day after to-morrow. I'll sit here all the time.... [Jumps up] I ask you: Have I got to pay the interest to-morrow, or haven't I? Or do you think I'm doing this for a joke?

POPOVA. Please don't shout! This isn't a stable!

SMIRNOV. I wasn't asking you about a stable, but whether I'd got my interest to pay to-morrow or not?

POPOVA. You don't know how to behave before women!

SMIRNOV. No, I do know how to behave before women!

POPOVA. No, you don't! You're a rude, ill-bred man! Decent people don't talk to a woman like that!

SMIRNOV. What a business! How do you want me to talk to you? In French, or what? [Loses his temper and lisps] *Madame, je vous prie*.... How happy I am that you don't pay me.... Ah, pardon. I have disturbed you! Such lovely weather to-day! And how well you look in mourning! [Bows.]

POPOVA. That's silly and rude.

SMIRNOV. [Teasing her] Silly and rude! I don't know how to behave before women! Madam, in my time I've seen more women than you've seen sparrows! Three times I've fought duels on account of women. I've refused twelve women, and nine have refused me! Yes! There was a time when I played the fool, scented myself, used honeyed words, wore jewellery, made beautiful bows. I used to love, to suffer, to sigh at the moon, to get sour, to thaw, to freeze.... I used to love passionately, madly, every blessed way, devil take me; I used to chatter like a magpie about emancipation, and wasted half my wealth on tender feelings, but now—you must excuse me! You won't get round me like that now! I've had enough! Black eyes, passionate eyes, ruby lips, dimpled cheeks, the moon, whispers, timid breathing—I wouldn't give a brass farthing for the lot, madam! Present company always excepted, all women, great or little, are insincere, crooked, backbiters, envious, liars to the marrow of their bones, vain, trivial, merciless, unreasonable, and, as far as this is concerned [taps his forehead] excuse my outspokenness, a sparrow can give ten points to any philosopher in petticoats you like to name! You look at one of these poetic creatures: all muslin, an ethereal demi-goddess, you have a million transports of joy, and you look into her soul—and see a common crocodile! [He grips the back of a chair; the chair creaks and breaks] But the most disgusting thing of all is that this crocodile for some reason or other imagines that its chef d'oeuvre, its privilege and monopoly, is its tender feelings. Why, confound it, hang me on that nail feet upwards, if you like, but have you met a woman who can love anybody except a lapdog? When she's in love, can she do anything but snivel and slobber? While a man is suffering and making sacrifices all her love expresses itself in her playing about with her scarf, and trying to hook him more firmly by the nose. You have the misfortune to be a woman, you know from yourself what is the nature of woman. Tell me truthfully, have you ever seen a woman who was sincere, faithful, and constant? You haven't! Only freaks and old women are faithful and constant! You'll meet a cat with a horn or a white woodcock sooner than a constant woman!

POPOVA. Then, according to you, who is faithful and constant in love? Is it the man?

SMIRNOV. Yes, the man!

POPOVA. The man! [Laughs bitterly] Men are faithful and constant in love! What an idea! [With heat] What right have you to talk like that? Men are faithful and constant! Since we are talking about it, I'll tell you that of all the men I knew and know, the best was my late husband.... I loved him passionately with all my being, as only a young and imaginative woman can love, I gave him my youth, my happiness, my life, my fortune, I breathed in him, I worshipped him as if I were a heathen, and... and what then? This best of men shamelessly deceived me at every step! After his death I found in his desk a whole drawerful of love-letters, and when he was alive—it's an awful thing to remember!—he used to leave me alone for weeks at a time, and make love to other women and betray me before my very eyes; he wasted my money, and made fun of my feelings.... And, in spite of all that, I loved him and was true to him. And not only that, but, now that he is dead, I am still true and constant to his memory. I have shut myself for ever within these four walls, and will wear these weeds to the very end....

SMIRNOV. [Laughs contemptuously] Weeds!... I don't understand what you take me for. As if I don't know why you wear that black domino and bury yourself between four walls! I should say I did! It's so mysterious, so poetic! When some junker [Note: So in the original.] or some tame poet goes past your windows he'll think: "There lives the mysterious Tamara who, for the love of her husband, buried herself between four walls." We know these games!

POPOVA. [Exploding] What? How dare you say all that to me?

SMIRNOV. You may have buried yourself alive, but you haven't forgotten to powder your face!

POPOVA. How dare you speak to me like that?

SMIRNOV. Please don't shout, I'm not your steward! You must allow me to call things by their real names. I'm not a woman, and I'm used to saying what I think straight out! Don't you shout, either!

POPOVA. I'm not shouting, it's you! Please leave me alone!

SMIRNOV. Pay me my money and I'll go.

POPOVA. I shan't give you any money!

SMIRNOV. Oh, no, you will.

POPOVA. I shan't give you a farthing, just to spite you. You leave me alone!

SMIRNOV. I have not the pleasure of being either your husband or your fiancé, so please don't make scenes. [Sits] I don't like it.

POPOVA. [Choking with rage] So you sit down?

SMIRNOV. I do.

POPOVA. I ask you to go away!

SMIRNOV. Give me my money.... [Aside] Oh, how angry I am! How angry I am!

POPOVA. I don't want to talk to impudent scoundrels! Get out of this! [Pause] Aren't you going? No?

SMIRNOV. No.

POPOVA. No?

SMIRNOV. No!

POPOVA. Very well then! [Rings, enter LUKA] Luka, show this gentleman out!

LUKA. [Approaches SMIRNOV] Would you mind going out, sir, as you're asked to! You needn't...

SMIRNOV. [Jumps up] Shut up! Who are you talking to? I'll chop you into pieces!

LUKA. [Clutches at his heart] Little fathers!... What people!... [Falls into a chair] Oh, I'm ill, I'm ill! I can't breathe!

POPOVA. Where's Dasha? Dasha! [Shouts] Dasha! Pelageya! Dasha! [Rings.]

LUKA. Oh! They've all gone out to pick fruit.... There's nobody at home! I'm ill! Water!

POPOVA. Get out of this, now.

SMIRNOV. Can't you be more polite?

POPOVA. [Clenches her fists and stamps her foot] You're a boor! A coarse bear! A Bourbon! A monster!

SMIRNOV. What? What did you say?

POPOVA. I said you are a bear, a monster!

SMIRNOV. [Approaching her] May I ask what right you have to insult me?

POPOVA. And suppose I am insulting you? Do you think I'm afraid of you?

SMIRNOV. And do you think that just because you're a poetic creature you can insult me with impunity? Eh? We'll fight it out!

LUKA. Little fathers!... What people!... Water!

SMIRNOV. Pistols!

POPOVA. Do you think I'm afraid of you just because you have large fists and a bull's throat? Eh? You Bourbon!

SMIRNOV. We'll fight it out! I'm not going to be insulted by anybody, and I don't care if you are a woman, one of the "softer sex," indeed!

POPOVA. [Trying to interrupt him] Bear! Bear! Bear!

SMIRNOV. It's about time we got rid of the prejudice that only men need pay for their insults. Devil take it, if you want equality of rights you can have it. We're going to fight it out!

POPOVA. With pistols? Very well!

SMIRNOV. This very minute.

POPOVA. This very minute! My husband had some pistols.... I'll bring them here. [Is going, but turns back] What pleasure it will give me to put a bullet into your thick head! Devil take you! [Exit.]

SMIRNOV. I'll bring her down like a chicken! I'm not a little boy or a sentimental puppy; I don't care about this "softer sex."

LUKA. Gracious little fathers!... [Kneels] Have pity on a poor old man, and go away from here! You've frightened her to death, and now you want to shoot her!

SMIRNOV. [Not hearing him] If she fights, well that's equality of rights, emancipation, and all that! Here the sexes are equal! I'll shoot her on principle! But what a woman! [Parodying her] "Devil take you! I'll put a bullet into your thick head." Eh? How she reddened, how her cheeks shone!... She accepted my challenge! My word, it's the first time in my life that I've seen....

LUKA. Go away, sir, and I'll always pray to God for you!

SMIRNOV. She is a woman! That's the sort I can understand! A real woman! Not a sour-faced jellybag, but fire, gunpowder, a rocket! I'm even sorry to have to kill her!

LUKA. [Weeps] Dear... dear sir, do go away!

SMIRNOV. I absolutely like her! Absolutely! Even though her cheeks are dimpled, I like her! I'm almost ready to let the debt go... and I'm not angry any longer.... Wonderful woman!

[Enter POPOVA with pistols.]

POPOVA. Here are the pistols.... But before we fight you must show me how to fire. I've never held a pistol in my hands before.

LUKA. Oh, Lord, have mercy and save her.... I'll go and find the coachman and the gardener.... Why has this infliction come on us.... [Exit.]

SMIRNOV. [Examining the pistols] You see, there are several sorts of pistols.... There are Mortimer pistols, specially made for duels, they fire a percussion-cap. These are Smith and Wesson revolvers, triple action, with extractors.... These are excellent pistols. They can't cost less than ninety roubles the pair.... You must hold the revolver like this.... [Aside] Her eyes, her eyes! What an inspiring woman!

POPOVA. Like this?

SMIRNOV. Yes, like this.... Then you cock the trigger, and take aim like this.... Put your head back a little! Hold your arm out properly.... Like that.... Then you press this thing with your finger—and that's all. The great thing is to keep cool and aim steadily.... Try not to jerk your arm.

POPOVA. Very well.... It's inconvenient to shoot in a room, let's go into the garden.

SMIRNOV. Come along then. But I warn you, I'm going to fire in the air.

POPOVA. That's the last straw! Why?

SMIRNOV. Because... because... it's my affair.

POPOVA. Are you afraid? Yes? Ah! No, sir, you don't get out of it! You come with me! I shan't have any peace until I've made a hole in your forehead... that forehead which I hate so much! Are you afraid?

SMIRNOV. Yes, I am afraid.

POPOVA. You lie! Why won't you fight?

SMIRNOV. Because... because you... because I like you.

POPOVA. [Laughs] He likes me! He dares to say that he likes me! [Points to the door] That's the way.

SMIRNOV. [Loads the revolver in silence, takes his cap and goes to the door. There he stops for half a minute, while they look at each other in silence, then he hesitatingly approaches POPOVA] Listen.... Are you still angry? I'm devilishly annoyed, too... but, do you understand... how can I express myself?... The fact is, you see, it's like this, so to speak.... [Shouts] Well, is it my fault that I like you? [He snatches at the back of a chair; the chair creaks and breaks] Devil take it, how I'm smashing up your furniture! I like you! Do you understand? I... I almost love you!

POPOVA. Get away from me—I hate you!

SMIRNOV. God, what a woman! I've never in my life seen one like her! I'm lost! Done for! Fallen into a mousetrap, like a mouse!

POPOVA. Stand back, or I'll fire!

SMIRNOV. Fire, then! You can't understand what happiness it would be to die before those beautiful eyes, to be shot by a revolver held in that little, velvet hand.... I'm out of my senses! Think, and make up your mind at once, because if I go out we shall never see each other again! Decide now.... I am a landowner, of respectable character, have an income of ten thousand a year. I can put a bullet through a coin tossed into the air as it comes down.... I own some fine horses.... Will you be my wife?

POPOVA. [Indignantly shakes her revolver] Let's fight! Let's go out!

SMIRNOV. I'm mad.... I understand nothing. [Yells] Waiter, water!

POPOVA. [Yells] Let's go out and fight!

SMIRNOV. I'm off my head, I'm in love like a boy, like a fool! [Snatches her hand, she screams with pain] I love you! [Kneels] I love you as I've never loved before! I've refused twelve women, nine have refused me, but I never loved one of them as I love you.... I'm weak, I'm wax, I've melted.... I'm on my knees like a fool, offering you my hand.... Shame, shame! I haven't been in love for five years, I'd taken a vow, and now all of a sudden I'm in love, like a fish out of water! I offer you my hand. Yes or no? You don't want me? Very well! [Gets up and quickly goes to the door.]

POPOVA. Stop.

SMIRNOV. [Stops] Well?

POPOVA. Nothing, go away.... No, stop.... No, go away, go away! I hate you! Or no.... Don't go away! Oh, if you knew how angry I am, how angry I am! [Throws her revolver on the table] My fingers have swollen because of all this.... [Tears her handkerchief in temper] What are you waiting for? Get out!

SMIRNOV. Good-bye.

POPOVA. Yes, yes, go away!... [Yells] Where are you going? Stop.... No, go away. Oh, how angry I am! Don't come near me, don't come near me!

SMIRNOV. [Approaching her] How angry I am with myself! I'm in love like a student, I've been on my knees.... [Rudely] I love you! What do I want to fall in love with you for? To-morrow I've got to pay the interest, and begin mowing, and here you.... [Puts his arms around her] I shall never forgive myself for this....

POPOVA. Get away from me! Take your hands away! I hate you! Let's go and fight!

[A prolonged kiss. Enter LUKA with an axe, the GARDENER with a rake, the COACHMAN with a pitchfork, and WORKMEN with poles.]

LUKA. [Catches sight of the pair kissing] Little fathers! [Pause.]

POPOVA. [Lowering her eyes] Luka, tell them in the stables that Toby isn't to have any oats at all to-day.

Curtain.

A TRAGEDIAN IN SPITE OF HIMSELF

CHARACTERS

IVAN IVANOVITCH TOLKACHOV, the father of a family
ALEXEY ALEXEYEVITCH MURASHKIN, his friend

The scene is laid in St. Petersburg, in MURASHKIN'S flat

[MURASHKIN'S study. Comfortable furniture. MURASHKIN is seated at his desk. Enter TOLKACHOV holding in his hands a glass globe for a lamp, a toy bicycle, three hat-boxes, a large parcel containing a dress, a bin-case of beer, and several little parcels. He looks round stupidly and lets himself down on the sofa in exhaustion.]

MURASHKIN. How do you do, Ivan Ivanovitch? Delighted to see you! What brings you here?

TOLKACHOV. [Breathing heavily] My dear good fellow... I want to ask you something.... I implore you lend me a revolver till to-morrow. Be a friend!

MURASHKIN. What do you want a revolver for?

TOLKACHOV. I must have it.... Oh, little fathers!... give me some water... water quickly!... I must have it... I've got to go through a dark wood to-night, so in case of accidents... do, please, lend it to me.

MURASHKIN. Oh, you liar, Ivan Ivanovitch! What the devil have you got to do in a dark wood? I expect you are up to something. I can see by your face that you are up to something. What's the matter with you? Are you ill?

TOLKACHOV. Wait a moment, let me breathe.... Oh little mothers! I am dog-tired. I've got a feeling all over me, and in my head as well, as if I've been roasted on a spit. I can't stand it any longer. Be a friend, and don't ask me any questions or insist on details; just give me the revolver! I beseech you!

MURASHKIN. Well, really! Ivan Ivanovitch, what cowardice is this? The father of a family and a Civil Servant holding a responsible post! For shame!

TOLKACHOV. What sort of a father of a family am I! I am a martyr. I am a beast of burden, a nigger, a slave, a rascal who keeps on waiting here for something to happen instead of starting off for the next world. I am a rag, a fool, an idiot. Why am I alive? What's the use? [Jumps up] Well now, tell me why am I alive? What's the purpose of this uninterrupted series of mental and physical sufferings? I understand being a martyr to an idea, yes! But to be a martyr to the devil knows what, skirts and lamp-globes, no! I humbly decline! No, no, no! I've had enough! Enough!

MURASHKIN. Don't shout, the neighbours will hear you!

TOLKACHOV. Let your neighbours hear; it's all the same to me! If you don't give me a revolver somebody else will, and there will be an end of me anyway! I've made up my mind!

MURASHKIN. Hold on, you've pulled off a button. Speak calmly. I still don't understand what's wrong with your life.

TOLKACHOV. What's wrong? You ask me what's wrong? Very well, I'll tell you! Very well! I'll tell you everything, and then perhaps my soul will be lighter. Let's sit down. Now listen... Oh, little mothers, I am out of breath!... Just let's take to-day as an instance. Let's take to-day. As you know, I've got to work at the Treasury from ten to four. It's hot, it's stuffy, there are flies, and, my dear fellow, the very dickens of a chaos. The Secretary is on leave, Khrapov has gone to get married, and the smaller fry is mostly in the country, making love or occupied with amateur theatricals. Everybody is so sleepy, tired, and done up that you can't get any sense out of them. The Secretary's duties are in the hands of an individual who is deaf in the left ear and in love; the public has lost its memory; everybody is running about angry and raging, and there is such a hullabaloo that you can't hear yourself speak. Confusion and smoke everywhere. And my work is deathly: always the same, always the same—first a correction, then a reference back, another correction, another reference back; it's all as monotonous as the waves of the sea. One's eyes, you understand, simply crawl out of one's head. Give me some water.... You come out a broken, exhausted man. You would like to dine and fall asleep, but you don't!—You remember that you live in the country—that is, you are a slave, a rag, a bit of string, a bit of limp flesh, and you've got to run round and do errands. Where we live a pleasant custom has grown up: when a man goes to town every wretched female inhabitant, not to mention one's own wife, has the power and the right to give him a crowd of commissions. The wife orders you to run into the modiste's and curse her for making a bodice too wide across the chest and too narrow across the shoulders; little Sonya wants a new pair of shoes; your sister-in-law wants some scarlet silk like the pattern at twenty copecks and three arshins long.... Just wait; I'll read you. [Takes a note out of his pocket and reads] A globe for the lamp; one pound of pork sausages; five copecks' worth of cloves and cinnamon; castor-oil for Misha; ten pounds of granulated sugar. To bring with you from home: a copper jar for the sugar; carbolic acid; insect powder, ten copecks' worth; twenty bottles of beer; vinegar; and corsets for

Mlle. Shanceau at No. 82.... Ouf! And to bring home Misha's winter coat and goloshes. That is the order of my wife and family. Then there are the commissions of our dear friends and neighbours —devil take them! To-morrow is the name-day of Volodia Vlasin; I have to buy a bicycle for him. The wife of Lieutenant-Colonel Virkhin is in an interesting condition, and I am therefore bound to call in at the midwife's every day and invite her to come. And so on, and so on. There are five notes in my pocket and my handkerchief is all knots. And so, my dear fellow, you spend the time between your office and your train, running about the town like a dog with your tongue hanging out, running and running and cursing life. From the clothier's to the chemist's, from the chemist's to the modiste's, from the modiste's to the pork butcher's, and then back again to the chemist's. In one place you stumble, in a second you lose your money, in a third you forget to pay and they raise a hue and cry after you, in a fourth you tread on the train of a lady's dress.... Tfoo! You get so shaken up from all this that your bones ache all night and you dream of crocodiles. Well, you've made all your purchases, but how are you to pack all these things? For instance, how are you to put a heavy copper jar together with the lamp-globe or the carbolic acid with the tea? How are you to make a combination of beer-bottles and this bicycle? It's the labours of Hercules, a puzzle, a rebus! Whatever tricks you think of, in the long run you're bound to smash or scatter something, and at the station and in the train you have to stand with your arms apart, holding up some parcel or other under your chin, with parcels, cardboard boxes, and such-like rubbish all over you. The train starts, the passengers begin to throw your luggage about on all sides: you've got your things on somebody else's seat. They yell, they call for the conductor, they threaten to have you put out, but what can I do? I just stand and blink my eyes like a whacked donkey. Now listen to this. I get home. You think I'd like to have a nice little drink after my righteous labours and a good square meal —isn't that so?—but there is no chance of that. My spouse has been on the look-out for me for some time. You've hardly started on your soup when she has her claws into you, wretched slave that you are—and wouldn't you like to go to some amateur theatricals or to a dance? You can't protest. You are a husband, and the word husband when translated into the language of summer residents in the country means a dumb beast which you can load to any extent without fear of the interference of the Society for the Prevention of Cruelty to Animals. So you go and blink at "A Family Scandal" or something, you applaud when your wife tells you to, and you feel worse and worse and worse until you expect an apoplectic fit to happen any moment. If you go to a dance you have to find partners for your wife, and if there is a shortage of them then you dance the quadrilles yourself. You get back from the theatre or the dance after midnight, when you are no longer a man but a useless, limp rag. Well, at last you've got what you want; you unrobe and get into bed. It's excellent—you can close your eyes and sleep.... Everything is so nice, poetic, and warm, you understand; there are no children squealing behind the wall, and you've got rid of your wife, and your conscience is clear—what more can you want? You fall asleep—and suddenly... you hear a buzz!... Gnats! [Jumps up] Gnats! Be they triply accursed Gnats! [Shakes his fist] Gnats! It's one of the plagues of Egypt, one of the tortures of the Inquisition! Buzz! It sounds so pitiful, so pathetic, as if it's begging your pardon, but the villain stings so that you have to scratch yourself for an hour after. You smoke, and go for them, and cover yourself from head to foot, but it is no good! At last you have to sacrifice yourself and let the cursed things devour you. You've no sooner got used to the gnats when another plague begins: downstairs your wife begins practising sentimental songs with her two friends. They sleep by day and rehearse for amateur concerts by night. Oh, my God! Those tenors are a torture with which no gnats on earth can compare. [He sings] "Oh, tell me not my youth has ruined you." "Before thee do I stand enchanted." Oh, the beastly things! They've about killed me! So as to deafen myself a little I do this: I drum on my ears. This goes on till four o'clock. Oh, give me some more water, brother!... I can't... Well, not having slept, you get up at six o'clock in the morning and off you go to the station. You run so as not to be late, and it's muddy, foggy, cold—brr! Then you get to town and start all over again. So there, brother. It's a horrible life; I wouldn't wish one like it for my enemy. You understand—I'm ill! Got asthma, heartburn—I'm always afraid of something. I've got indigestion, everything is thick before me... I've become a regular psychopath.... [Looking round] Only, between ourselves, I want to go down to see Chechotte or Merzheyevsky. There's some devil in me, brother. In moments of despair and suffering, when the gnats are stinging or the tenors sing, everything suddenly grows dim; you jump up and race round the whole house like a lunatic and shout, "I want blood! Blood!" And really all the time you do want to let a knife into somebody or hit him over the head with a chair. That's what life in a summer villa leads to! And nobody has any sympathy for me, and everybody seems to think it's all as it should be. People even laugh. But understand, I am a living being and I want to live! This isn't farce, it's tragedy! I say, if you don't give me your revolver, you might at any rate sympathize.

MURASHKIN. I do sympathize.

TOLKACHOV. I see how much you sympathize.... Good-bye. I've got to buy some anchovies and some sausage... and some tooth-powder, and then to the station.

MURASHKIN. Where are you living?

TOLKACHOV. At Carrion River.

MURASHKIN. [Delighted] Really? Then you'll know Olga Pavlovna Finberg, who lives there?

TOLKACHOV. I know her. We are even acquainted.

MURASHKIN. How perfectly splendid! That's so convenient, and it would be so good of you...

TOLKACHOV. What's that?

MURASHKIN. My dear fellow, wouldn't you do one little thing for me? Be a friend! Promise me now.

TOLKACHOV. What's that?

MURASHKIN. It would be such a friendly action! I implore you, my dear man. In the first place, give Olga Pavlovna my very kind regards. In the second place, there's a little thing I'd like you to take down to her. She asked me to get a sewing-machine but I haven't anybody to send it down to her by.... You take it, my dear! And you might at the same time take down this canary in its cage... only be careful, or you'll break the door.... What are you looking at me like that for?

TOLKACHOV. A sewing-machine... a canary in a cage... siskins, chaffinches...

MURASHKIN. Ivan Ivanovitch, what's the matter with you? Why are you turning purple?

TOLKACHOV. [Stamping] Give me the sewing-machine! Where's the bird-cage? Now get on top yourself! Eat me! Tear me to pieces! Kill me! [Clenching his fists] I want blood! Blood! Blood!

MURASHKIN. You've gone mad!

TOLKACHOV. [Treading on his feet] I want blood! Blood!

MURASHKIN. [In horror] He's gone mad! [Shouts] Peter! Maria! Where are you? Help!

TOLKACHOV. [Chasing him round the room] I want blood! Blood!

Curtain.

THE ANNIVERSARY

CHARACTERS

ANDREY ANDREYEVITCH SHIPUCHIN, Chairman of the N—— Joint Stock

Bank, a middle-aged man, with a monocle
TATIANA ALEXEYEVNA, his wife, aged 25
KUSMA NICOLAIEVITCH KHIRIN, the bank's aged book-keeper
NASTASYA FYODOROVNA MERCHUTKINA, an old woman wearing an old-fashioned cloak
DIRECTORS OF THE BANK
EMPLOYEES OF THE BANK

The action takes place at the Bank

[The private office of the Chairman of Directors. On the left is a door, leading into the public department. There are two desks. The furniture aims at a deliberately luxurious effect, with armchairs covered in velvet, flowers, statues, carpets, and a telephone. It is midday. KHIRIN is alone; he wears long felt boots, and is shouting through the door.]

KHIRIN. Send out to the chemist for 15 copecks' worth of valerian drops, and tell them to bring some drinking water into the Directors' office! This is the hundredth time I've asked! [Goes to a desk] I'm absolutely tired out. This is the fourth day I've been working, without a chance of shutting my eyes. From morning to evening I work here, from evening to morning at home. [Coughs] And I've got an inflammation all over me. I'm hot and cold, and I cough, and my legs ache, and there's something dancing before my eyes. [Sits] Our scoundrel of a Chairman, the brute, is going to read a report at a general meeting. "Our Bank, its Present and Future." You'd think he was a Gambetta.... [At work] Two... one... one... six... nought... seven.... Next, six... nought... one... six.... He just wants to throw dust into people's eyes, and so I sit here and work for him like a galley-slave! This report of his is poetic fiction and nothing more, and here I've got to sit day after day and add figures, devil take his soul! [Rattles on his counting-frame] I can't stand it! [Writing] That is, one... three... seven... two... one... nought.... He promised to reward me for my work. If everything goes well to-day and the public is properly put into blinkers, he's promised me a gold charm and 300 roubles bonus.... We'll see. [Works] Yes, but if my work all goes for nothing, then you'd better look out.... I'm very excitable.... If I lose my temper I'm capable of committing some crime, so look out! Yes!

[Noise and applause behind the scenes. SHIPUCHIN'S voice: "Thank you! Thank you! I am extremely grateful." Enter SHIPUCHIN. He wears a frockcoat and white tie; he carries an album which has been just presented to him.]

SHIPUCHIN. [At the door, addresses the outer office] This present, my dear colleagues, will be preserved to the day of my death, as a memory of the happiest days of my life! Yes, gentlemen! Once more, I thank you! [Throws a kiss into the air and turns to KHIRIN] My dear, my respected Kusma Nicolaievitch!

[All the time that SHIPUCHIN is on the stage, clerks intermittently come in with papers for his signature and go out.]

KHIRIN. [Standing up] I have the honour to congratulate you, Andrey Andreyevitch, on the fiftieth anniversary of our Bank, and hope that...

SHIPUCHIN. [Warmly shakes hands] Thank you, my dear sir! Thank you! I think that in view of the unique character of the day, as it is an anniversary, we may kiss each other!... [They kiss] I am very, very glad! Thank you for your service... for everything! If, in the course of the time during which I have had the honour to be Chairman of this Bank anything useful has been done, the credit is due, more than to anybody else, to my colleagues. [Sighs] Yes, fifteen years! Fifteen years as my name's Shipuchin! [Changes his tone] Where's my report? Is it getting on?

KHIRIN. Yes; there's only five pages left.

SHIPUCHIN. Excellent. Then it will be ready by three?

KHIRIN. If nothing occurs to disturb me, I'll get it done. Nothing of any importance is now left.

SHIPUCHIN. Splendid. Splendid, as my name's Shipuchin! The general meeting will be at four. If you please, my dear fellow. Give me the first half, I'll peruse it.... Quick.... [Takes the report] I base enormous hopes on this report. It's my *profession de foi*, or, better still, my firework. [Note: The actual word employed.] My firework, as my name's Shipuchin! [Sits and reads the report to himself] I'm hellishly tired.... My gout kept on giving me trouble last night, all the morning I was running about, and then these excitements, ovations, agitations... I'm tired!

KHIRIN. Two... nought... nought... three... nine... two... nought. I can't see straight after all these figures.... Three... one... six... four... one... five.... [Uses the counting-frame.]

SHIPUCHIN. Another unpleasantness.... This morning your wife came to see me and complained about you once again. Said that last night you threatened her and her sister with a knife. Kusma Nicolaievitch, what do you mean by that? Oh, oh!

KHIRIN. [Rudely] As it's an anniversary, Andrey Andreyevitch, I'll ask for a special favour. Please, even if it's only out of respect for my toil, don't interfere in my family life. Please!

SHIPUCHIN. [Sighs] Yours is an impossible character, Kusma Nicolaievitch! You're an excellent and respected man, but you behave to women like some scoundrel. Yes, really. I don't understand why you hate them so?

KHIRIN. I wish I could understand why you love them so! [Pause.]

SHIPUCHIN. The employees have just presented me with an album; and the Directors, as I've heard, are going to give me an address and a silver loving-cup.... [Playing with his monocle] Very nice, as my name's Shipuchin! It isn't excessive. A certain pomp is essential to the reputation of the Bank, devil take it! You know everything, of course.... I composed the address myself, and I bought the cup myself, too.... Well, then there was 45 roubles for the cover of the address, but you can't do without that. They'd never have thought of it for themselves. [Looks round] Look at the furniture! Just look at it! They say I'm stingy, that all I want is that the locks on the doors should be polished, that the employees should wear fashionable ties, and that a fat hall-porter should stand by the door. No, no, sirs. Polished locks and a fat porter mean a good deal. I can behave as I like at home, eat and sleep like a pig, get drunk....

KHIRIN. Please don't make hints.

SHIPUCHIN. Nobody's making hints! What an impossible character yours is.... As I was saying, at home I can live like a tradesman, a *parvenu*, and be up to any games I like, but here everything must be *en grand*. This is a Bank! Here every detail must *imponiren*, so to speak, and have a majestic appearance. [He picks up a paper from the floor and throws it into the fireplace] My service to the Bank has been just this—I've raised its reputation. A thing of immense importance is tone! Immense, as my name's Shipuchin! [Looks over KHIRIN] My dear man, a deputation of shareholders may come here any moment, and there you are in felt boots, wearing a scarf... in some absurdly coloured jacket.... You might have put on a frock-coat, or at any rate a dark jacket....

KHIRIN. My health matters more to me than your shareholders. I've an inflammation all over me.

SHIPUCHIN. [Excitedly] But you will admit that it's untidy! You spoil the *ensemble*!

KHIRIN. If the deputation comes I can go and hide myself. It won't matter if... seven... one... seven... two... one... five... nought. I don't like untidiness myself.... Seven... two... nine... [Uses the counting-frame] I can't stand untidiness! It would have been wiser of you not to have invited ladies to to-day's anniversary dinner....

SHIPUCHIN. Oh, that's nothing.

KHIRIN. I know that you're going to have the hall filled with them to-night to make a good show, but you look out, or they'll spoil everything. They cause all sorts of mischief and disorder.

SHIPUCHIN. On the contrary, feminine society elevates!

KHIRIN. Yes.... Your wife seems intelligent, but on the Monday of last week she let something off that upset me for two days. In front of a lot of people she suddenly asks: "Is it true that at our Bank my husband bought up a lot of the shares of the Driazhsky-Priazhsky Bank, which have been falling on exchange? My husband is so annoyed about it!" This in front of people. Why do you tell them everything, I don't understand. Do you want them to get you into serious trouble?

SHIPUCHIN. Well, that's enough, enough! All that's too dull for an anniversary. Which reminds me, by the way. [Looks at the time] My wife ought to be here soon. I really ought to have gone to the station, to meet the poor little thing, but there's no time.... and I'm tired. I must say I'm not glad of her! That is to say, I am glad, but I'd be gladder if she only stayed another couple of days with her mother. She'll want me to spend the whole evening with her to-night, whereas we have arranged a little excursion for ourselves.... [Shivers] Oh, my nerves have already started dancing me about. They are so strained that I think the very smallest trifle would be enough to make me break into tears! No, I must be strong, as my name's Shipuchin!

[Enter TATIANA ALEXEYEVNA SHIPUCHIN in a waterproof, with a little travelling satchel slung across her shoulder.]

SHIPUCHIN. Ah! In the nick of time!

TATIANA ALEXEYEVNA. Darling!

[Runs to her husband: a prolonged kiss.]

SHIPUCHIN. We were only speaking of you just now! [Looks at his watch.]

TATIANA ALEXEYEVNA. [Panting] Were you very dull without me? Are you well? I haven't been home yet, I came here straight from the station. I've a lot, a lot to tell you.... I couldn't wait.... I shan't take off my clothes, I'll only stay a minute. [To KHIRIN] Good morning, Kusma Nicolaievitch! [To her husband] Is everything all right at home?

SHIPUCHIN. Yes, quite. And, you know, you've got to look plumper and better this week.... Well, what sort of a time did you have?

TATIANA ALEXEYEVNA. Splendid. Mamma and Katya send their regards. Vassili Andreitch sends you a kiss. [Kisses him] Aunt sends you a jar of jam, and is annoyed because you don't write. Zina sends you a kiss. [Kisses.] Oh, if you knew what's happened. If you only knew! I'm even frightened to tell you! Oh, if you only knew! But I see by your eyes that you're sorry I came!

SHIPUCHIN. On the contrary.... Darling.... [Kisses her.]

[KHIRIN coughs angrily.]

TATIANA ALEXEYEVNA. Oh, poor Katya, poor Katya! I'm so sorry for her, so sorry for her.

SHIPUCHIN. This is the Bank's anniversary to-day, darling, we may get a deputation of the shareholders at any moment, and you're not dressed.

TATIANA ALEXEYEVNA. Oh, yes, the anniversary! I congratulate you, gentlemen. I wish you.... So it means that to-day's the day of the meeting, the dinner.... That's good. And do you remember that beautiful address which you spent such a long time composing for the shareholders? Will it be read to-day?

[KHIRIN coughs angrily.]

SHIPUCHIN. [Confused] My dear, we don't talk about these things. You'd really better go home.

TATIANA ALEXEYEVNA. In a minute, in a minute. I'll tell you everything in one minute and go. I'll tell you from the very beginning. Well.... When you were seeing me off, you remember I was sitting next to that stout lady, and I began to read. I don't like to talk in the train. I read for three stations and didn't say a word to anyone.... Well, then the evening set in, and I felt so mournful, you know, with such sad thoughts! A young man was sitting opposite me—not a bad-looking fellow, a brunette.... Well, we fell into conversation.... A sailor came along then, then some student or other.... [Laughs] I told them that I wasn't married... and they did look after me! We chattered till midnight, the brunette kept on telling the most awfully funny stories, and the sailor kept on singing. My chest began to ache from laughing. And when the sailor—oh, those sailors!—when he got to know my name was TATIANA, you know what he sang? [Sings in a bass voice] "Onegin don't let me conceal it, I love Tatiana madly!" [Note: From the Opera *Evgeni Onegin*—words by Pushkin.] [Roars with laughter.]

[KHIRIN coughs angrily.]

SHIPUCHIN. Tania, dear, you're disturbing Kusma Nicolaievitch. Go home, dear.... Later on....

TATIANA ALEXEYEVNA. No, no, let him hear if he wants to, it's awfully interesting. I'll end in a minute. Serezha came to meet me at the station. Some young man or other turns up, an inspector of taxes, I think... quite handsome, especially his eyes.... Serezha introduced me, and the three of us rode off together.... It was lovely weather....

[Voices behind the stage: "You can't, you can't! What do you want?" Enter MERCHUTKINA, waving her arms about.]

MERCHUTKINA. What are you dragging at me for. What else! I want him himself! [To SHIPUCHIN] I have the honour, your excellency... I am the wife of a civil servant, Nastasya Fyodorovna Merchutkina.

SHIPUCHIN. What do you want?

MERCHUTKINA. Well, you see, your excellency, my husband has been ill for five months, and while he was at home, getting better, he was suddenly dismissed for no reason, your excellency, and when I went to get his salary, they, you see, deducted 24 roubles 36 copecks from it. What for? I ask. They said, "Well, he drew it from the employees' account, and the others had to make it up." How can that be? How could he draw anything without my permission? No, your excellency! I'm a poor woman... my lodgers are all I have to live on.... I'm weak and defenceless.... Everybody does me some harm, and nobody has a kind word for me.

SHIPUCHIN. Excuse me. [Takes a petition from her and reads it standing.]

TATIANA ALEXEYEVNA. [To KHIRIN] Yes, but first we.... Last week I suddenly received a letter from my mother. She writes that a certain Grendilevsky has proposed to my sister Katya. A nice, modest, young man, but with no means of his own, and no assured position. And, unfortunately, just think of it, Katya is absolutely gone on him. What's to be done? Mamma writes telling me to come at once and influence Katya....

KHIRIN. [Angrily] Excuse me, you've made me lose my place! You go talking about your mamma and Katya, and I understand nothing; and I've lost my place.

TATIANA ALEXEYEVNA. What does that matter? You listen when a lady is talking to you! Why are you so angry to-day? Are you in love? [Laughs.]

SHIPUCHIN. [To MERCHUTKINA] Excuse me, but what is this? I can't make head or tail of it.

TATIANA ALEXEYEVNA. Are you in love? Aha! You're blushing!

SHIPUCHIN. [To his wife] Tanya, dear, do go out into the public office for a moment. I shan't be long.

TATIANA ALEXEYEVNA. All right. [Goes out.]

SHIPUCHIN. I don't understand anything of this. You've obviously come to the wrong place, madam. Your petition doesn't concern us at all. You should go to the department in which your husband was employed.

MERCHUTKINA. I've been there a good many times these five months, and they wouldn't even look at my petition. I'd given up all hopes, but, thanks to my son-in-law, Boris Matveyitch, I thought of coming to you. "You go, mother," he says, "and apply to Mr. Shipuchin, he's an influential man and can do anything." Help me, your excellency!

SHIPUCHIN. We can't do anything for you, Mrs. Merchutkina. You must understand that your husband, so far as I can gather, was in the employ of the Army Medical Department, while this is a private, commercial concern, a bank. Don't you understand that?

MERCHUTKINA. Your excellency, I can produce a doctor's certificate of my husband's illness. Here it is, just look at it....

SHIPUCHIN. [Irritated] That's all right; I quite believe you, but it's not our business. [Behind the scene, TATIANA ALEXEYEVNA'S laughter is heard, then a man's. SHIPUCHIN glances at the door] She's disturbing the employees. [To MERCHUTKINA] It's strange and it's even silly. Surely your husband knows where you ought to apply?

MERCHUTKINA. Your excellency, I don't let him know anything. He just cried out: "It isn't your business! Get out of this!" And...

SHIPUCHIN. Madam, I repeat, your husband was in the employ of the Army Medical Department, and this is a bank, a private, commercial concern.

MERCHUTKINA. Yes, yes, yes.... I understand, my dear. In that case, your excellency, just order them to pay me 15 roubles! I don't mind taking that to be going on with.

SHIPUCHIN. [Sighs] Ouf!

KHIRIN. Andrey Andreyevitch, I'll never finish the report at this rate!

SHIPUCHIN. One moment. [To MERCHUTKINA] I can't get any sense out of you. But do understand that your taking this business here is as absurd as if you took a divorce petition to a chemist's or into a gold assay office. [Knock at the door. The voice of TATIANA ALEXEYEVNA is heard, "Can I come in, Andrey?" SHIPUCHIN shouts] Just wait one minute, dear! [To MERCHUTKINA] What has it got to do with us if you haven't been paid? As it happens, madam, this is an anniversary to-day, we're busy... and somebody may be coming here at any moment.... Excuse me....

MERCHUTKINA. Your excellency, have pity on me, an orphan! I'm a weak, defenceless woman.... I'm tired to death.... I'm having trouble with my lodgers, and on account of my husband, and I've got the house to look after, and my son-in-law is out of work....

SHIPUCHIN. Mrs. Merchutkina, I... No, excuse me, I can't talk to you! My head's even in a whirl.... You are disturbing us and making us waste our time. [Sighs, aside] What a business, as my name's Shipuchin! [To KHIRIN] Kusma Nicolaievitch, will you please explain to Mrs. Merchutkina. [Waves his hand and goes out into public department.]

KHIRIN. [Approaching MERCHUTKINA, angrily] What do you want?

MERCHUTKINA. I'm a weak, defenceless woman.... I may look all right, but if you were to take me to pieces you wouldn't find a single healthy bit in me! I can hardly stand on my legs, and I've lost my appetite. I drank my coffee to-day and got no pleasure out of it.

KHIRIN. I ask you, what do you want?

MERCHUTKINA. Tell them, my dear, to give me 15 roubles, and a month later will do for the rest.

KHIRIN. But haven't you been told perfectly plainly that this is a bank!

MERCHUTKINA. Yes, yes.... And if you like I can show you the doctor's certificate.

KHIRIN. Have you got a head on your shoulders, or what?

MERCHUTKINA. My dear, I'm asking for what's mine by law. I don't want what isn't mine.

KHIRIN. I ask you, madam, have you got a head on your shoulders, or what? Well, devil take me, I haven't any time to talk to you! I'm busy.... [Points to the door] That way, please!

MERCHUTKINA. [Surprised] And where's the money?

KHIRIN. You haven't a head, but this [Taps the table and then points to his forehead.]

MERCHUTKINA. [Offended] What? Well, never mind, never mind.... You can do that to your own wife, but I'm the wife of a civil servant.... You can't do that to me!

KHIRIN. [Losing his temper] Get out of this!

MERCHUTKINA. No, no, no... none of that!

KHIRIN. If you don't get out this second, I'll call for the hall-porter! Get out! [Stamping.]

MERCHUTKINA. Never mind, never mind! I'm not afraid! I've seen the like of you before! Miser!

KHIRIN. I don't think I've ever seen a more awful woman in my life.... Ouf! It's given me a headache.... [Breathing heavily] I tell you once more... do you hear me? If you don't get out of this, you old devil, I'll grind you into powder! I've got such a character that I'm perfectly capable of laming you for life! I can commit a crime!

MERCHUTKINA. I've heard barking dogs before. I'm not afraid. I've seen the like of you before.

KHIRIN. [In despair] I can't stand it! I'm ill! I can't! [Sits down at his desk] They've let the Bank get filled with women, and I can't finish my report! I can't.

MERCHUTKINA. I don't want anybody else's money, but my own, according to law. You ought to be ashamed of yourself! Sitting in a government office in felt boots....

[Enter SHIPUCHIN and TATIANA ALEXEYEVNA.]

TATIANA ALEXEYEVNA. [Following her husband] We spent the evening at the Berezhnitskys. Katya was wearing a sky-blue frock of foulard silk, cut low at the neck.... She looks very well with her hair done over her head, and I did her hair myself.... She was perfectly fascinating....

SHIPUCHIN. [Who has had enough of it already] Yes, yes... fascinating.... They may be here any moment....

MERCHUTKINA. Your excellency!

SHIPUCHIN. [Dully] What else? What do you want?

MERCHUTKINA. Your excellency! [Points to KHIRIN] This man... this man tapped the table with his finger, and then his head.... You told him to look after my affair, but he insults me and says all sorts of things. I'm a weak, defenceless woman....

SHIPUCHIN. All right, madam, I'll see to it... and take the necessary steps.... Go away now... later on! [Aside] My gout's coming on!

KHIRIN. [In a low tone to SHIPUCHIN] Andrey Andreyevitch, send for the hall-porter and have her turned out neck and crop! What else can we do?

SHIPUCHIN. [Frightened] No, no! She'll kick up a row and we aren't the only people in the building.

MERCHUTKINA. Your excellency.

KHIRIN. [In a tearful voice] But I've got to finish my report! I won't have time! I won't!

MERCHUTKINA. Your excellency, when shall I have the money? I want it now.

SHIPUCHIN. [Aside, in dismay] A re-mark-ab-ly beastly woman! [Politely] Madam, I've already told you, this is a bank, a private, commercial concern.

MERCHUTKINA. Be a father to me, your excellency.... If the doctor's certificate isn't enough, I can get you another from the police. Tell them to give me the money!

SHIPUCHIN. [Panting] Ouf!

TATIANA ALEXEYEVNA. [To MERCHUTKINA] Mother, haven't you already been told that you're disturbing them? What right have you?

MERCHUTKINA. Mother, beautiful one, nobody will help me. All I do is to eat and drink, and just now I didn't enjoy my coffee at all.

SHIPUCHIN. [Exhausted] How much do you want?

MERCHUTKINA. 24 roubles 36 copecks.

SHIPUCHIN. All right! [Takes a 25-rouble note out of his pocket-book and gives it to her] Here are 25 roubles. Take it and... go!

[KHIRIN coughs angrily.]

MERCHUTKINA. I thank you very humbly, your excellency. [Hides the money.]

TATIANA ALEXEYEVNA. [Sits by her husband] It's time I went home.... [Looks at watch] But I haven't done yet.... I'll finish in one minute and go away.... What a time we had! Yes, what a time! We went to spend the evening at the Berezhnitskys.... It was all right, quite fun, but nothing in particular.... Katya's devoted Grendilevsky was there, of course.... Well, I talked to Katya, cried, and induced her to talk to Grendilevsky and refuse him. Well, I thought, everything's, settled the best possible way; I've quieted mamma down, saved Katya, and can be quiet myself.... What do you think? Katya and I were going along the avenue, just before supper, and suddenly... [Excitedly] And suddenly we heard a shot.... No, I can't talk about it calmly! [Waves her handkerchief] No, I can't!

SHIPUCHIN. [Sighs] Ouf!

TATIANA ALEXEYEVNA. [Weeps] We ran to the summer-house, and there... there poor Grendilevsky was lying... with a pistol in his hand....

SHIPUCHIN. No, I can't stand this! I can't stand it! [To MERCHUTKINA] What else do you want?

MERCHUTKINA. Your excellency, can't my husband go back to his job?

TATIANA ALEXEYEVNA. [Weeping] He'd shot himself right in the heart... here.... And the poor man had fallen down senseless.... And he was awfully frightened, as he lay there... and asked for a doctor. A doctor came soon... and saved the unhappy man....

MERCHUTKINA. Your excellency, can't my husband go back to his job?

SHIPUCHIN. No, I can't stand this! [Weeps] I can't stand it! [Stretches out both his hands in despair to KHIRIN] Drive her away! Drive her away, I implore you!

KHIRIN. [Goes up to TATIANA ALEXEYEVNA] Get out of this!

SHIPUCHIN. Not her, but this one... this awful woman.... [Points] That one!

KHIRIN. [Not understanding, to TATIANA ALEXEYEVNA] Get out of this! [Stamps] Get out!

TATIANA ALEXEYEVNA. What? What are you doing? Have you taken leave of your senses?

SHIPUCHIN. It's awful? I'm a miserable man! Drive her out! Out with her!

KHIRIN. [To TATIANA ALEXEYEVNA] Out of it! I'll cripple you! I'll knock you out of shape! I'll break the law!

TATIANA ALEXEYEVNA. [Running from him; he chases her] How dare you! You impudent fellow! [Shouts] Andrey! Help! Andrey! [Screams.]

SHIPUCHIN. [Chasing them] Stop! I implore you! Not such a noise? Have pity on me!

KHIRIN. [Chasing MERCHUTKINA] Out of this! Catch her! Hit her! Cut her into pieces!

SHIPUCHIN. [Shouts] Stop! I ask you! I implore you!

MERCHUTKINA. Little fathers... little fathers! [Screams] Little fathers!...

TATIANA ALEXEYEVNA. [Shouts] Help! Help!... Oh, oh... I'm sick, I'm sick! [Jumps on to a chair, then falls on to the sofa and groans as if in a faint.]

KHIRIN. [Chasing MERCHUTKINA] Hit her! Beat her! Cut her to pieces!

MERCHUTKINA. Oh, oh... little fathers, it's all dark before me! Ah! [Falls senseless into SHIPUCHIN'S arms. There is a knock at the door; a VOICE announces THE DEPUTATION] The deputation... reputation... occupation...

KHIRIN. [Stamps] Get out of it, devil take me! [Turns up his sleeves] Give her to me: I may break the law!

[A deputation of five men enters; they all wear frockcoats. One carries the velvet-covered address, another, the loving-cup. Employees look in at the door, from the public department. TATIANA ALEXEYEVNA on the sofa, and MERCHUTKINA in SHIPUCHIN'S arms are both groaning.]

ONE OF THE DEPUTATION. [Reads aloud] "Deeply respected and dear Andrey Andreyevitch! Throwing a retrospective glance at the past history of our financial administration, and reviewing in our minds its gradual development, we receive an extremely satisfactory impression. It is true that in the first period of its existence, the inconsiderable amount of its capital, and the absence of serious operations of any description, and also the indefinite aims of this bank, made us attach an extreme importance to the question raised by Hamlet, 'To be or not to be,' and at one time there were even voices to be heard demanding our liquidation. But at that moment you become the head of our concern. Your knowledge, energies, and your native tact were the causes of extraordinary success and widespread extension. The reputation of the bank... [Coughs] reputation of the bank..."

MERCHUTKINA. [Groans] Oh! Oh!

TATIANA ALEXEYEVNA. [Groans] Water! Water!

THE MEMBER OF THE DEPUTATION. [Continues] The reputation [Coughs]... the reputation of the bank has been raised by you to such a height that we are now the rivals of the best foreign concerns.

SHIPUCHIN. Deputation... reputation... occupation.... Two friends that had a walk at night, held converse by the pale moonlight.... Oh tell me not, that youth is vain, that jealousy has turned my brain.

THE MEMBER OF THE DEPUTATION. [Continues in confusion] "Then, throwing an objective glance at the present condition of things, we, deeply respected and dear Andrey Andreyevitch... [Lowering his voice] In that case, we'll do it later on.... Yes, later on...." [DEPUTATION goes out in confusion.]

Curtain.

THE THREE SISTERS

A DRAMA IN FOUR ACTS

CHARACTERS

ANDREY SERGEYEVITCH PROSOROV
NATALIA IVANOVA (NATASHA), his fiancée, later his wife (28)
His sisters:
OLGA
MASHA
IRINA
FEODOR ILITCH KULIGIN, high school teacher, married to MASHA (20)
ALEXANDER IGNATEYEVITCH VERSHININ, lieutenant-colonel in charge of a battery (42)
NICOLAI LVOVITCH TUZENBACH, baron, lieutenant in the army (30)
VASSILI VASSILEVITCH SOLENI, captain
IVAN ROMANOVITCH CHEBUTIKIN, army doctor (60)
ALEXEY PETROVITCH FEDOTIK, sub-lieutenant
VLADIMIR CARLOVITCH RODE, sub-lieutenant
FERAPONT, door-keeper at local council offices, an old man
ANFISA, nurse (80)

The action takes place in a provincial town.

[Ages are stated in brackets.]

ACT I

[In PROSOROV'S house. A sitting-room with pillars; behind is seen a large dining-room. It is midday, the sun is shining brightly outside. In the dining-room the table is being laid for lunch.]

[OLGA, in the regulation blue dress of a teacher at a girl's high school, is walking about correcting exercise books; MASHA, in a black dress, with a hat on her knees, sits and reads a book; IRINA, in white, stands about, with a thoughtful expression.]

OLGA. It's just a year since father died last May the fifth, on your name-day, Irina. It was very cold then, and snowing. I thought I would never survive it, and you were in a dead faint. And now a year has gone by and we are already thinking about it without pain, and you are wearing a white dress and your face is happy. [Clock strikes twelve] And the clock struck just the same way then. [Pause] I remember that there was music at the funeral, and they fired a volley in the cemetery. He was a general in command of a brigade but there were few people present. Of course, it was raining then, raining hard, and snowing.

IRINA. Why think about it!

[BARON TUZENBACH, CHEBUTIKIN and SOLENI appear by the table in the dining-room, behind the pillars.]

OLGA. It's so warm to-day that we can keep the windows open, though the birches are not yet in flower. Father was put in command of a brigade, and he rode out of Moscow with us eleven years ago. I remember perfectly that it was early in May and that everything in Moscow was flowering then. It was warm too, everything was bathed in sunshine. Eleven years have gone, and I remember everything as if we rode out only yesterday. Oh, God! When I awoke this morning and saw all the light and the spring, joy entered my heart, and I longed passionately to go home.

CHEBUTIKIN. Will you take a bet on it?

TUZENBACH. Oh, nonsense.

[MASHA, lost in a reverie over her book, whistles softly.]

OLGA. Don't whistle, Masha. How can you! [Pause] I'm always having headaches from having to go to the High School every day and then teach till evening. Strange thoughts come to me, as if I were already an old woman. And really, during these four years that I have been working here, I have been feeling as if every day my strength and youth have been squeezed out of me, drop by drop. And only one desire grows and gains in strength...

IRINA. To go away to Moscow. To sell the house, drop everything here, and go to Moscow...

OLGA. Yes! To Moscow, and as soon as possible.

[CHEBUTIKIN and TUZENBACH laugh.]

IRINA. I expect Andrey will become a professor, but still, he won't want to live here. Only poor Masha must go on living here.

OLGA. Masha can come to Moscow every year, for the whole summer.

[MASHA is whistling gently.]

IRINA. Everything will be arranged, please God. [Looks out of the window] It's nice out to-day. I don't know why I'm so happy: I remembered this morning that it was my name-day, and I suddenly felt glad and remembered my childhood, when mother was still with us. What beautiful thoughts I had, what thoughts!

OLGA. You're all radiance to-day, I've never seen you look so lovely. And Masha is pretty, too. Andrey wouldn't be bad-looking, if he wasn't so stout; it does spoil his appearance. But I've grown old and very thin, I suppose it's because I get angry with the girls at school. To-day I'm free. I'm at home. I haven't got a headache, and I feel younger than I was yesterday. I'm only twenty-eight.... All's well, God is everywhere, but it seems to me that if only I were married and could stay at home all day, it would be even better. [Pause] I should love my husband.

TUZENBACH. [To SOLENI] I'm tired of listening to the rot you talk. [Entering the sitting-room] I forgot to say that Vershinin, our new lieutenant-colonel of artillery, is coming to see us to-day. [Sits down to the piano.]

OLGA. That's good. I'm glad.

IRINA. Is he old?

TUZENBACH. Oh, no. Forty or forty-five, at the very outside. [Plays softly] He seems rather a good sort. He's certainly no fool, only he likes to hear himself speak.

IRINA. Is he interesting?

TUZENBACH. Oh, he's all right, but there's his wife, his mother-in-law, and two daughters. This is his second wife. He pays calls and tells everybody that he's got a wife and two daughters. He'll tell you so here. The wife isn't all there, she does her hair like a flapper and gushes extremely. She talks philosophy and tries to commit suicide every now and again, apparently in order to annoy her husband. I should have left her long ago, but he bears up patiently, and just grumbles.

SOLENI. [Enters with CHEBUTIKIN from the dining-room] With one hand I can only lift fifty-four pounds, but with both hands I can lift 180, or even 200 pounds. From this I conclude that two men are not twice as strong as one, but three times, perhaps even more....

CHEBUTIKIN. [Reads a newspaper as he walks] If your hair is coming out... take an ounce of naphthaline and hail a bottle of spirit... dissolve and use daily.... [Makes a note in his pocket diary] When found make a note of! Not that I want it though.... [Crosses it out] It doesn't matter.

IRINA. Ivan Romanovitch, dear Ivan Romanovitch!

CHEBUTIKIN. What does my own little girl want?

IRINA. Ivan Romanovitch, dear Ivan Romanovitch! I feel as if I were sailing under the broad blue sky with great white birds around me. Why is that? Why?

CHEBUTIKIN. [Kisses her hands, tenderly] My white bird....

IRINA. When I woke up to-day and got up and dressed myself, I suddenly began to feel as if everything in this life was open to me, and that I knew how I must live. Dear Ivan Romanovitch, I know everything. A man must work, toil in the sweat of his brow, whoever he may be, for that is the meaning and object of his life, his happiness, his enthusiasm. How fine it is to be a workman who gets up at daybreak and breaks stones in the street, or a shepherd, or a schoolmaster, who teaches children, or an engine-driver on the railway.... My God, let alone a man, it's better to be an ox, or just a horse, so long as it can work, than a young woman who wakes up at twelve o'clock, has her coffee in bed, and then spends two hours dressing.... Oh it's awful! Sometimes when it's hot, your thirst can be just as tiresome as my need for work. And if I don't get up early in future and work, Ivan Romanovitch, then you may refuse me your friendship.

CHEBUTIKIN. [Tenderly] I'll refuse, I'll refuse....

OLGA. Father used to make us get up at seven. Now Irina wakes at seven and lies and meditates about something till nine at least. And she looks so serious! [Laughs.]

IRINA. You're so used to seeing me as a little girl that it seems queer to you when my face is serious. I'm twenty!

TUZENBACH. How well I can understand that craving for work, oh God! I've never worked once in my life. I was born in Petersburg, a chilly, lazy place, in a family which never knew what work or worry meant. I remember that when I used to come home from my regiment, a footman used to have to pull off my boots while I fidgeted and my mother looked on in adoration and wondered why other people didn't see me in the same light. They shielded me from work; but only just in time! A new age is dawning, the people are marching on us all, a powerful, health-giving storm is gathering, it is drawing near, soon it will be upon us and it will drive away laziness, indifference, the prejudice against labour, and rotten dullness from our society. I shall work, and in twenty-five or thirty years, every man will have to work. Every one!

CHEBUTIKIN. I shan't work.

TUZENBACH. You don't matter.

SOLENI. In twenty-five years' time, we shall all be dead, thank the Lord. In two or three years' time apoplexy will carry you off, or else I'll blow your brains out, my pet. [Takes a scent-bottle out of his pocket and sprinkles his chest and hands.]

CHEBUTIKIN. [Laughs] It's quite true, I never have worked. After I came down from the university I never stirred a finger or opened a book, I just read the papers.... [Takes another newspaper out of his pocket] Here we are.... I've learnt from the papers that there used to be one, Dobrolubov [Note: Dobroluboy (1836-81), in spite of the shortness of his career, established himself as one of the classic literary critics of Russia], for instance, but what he wrote—I don't know... God only knows.... [Somebody is heard tapping on the floor from below] There.... They're calling me downstairs, somebody's come to see me. I'll be back in a minute... won't be long.... [Exit hurriedly, scratching his beard.]

IRINA. He's up to something.

TUZENBACH. Yes, he looked so pleased as he went out that I'm pretty certain he'll bring you a present in a moment.

IRINA. How unpleasant!

OLGA. Yes, it's awful. He's always doing silly things.

MASHA.

> *"There stands a green oak by the sea.*
> *And a chain of bright gold is around it...*
> *And a chain of bright gold is around it...."*

[Gets up and sings softly.]

OLGA. You're not very bright to-day, Masha. [MASHA sings, putting on her hat] Where are you off to?

MASHA. Home.

IRINA. That's odd....

TUZENBACH. On a name-day, too!

MASHA. It doesn't matter. I'll come in the evening. Good-bye, dear. [Kisses MASHA] Many happy returns, though I've said it before. In the old days when father was alive, every time we had a name-day, thirty or forty officers used to come, and there was lots of noise and fun, and to-day there's only a man and a half, and it's as quiet as a desert... I'm off... I've got the hump to-day, and am not at all cheerful, so don't you mind me. [Laughs through her tears] We'll have a talk later on, but good-bye for the present, my dear; I'll go somewhere.

IRINA. [Displeased] You are queer....

OLGA. [Crying] I understand you, Masha.

SOLENI. When a man talks philosophy, well, it is philosophy or at any rate sophistry; but when a woman, or two women, talk philosophy—it's all my eye.

MASHA. What do you mean by that, you very awful man?

SOLENI. Oh, nothing. You came down on me before I could say... help! [Pause.]

MASHA. [Angrily, to OLGA] Don't cry!

[Enter ANFISA and FERAPONT with a cake.]

ANFISA. This way, my dear. Come in, your feet are clean. [To IRINA] From the District Council, from Mihail Ivanitch Protopopov... a cake.

IRINA. Thank you. Please thank him. [Takes the cake.]

FERAPONT. What?

IRINA. [Louder] Please thank him.

OLGA. Give him a pie, nurse. Ferapont, go, she'll give you a pie.

FERAPONT. What?

ANFISA. Come on, gran'fer, Ferapont Spiridonitch. Come on. [Exeunt.]

MASHA. I don't like this Mihail Potapitch or Ivanitch, Protopopov. We oughtn't to invite him here.

IRINA. I never asked him.

MASHA. That's all right.

[Enter CHEBUTIKIN followed by a soldier with a silver samovar; there is a rumble of dissatisfied surprise.]

OLGA. [Covers her face with her hands] A samovar! That's awful! [Exit into the dining-room, to the table.]

IRINA. My dear Ivan Romanovitch, what are you doing!

TUZENBACH. [Laughs] I told you so!

MASHA. Ivan Romanovitch, you are simply shameless!

CHEBUTIKIN. My dear good girl, you are the only thing, and the dearest thing I have in the world. I'll soon be sixty. I'm an old man, a lonely worthless old man. The only good thing in me is my love for you, and if it hadn't been for that, I would have been dead long ago.... [To IRINA] My dear little girl, I've known you since the day of your birth, I've carried you in my arms... I loved your dead mother....

MASHA. But your presents are so expensive!

CHEBUTIKIN. [Angrily, through his tears] Expensive presents.... You really, are!... [To the orderly] Take the samovar in there.... [Teasing] Expensive presents!

[The orderly goes into the dining-room with the samovar.]

ANFISA. [Enters and crosses stage] My dear, there's a strange Colonel come! He's taken off his coat already. Children, he's coming here. Irina darling, you'll be a nice and polite little girl, won't you.... Should have lunched a long time ago.... Oh, Lord.... [Exit.]

TUZENBACH. It must be Vershinin. [Enter VERSHININ] Lieutenant-Colonel Vershinin!

VERSHININ. [To MASHA and IRINA] I have the honour to introduce myself, my name is Vershinin. I am very glad indeed to be able to come at last. How you've grown! Oh! oh!

IRINA. Please sit down. We're very glad you've come.

VERSHININ. [Gaily] I am glad, very glad! But there are three sisters, surely. I remember—three little girls. I forget your faces, but your father, Colonel Prosorov, used to have three little girls, I remember that perfectly, I saw them with my own eyes. How time does fly! Oh, dear, how it flies!

TUZENBACH. Alexander Ignateyevitch comes from Moscow.

IRINA. From Moscow? Are you from Moscow?

VERSHININ. Yes, that's so. Your father used to be in charge of a battery there, and I was an officer in the same brigade. [To MASHA] I seem to remember your face a little.

MASHA. I don't remember you.

IRINA. Olga! Olga! [Shouts into the dining-room] Olga! Come along! [OLGA enters from the dining-room] Lieutenant Colonel Vershinin comes from Moscow, as it happens.

VERSHININ. I take it that you are Olga Sergeyevna, the eldest, and that you are Maria... and you are Irina, the youngest....

OLGA. So you come from Moscow?

VERSHININ. Yes. I went to school in Moscow and began my service there; I was there for a long time until at last I got my battery and moved over here, as you see. I don't really remember you, I only remember that there used to be three sisters. I remember your father well; I have only to shut my eyes to see him as he was. I used to come to your house in Moscow....

OLGA. I used to think I remembered everybody, but...

VERSHININ. My name is Alexander Ignateyevitch.

IRINA. Alexander Ignateyevitch, you've come from Moscow. That is really quite a surprise!

OLGA. We are going to live there, you see.

IRINA. We think we may be there this autumn. It's our native town, we were born there. In Old Basmanni Road.... [They both laugh for joy.]

MASHA. We've unexpectedly met a fellow countryman. [Briskly] I remember: Do you remember, Olga, they used to speak at home of a "lovelorn Major." You were only a Lieutenant then, and in love with somebody, but for some reason they always called you a Major for fun.

VERSHININ. [Laughs] That's it... the lovelorn Major, that's got it!

MASHA. You only wore moustaches then. You have grown older! [Through her tears] You have grown older!

VERSHININ. Yes, when they used to call me the lovelorn Major, I was young and in love. I've grown out of both now.

OLGA. But you haven't a single white hair yet. You're older, but you're not yet old.

VERSHININ. I'm forty-two, anyway. Have you been away from Moscow long?

IRINA. Eleven years. What are you crying for, Masha, you little fool.... [Crying] And I'm crying too.

MASHA. It's all right. And where did you live?

VERSHININ. Old Basmanni Road.

OLGA. Same as we.

VERSHININ. Once I used to live in German Street. That was when the Red Barracks were my headquarters. There's an ugly bridge in between, where the water rushes underneath. One gets melancholy when one is alone there. [Pause] Here the river is so wide and fine! It's a splendid river!

OLGA. Yes, but it's so cold. It's very cold here, and the midges....

VERSHININ. What are you saying! Here you've got such a fine healthy Russian climate. You've a forest, a river... and birches. Dear, modest birches, I like them more than any other tree. It's good to live here. Only it's odd that the railway station should be thirteen miles away.... Nobody knows why.

SOLENI. I know why. [All look at him] Because if it was near it wouldn't be far off, and if it's far off, it can't be near. [An awkward pause.]

TUZENBACH. Funny man.

OLGA. Now I know who you are. I remember.

VERSHININ. I used to know your mother.

CHEBUTIKIN. She was a good woman, rest her soul.

IRINA. Mother is buried in Moscow.

OLGA. At the Novo-Devichi Cemetery.

MASHA. Do you know, I'm beginning to forget her face. We'll be forgotten in just the same way.

VERSHININ. Yes, they'll forget us. It's our fate, it can't be helped. A time will come when everything that seems serious, significant, or very important to us will be forgotten, or considered trivial. [Pause] And the curious thing is that we can't possibly find out what will come to be regarded as great and important, and what will be feeble, or silly. Didn't the discoveries of Copernicus, or Columbus, say, seem unnecessary and ludicrous at first, while wasn't it thought that some rubbish written by a fool, held all the truth? And it may so happen that our present existence, with which we are so satisfied, will in time appear strange, inconvenient, stupid, unclean, perhaps even sinful....

TUZENBACH. Who knows? But on the other hand, they may call our life noble and honour its memory. We've abolished torture and capital punishment, we live in security, but how much suffering there is still!

SOLENI. [In a feeble voice] There, there.... The Baron will go without his dinner if you only let him talk philosophy.

TUZENBACH. Vassili Vassilevitch, kindly leave me alone. [Changes his chair] You're very dull, you know.

SOLENI. [Feebly] There, there, there.

TUZENBACH. [To VERSHININ] The sufferings we see to-day—there are so many of them!—still indicate a certain moral improvement in society.

VERSHININ. Yes, yes, of course.

CHEBUTIKIN. You said just now, Baron, that they may call our life noble; but we are very petty.... [Stands up] See how little I am. [Violin played behind.]

MASHA. That's Andrey playing—our brother.

IRINA. He's the learned member of the family. I expect he will be a professor some day. Father was a soldier, but his son chose an academic career for himself.

MASHA. That was father's wish.

OLGA. We ragged him to-day. We think he's a little in love.

IRINA. To a local lady. She will probably come here to-day.

MASHA. You should see the way she dresses! Quite prettily, quite fashionably too, but so badly! Some queer bright yellow skirt with a wretched little fringe and a red bodice. And such a complexion! Andrey isn't in love. After all he has taste, he's simply making fun of us. I heard yesterday that she was going to marry Protopopov, the chairman of the Local Council. That would do her nicely.... [At the side door] Andrey, come here! Just for a minute, dear! [Enter ANDREY.]

OLGA. My brother, Andrey Sergeyevitch.

VERSHININ. My name is Vershinin.

ANDREY. Mine is Prosorov. [Wipes his perspiring hands] You've come to take charge of the battery?

OLGA. Just think, Alexander Ignateyevitch comes from Moscow.

ANDREY. That's all right. Now my little sisters won't give you any rest.

VERSHININ. I've already managed to bore your sisters.

IRINA. Just look what a nice little photograph frame Andrey gave me to-day. [Shows it] He made it himself.

VERSHININ. [Looks at the frame and does not know what to say] Yes.... It's a thing that...

IRINA. And he made that frame there, on the piano as well. [Andrey waves his hand and walks away.]

OLGA. He's got a degree, and plays the violin, and cuts all sorts of things out of wood, and is really a domestic Admirable Crichton. Don't go away, Andrey! He's got into a habit of always going away. Come here!

[MASHA and IRINA take his arms and laughingly lead him back.]

MASHA. Come on, come on!

ANDREY. Please leave me alone.

MASHA. You are funny. Alexander Ignateyevitch used to be called the lovelorn Major, but he never minded.

VERSHININ. Not the least.

MASHA. I'd like to call you the lovelorn fiddler!

IRINA. Or the lovelorn professor!

OLGA. He's in love! little Andrey is in love!

IRINA. [Applauds] Bravo, Bravo! Encore! Little Andrey is in love.

CHEBUTIKIN. [Goes up behind ANDREY and takes him round the waist with both arms] Nature only brought us into the world that we should love! [Roars with laughter, then sits down and reads a newspaper which he takes out of his pocket.]

ANDREY. That's enough, quite enough.... [Wipes his face] I couldn't sleep all night and now I can't quite find my feet, so to speak. I read until four o'clock, then tried to sleep, but nothing happened. I thought about one thing and another, and then it dawned and the sun crawled into my bedroom. This summer, while I'm here, I want to translate a book from the English....

VERSHININ. Do you read English?

ANDREY. Yes father, rest his soul, educated us almost violently. It may seem funny and silly, but it's nevertheless true, that after his death I began to fill out and get rounder, as if my body had had some great pressure taken off it. Thanks to father, my sisters and I know French, German, and English, and Irina knows Italian as well. But we paid dearly for it all!

MASHA. A knowledge of three languages is an unnecessary luxury in this town. It isn't even a luxury but a sort of useless extra, like a sixth finger. We know a lot too much.

VERSHININ. Well, I say! [Laughs] You know a lot too much! I don't think there can really be a town so dull and stupid as to have no place for a clever, cultured person. Let us suppose even that among the hundred thousand inhabitants of this backward and uneducated town, there are only three persons like yourself. It stands to reason that you won't be able to conquer that dark mob around you; little by little as you grow older you will be bound to give way and lose yourselves in this crowd of a hundred thousand human beings; their life will suck you up in itself, but still, you won't disappear having influenced nobody; later on, others like you will come, perhaps six of them, then twelve, and so on, until at last your sort will be in the majority. In two or three hundred years' time life on this earth will be unimaginably beautiful and wonderful. Mankind needs such a life, and if it is not ours to-day then we must look ahead for it, wait, think, prepare for it. We must see and know more than our fathers and grandfathers saw and knew. [Laughs] And you complain that you know too much.

MASHA. [Takes off her hat] I'll stay to lunch.

IRINA. [Sighs] Yes, all that ought to be written down.

[ANDREY has gone out quietly.]

TUZENBACH. You say that many years later on, life on this earth will be beautiful and wonderful. That's true. But to share in it now, even though at a distance, we must prepare by work....

VERSHININ. [Gets up] Yes. What a lot of flowers you have. [Looks round] It's a beautiful flat. I envy you! I've spent my whole life in rooms with two chairs, one sofa, and fires which always smoke. I've never had flowers like these in my life.... [Rubs his hands] Well, well!

TUZENBACH. Yes, we must work. You are probably thinking to yourself: the German lets himself go. But I assure you I'm a Russian, I can't even speak German. My father belonged to the Orthodox Church.... [Pause.]

VERSHININ. [Walks about the stage] I often wonder: suppose we could begin life over again, knowing what we were doing? Suppose we could use one life, already ended, as a sort of rough draft for another? I think that every one of us would try, more than anything else, not to repeat himself, at the very least he would rearrange his manner of life, he would make sure of rooms like these, with flowers and light... I have a wife and two daughters, my wife's health is delicate and so on and so on, and if I had to begin life all over again I would not marry.... No, no!

[Enter KULIGIN in a regulation jacket.]

KULIGIN. [Going up to IRINA] Dear sister, allow me to congratulate you on the day sacred to your good angel and to wish you, sincerely and from the bottom of my heart, good health and all that one can wish for a girl of your years. And then let me offer you this book as a present. [Gives it to her] It is the history of our High School during the last fifty years, written by myself. The book is worthless, and written because I had nothing to do, but read it all the same. Good day, gentlemen! [To VERSHININ] My name is Kuligin, I am a master of the local High School. [Note: He adds that he is a *Nadvorny Sovetnik* (almost the same as a German *Hofrat*), an undistinguished civilian title with no English equivalent.] [To IRINA] In this book you will find a list of all those who have taken the full course at our High School during these fifty years. *Feci quod potui, faciant meliora potentes*. [Kisses MASHA.]

IRINA. But you gave me one of these at Easter.

KULIGIN. [Laughs] I couldn't have, surely! You'd better give it back to me in that case, or else give it to the Colonel. Take it, Colonel. You'll read it some day when you're bored.

VERSHININ. Thank you. [Prepares to go] I am extremely happy to have made the acquaintance of...

OLGA. Must you go? No, not yet?

IRINA. You'll stop and have lunch with us. Please do.

OLGA. Yes, please!

VERSHININ. [Bows] I seem to have dropped in on your name-day. Forgive me, I didn't know, and I didn't offer you my congratulations. [Goes with OLGA into the dining-room.]

KULIGIN. To-day is Sunday, the day of rest, so let us rest and rejoice, each in a manner compatible with his age and disposition. The carpets will have to be taken up for the summer and put away till the winter... Persian powder or naphthaline.... The Romans were healthy because they knew both how to work and how to rest, they had *mens sana in corpore sano*. Their life ran along certain recognized patterns. Our director says: "The chief thing about each life is its pattern. Whoever loses his pattern is lost himself"—and it's just the same in our daily life. [Takes MASHA by the waist, laughing] Masha loves me. My wife loves me. And you ought to put the window curtains away with the carpets.... I'm feeling awfully pleased with life to-day. Masha, we've got to be at the director's at four. They're getting up a walk for the pedagogues and their families.

MASHA. I shan't go.

KULIGIN. [Hurt] My dear Masha, why not?

MASHA. I'll tell you later.... [Angrily] All right, I'll go, only please stand back.... [Steps away.]

KULIGIN. And then we're to spend the evening at the director's. In spite of his ill-health that man tries, above everything else, to be sociable. A splendid, illuminating personality. A wonderful man. After yesterday's committee he said to me: "I'm tired, Feodor Ilitch, I'm tired!" [Looks at the clock, then at his watch] Your clock is seven minutes fast. "Yes," he said, "I'm tired." [Violin played off.]

OLGA. Let's go and have lunch! There's to be a masterpiece of baking!

KULIGIN. Oh my dear Olga, my dear. Yesterday I was working till eleven o'clock at night, and got awfully tired. To-day I'm quite happy. [Goes into dining-room] My dear...

CHEBUTIKIN. [Puts his paper into his pocket, and combs his beard] A pie? Splendid!

MASHA. [Severely to CHEBUTIKIN] Only mind; you're not to drink anything to-day. Do you hear? It's bad for you.

CHEBUTIKIN. Oh, that's all right. I haven't been drunk for two years. And it's all the same, anyway!

MASHA. You're not to dare to drink, all the same. [Angrily, but so that her husband should not hear] Another dull evening at the Director's, confound it!

TUZENBACH. I shouldn't go if I were you.... It's quite simple.

CHEBUTIKIN. Don't go.

MASHA. Yes, "don't go...." It's a cursed, unbearable life.... [Goes into dining-room.]

CHEBUTIKIN. [Follows her] It's not so bad.

SOLENI. [Going into the dining-room] There, there, there....

TUZENBACH. Vassili Vassilevitch, that's enough. Be quiet!

SOLENI. There, there, there....

KULIGIN. [Gaily] Your health, Colonel! I'm a pedagogue and not quite at home here. I'm Masha's husband.... She's a good sort, a very good sort.

VERSHININ. I'll have some of this black vodka.... [Drinks] Your health! [To OLGA] I'm very comfortable here!

[Only IRINA and TUZENBACH are now left in the sitting-room.]

IRINA. Masha's out of sorts to-day. She married when she was eighteen, when he seemed to her the wisest of men. And now it's different. He's the kindest man, but not the wisest.

OLGA. [Impatiently] Andrey, when are you coming?

ANDREY. [Off] One minute. [Enters and goes to the table.]

TUZENBACH. What are you thinking about?

IRINA. I don't like this Soleni of yours and I'm afraid of him. He only says silly things.

TUZENBACH. He's a queer man. I'm sorry for him, though he vexes me. I think he's shy. When there are just the two of us he's quite all right and very good company; when other people are about he's rough and hectoring. Don't let's go in, let them have their meal without us. Let me stay with you. What are you thinking of? [Pause] You're twenty. I'm not yet thirty. How many years are there left to us, with their long, long lines of days, filled with my love for you....

IRINA. Nicolai Lvovitch, don't speak to me of love.

TUZENBACH. [Does not hear] I've a great thirst for life, struggle, and work, and this thirst has united with my love for you, Irina, and you're so beautiful, and life seems so beautiful to me! What are you thinking about?

IRINA. You say that life is beautiful. Yes, if only it seems so! The life of us three hasn't been beautiful yet; it has been stifling us as if it was weeds... I'm crying. I oughtn't.... [Dries her tears, smiles] We must work, work. That is why we are unhappy and look at the world so sadly; we don't know what work is. Our parents despised work....

[Enter NATALIA IVANOVA; she wears a pink dress and a green sash.]

NATASHA. They're already at lunch... I'm late... [Carefully examines herself in a mirror, and puts herself straight] I think my hair's done all right.... [Sees IRINA] Dear Irina Sergeyevna, I congratulate you! [Kisses her firmly and at length] You've so many visitors, I'm really ashamed.... How do you do, Baron!

OLGA. [Enters from dining-room] Here's Natalia Ivanovna. How are you, dear! [They kiss.]

NATASHA. Happy returns. I'm awfully shy, you've so many people here.

OLGA. All our friends. [Frightened, in an undertone] You're wearing a green sash! My dear, you shouldn't!

NATASHA. Is it a sign of anything?

OLGA. No, it simply doesn't go well... and it looks so queer.

NATASHA. [In a tearful voice] Yes? But it isn't really green, it's too dull for that. [Goes into dining-room with OLGA.]

[They have all sat down to lunch in the dining-room, the sitting-room is empty.]

KULIGIN. I wish you a nice fiancée, Irina. It's quite time you married.

CHEBUTIKIN. Natalia Ivanovna, I wish you the same.

KULIGIN. Natalia Ivanovna has a fiancé already.

MASHA. [Raps with her fork on a plate] Let's all get drunk and make life purple for once!

KULIGIN. You've lost three good conduct marks.

VERSHININ. This is a nice drink. What's it made of?

SOLENI. Blackbeetles.

IRINA. [Tearfully] Phoo! How disgusting!

OLGA. There is to be a roast turkey and a sweet apple pie for dinner. Thank goodness I can spend all day and the evening at home. You'll come in the evening, ladies and gentlemen....

VERSHININ. And please may I come in the evening!

IRINA. Please do.

NATASHA. They don't stand on ceremony here.

CHEBUTIKIN. Nature only brought us into the world that we should love! [Laughs.]

ANDREY. [Angrily] Please don't! Aren't you tired of it?

[Enter FEDOTIK and RODE with a large basket of flowers.]

FEDOTIK. They're lunching already.

RODE. [Loudly and thickly] Lunching? Yes, so they are....

FEDOTIK. Wait a minute! [Takes a photograph] That's one. No, just a moment.... [Takes another] That's two. Now we're ready!

[They take the basket and go into the dining-room, where they have a noisy reception.]

RODE. [Loudly] Congratulations and best wishes! Lovely weather to-day, simply perfect. Was out walking with the High School students all the morning. I take their drills.

FEDOTIK. You may move, Irina Sergeyevna! [Takes a photograph] You look well to-day. [Takes a humming-top out of his pocket] Here's a humming-top, by the way. It's got a lovely note!

IRINA. How awfully nice!

MASHA.

> "There stands a green oak by the sea,
> And a chain of bright gold is around it...
> And a chain of bright gold is around it..."

[Tearfully] What am I saying that for? I've had those words running in my head all day....

KULIGIN. There are thirteen at table!

RODE. [Aloud] Surely you don't believe in that superstition? [Laughter.]

KULIGIN. If there are thirteen at table then it means there are lovers present. It isn't you, Ivan Romanovitch, hang it all.... [Laughter.]

CHEBUTIKIN. I'm a hardened sinner, but I really don't see why Natalia Ivanovna should blush....

[Loud laughter; NATASHA runs out into the sitting-room, followed by ANDREY.]

ANDREY. Don't pay any attention to them! Wait... do stop, please....

NATASHA. I'm shy... I don't know what's the matter with me and they're all laughing at me. It wasn't nice of me to leave the table like that, but I can't... I can't. [Covers her face with her hands.]

ANDREY. My dear, I beg you. I implore you not to excite yourself. I assure you they're only joking, they're kind people. My dear, good girl, they're all kind and sincere people, and they like both you and me. Come here to the window, they can't see us here.... [Looks round.]

NATASHA. I'm so unaccustomed to meeting people!

ANDREY. Oh your youth, your splendid, beautiful youth! My darling, don't be so excited! Believe me, believe me... I'm so happy, my soul is full of love, of ecstasy.... They don't see us! They can't! Why, why or when did I fall in love with you—Oh, I can't understand anything. My dear, my pure darling, be my wife! I love you, love you... as never before.... [They kiss.]

[Two officers come in and, seeing the lovers kiss, stop in astonishment.]

Curtain.

ACT II

[Scene as before. It is 8 p.m. Somebody is heard playing a concertina outside in' the street. There is no fire. NATALIA IVANOVNA enters in indoor dress carrying a candle; she stops by the door which leads into ANDREY'S room.]

NATASHA. What are you doing, Andrey? Are you reading? It's nothing, only I.... [She opens another door, and looks in, then closes it] Isn't there any fire....

ANDREY. [Enters with book in hand] What are you doing, Natasha?

NATASHA. I was looking to see if there wasn't a fire. It's Shrovetide, and the servant is simply beside herself; I must look out that something doesn't happen. When I came through the dining-room yesterday midnight, there was a candle burning. I couldn't get her to tell me who had lighted it. [Puts down her candle] What's the time?

ANDREY. [Looks at his watch] A quarter past eight.

NATASHA. And Olga and Irina aren't in yet. The poor things are still at work. Olga at the teacher's council, Irina at the telegraph office.... [Sighs] I said to your sister this morning, "Irina, darling, you must take care of yourself." But she pays no attention. Did you say it was a quarter past eight? I am afraid little Bobby is quite ill. Why is he so cold? He was feverish yesterday, but to-day he is quite cold... I am so frightened!

ANDREY. It's all right, Natasha. The boy is well.

NATASHA. Still, I think we ought to put him on a diet. I am so afraid. And the entertainers were to be here after nine; they had better not come, Audrey.

ANDREY. I don't know. After all, they were asked.

NATASHA. This morning, when the little boy woke up and saw me he suddenly smiled; that means he knew me. "Good morning, Bobby!" I said, "good morning, darling." And he laughed. Children understand, they understand very well. So I'll tell them, Andrey dear, not to receive the entertainers.

ANDREY. [Hesitatingly] But what about my sisters. This is their flat.

NATASHA. They'll do as I want them. They are so kind.... [Going] I ordered sour milk for supper. The doctor says you must eat sour milk and nothing else, or you won't get thin. [Stops] Bobby is so cold. I'm afraid his room is too cold for him. It would be nice to put him into another room till the warm weather comes. Irina's room, for instance, is just right for a child: it's dry and has the sun all day. I must tell her, she can share Olga's room. It isn't as if she was at home in the daytime, she only sleeps here.... [A pause] Andrey, darling, why are you so silent?

ANDREY. I was just thinking.... There is really nothing to say....

NATASHA. Yes... there was something I wanted to tell you.... Oh, yes. Ferapont has come from the Council offices, he wants to see you.

ANDREY. [Yawns] Call him here.

[NATASHA goes out; ANDREY reads his book, stooping over the candle she has left behind. FERAPONT enters; he wears a tattered old coat with the collar up. His ears are muffled.]

ANDREY. Good morning, grandfather. What have you to say?

FERAPONT. The Chairman sends a book and some documents or other. Here.... [Hands him a book and a packet.]

ANDREY. Thank you. It's all right. Why couldn't you come earlier? It's past eight now.

FERAPONT. What?

ANDREY. [Louder]. I say you've come late, it's past eight.

FERAPONT. Yes, yes. I came when it was still light, but they wouldn't let me in. They said you were busy. Well, what was I to do. If you're busy, you're busy, and I'm in no hurry. [He thinks that ANDREY is asking him something] What?

ANDREY. Nothing. [Looks through the book] To-morrow's Friday. I'm not supposed to go to work, but I'll come—all the same... and do some work. It's dull at home. [Pause] Oh, my dear old man, how strangely life changes, and how it deceives! To-day, out of sheer boredom, I took up this book—old university lectures, and I couldn't help laughing. My God, I'm secretary of the local district council, the council which has Protopopov for its chairman, yes, I'm the secretary, and the summit of my ambitions is—to become a member of the council! I to be a member of the local district council, I, who dream every night that I'm a professor of Moscow University, a famous scholar of whom all Russia is proud!

FERAPONT. I can't tell... I'm hard of hearing....

ANDREY. If you weren't, I don't suppose I should talk to you. I've got to talk to somebody, and my wife doesn't understand me, and I'm a bit afraid of my sisters—I don't know why unless it is that they may make fun of me and make me feel ashamed... I don't drink, I don't like public-houses, but how I should like to be sitting just now in Tyestov's place in Moscow, or at the Great Moscow, old fellow!

FERAPONT. Moscow? That's where a contractor was once telling that some merchants or other were eating pancakes; one ate forty pancakes and he went and died, he was saying. Either forty or fifty, I forget which.

ANDREY. In Moscow you can sit in an enormous restaurant where you don't know anybody and where nobody knows you, and you don't feel all the same that you're a stranger. And here you know everybody and everybody knows you, and you're a stranger... and a lonely stranger.

FERAPONT. What? And the same contractor was telling—perhaps he was lying—that there was a cable stretching right across Moscow.

ANDREY. What for?

FERAPONT. I can't tell. The contractor said so.

ANDREY. Rubbish. [He reads] Were you ever in Moscow?

FERAPONT. [After a pause] No. God did not lead me there. [Pause] Shall I go?

ANDREY. You may go. Good-bye. [FERAPONT goes] Good-bye. [Reads] You can come to-morrow and fetch these documents.... Go along.... [Pause] He's gone. [A ring] Yes, yes.... [Stretches himself and slowly goes into his own room.]

[Behind the scene the nurse is singing a lullaby to the child. MASHA and VERSHININ come in. While they talk, a maidservant lights candles and a lamp.]

MASHA. I don't know. [Pause] I don't know. Of course, habit counts for a great deal. After father's death, for instance, it took us a long time to get used to the absence of orderlies. But, apart from habit, it seems to me in all fairness that, however it may be in other towns, the best and most-educated people are army men.

VERSHININ. I'm thirsty. I should like some tea.

MASHA. [Glancing at her watch] They'll bring some soon. I was given in marriage when I was eighteen, and I was afraid of my husband because he was a teacher and I'd only just left school. He then seemed to me frightfully wise and learned and important. And now, unfortunately, that has changed.

VERSHININ. Yes... yes.

MASHA. I don't speak of my husband, I've grown used to him, but civilians in general are so often coarse, impolite, uneducated. Their rudeness offends me, it angers me. I suffer when I see that a man isn't quite sufficiently refined, or delicate, or polite. I simply suffer agonies when I happen to be among schoolmasters, my husband's colleagues.

VERSHININ. Yes.... It seems to me that civilians and army men are equally interesting, in this town, at any rate. It's all the same! If you listen to a member of the local intelligentsia, whether to civilian or military, he will tell you that he's sick of his wife, sick of his house, sick of his estate, sick of his horses.... We Russians are extremely gifted in the direction of thinking on an exalted plane, but, tell me, why do we aim so low in real life? Why?

MASHA. Why?

VERSHININ. Why is a Russian sick of his children, sick of his wife? And why are his wife and children sick of him?

MASHA. You're a little downhearted to-day.

VERSHININ. Perhaps I am. I haven't had any dinner, I've had nothing since the morning. My daughter is a little unwell, and when my girls are ill, I get very anxious and my conscience tortures me because they have such a mother. Oh, if you had seen her to-day! What a trivial personality! We began quarrelling at seven in the morning and at nine I slammed the door and went out. [Pause] I never speak of her, it's strange that I bear my complaints to you alone. [Kisses her hand] Don't be angry with me. I haven't anybody but you, nobody at all.... [Pause.]

MASHA. What a noise in the oven. Just before father's death there was a noise in the pipe, just like that.

VERSHININ. Are you superstitious?

MASHA. Yes.

VERSHININ. That's strange. [Kisses her hand] You are a splendid, wonderful woman. Splendid, wonderful! It is dark here, but I see your sparkling eyes.

MASHA. [Sits on another chair] There is more light here.

VERSHININ. I love you, love you, love you... I love your eyes, your movements, I dream of them.... Splendid, wonderful woman!

MASHA. [Laughing] When you talk to me like that, I laugh; I don't know why, for I'm afraid. Don't repeat it, please.... [In an undertone] No, go on, it's all the same to me.... [Covers her face with her hands] Somebody's coming, let's talk about something else.

[IRINA and TUZENBACH come in through the dining-room.]

TUZENBACH. My surname is really triple. I am called Baron Tuzenbach-Krone-Altschauer, but I am Russian and Orthodox, the same as you. There is very little German left in me, unless perhaps it is the patience and the obstinacy with which I bore you. I see you home every night.

IRINA. How tired I am!

TUZENBACH. And I'll come to the telegraph office to see you home every day for ten or twenty years, until you drive me away. [He sees MASHA and VERSHININ; joyfully] Is that you? How do you do.

IRINA. Well, I am home at last. [To MASHA] A lady came to-day to telegraph to her brother in Saratov that her son died to-day, and she couldn't remember the address anyhow. So she sent the telegram without an address, just to Saratov. She was crying. And for some reason or other I was rude to her. "I've no time," I said. It was so stupid. Are the entertainers coming to-night?

MASHA. Yes.

IRINA. [Sitting down in an armchair] I want a rest. I am tired.

TUZENBACH. [Smiling] When you come home from your work you seem so young, and so unfortunate.... [Pause.]

IRINA. I am tired. No, I don't like the telegraph office, I don't like it.

MASHA. You've grown thinner.... [Whistles a little] And you look younger, and your face has become like a boy's.

TUZENBACH. That's the way she does her hair.

IRINA. I must find another job, this one won't do for me. What I wanted, what I hoped to get, just that is lacking here. Labour without poetry, without ideas.... [A knock on the floor] The doctor is knocking. [To TUZENBACH] Will you knock, dear. I can't... I'm tired.... [TUZENBACH knocks] He'll come in a minute. Something ought to be done. Yesterday the doctor and Andrey played cards at the club and lost money. Andrey seems to have lost 200 roubles.

MASHA. [With indifference] What can we do now?

IRINA. He lost money a fortnight ago, he lost money in December. Perhaps if he lost everything we should go away from this town. Oh, my God, I dream of Moscow every night. I'm just like a lunatic. [Laughs] We go there in June, and before June there's still... February, March, April, May... nearly half a year!

MASHA. Only Natasha mustn't get to know of these losses.

IRINA. I expect it will be all the same to her.

[CHEBUTIKIN, who has only just got out of bed—he was resting after dinner—comes into the dining-room and combs his beard. He then sits by the table and takes a newspaper from his pocket.]

MASHA. Here he is.... Has he paid his rent?

IRINA. [Laughs] No. He's been here eight months and hasn't paid a copeck. Seems to have forgotten.

MASHA. [Laughs] What dignity in his pose! [They all laugh. A pause.]

IRINA. Why are you so silent, Alexander Ignateyevitch?

VERSHININ. I don't know. I want some tea. Half my life for a tumbler of tea: I haven't had anything since morning.

CHEBUTIKIN. Irina Sergeyevna!

IRINA. What is it?

CHEBUTIKIN. Please come here, Venez ici. [IRINA goes and sits by the table] I can't do without you. [IRINA begins to play patience.]

VERSHININ. Well, if we can't have any tea, let's philosophize, at any rate.

TUZENBACH. Yes, let's. About what?

VERSHININ. About what? Let us meditate... about life as it will be after our time; for example, in two or three hundred years.

TUZENBACH. Well? After our time people will fly about in balloons, the cut of one's coat will change, perhaps they'll discover a sixth sense and develop it, but life will remain the same, laborious, mysterious, and happy. And in a thousand years' time, people will still be sighing: "Life is hard!"—and at the same time they'll be just as afraid of death, and unwilling to meet it, as we are.

VERSHININ. [Thoughtfully] How can I put it? It seems to me that everything on earth must change, little by little, and is already changing under our very eyes. After two or three hundred years, after a thousand—the actual time doesn't matter—a new and happy age will begin. We, of course, shall not take part in it, but we live and work and even suffer to-day that it should come. We create it—and in that one object is our destiny and, if you like, our happiness.

[MASHA laughs softly.]

TUZENBACH. What is it?

MASHA. I don't know. I've been laughing all day, ever since morning.

VERSHININ. I finished my education at the same point as you, I have not studied at universities; I read a lot, but I cannot choose my books and perhaps what I read is not at all what I should, but the longer I love, the more I want to know. My hair is turning white, I am nearly an old man now, but I know so little, oh, so little! But I think I know the things that matter most, and that are most real. I know them well. And I wish I could make you understand that there is no happiness for us, that there should not and cannot be.... We must only work and work, and happiness is only for our distant posterity. [Pause] If not for me, then for the descendants of my descendants.

[FEDOTIK and RODE come into the dining-room; they sit and sing softly, strumming on a guitar.]

TUZENBACH. According to you, one should not even think about happiness! But suppose I am happy!

VERSHININ. No.

TUZENBACH. [Moves his hands and laughs] We do not seem to understand each other. How can I convince you? [MASHA laughs quietly, TUZENBACH continues, pointing at her] Yes, laugh! [To VERSHININ] Not only after two or three centuries, but in a million years, life will still be as it was; life does not change, it remains for ever, following its own laws which do not concern us, or which, at any rate, you will never find out. Migrant birds, cranes for example, fly and fly, and whatever thoughts, high or low, enter their heads, they will still fly and not know why or where. They fly and will continue to fly, whatever philosophers come to life among them; they may philosophize as much as they like, only they will fly....

MASHA. Still, is there a meaning?

TUZENBACH. A meaning.... Now the snow is falling. What meaning? [Pause.]

MASHA. It seems to me that a man must have faith, or must search for a faith, or his life will be empty, empty.... To live and not to know why the cranes fly, why babies are born, why there are stars in the sky.... Either you must know why you live, or everything is trivial, not worth a straw. [A pause.]

VERSHININ. Still, I am sorry that my youth has gone.

MASHA. Gogol says: life in this world is a dull matter, my masters!

TUZENBACH. And I say it's difficult to argue with you, my masters! Hang it all.

CHEBUTIKIN. [Reading] Balzac was married at Berdichev. [IRINA is singing softly] That's worth making a note of. [He makes a note] Balzac was married at Berdichev. [Goes on reading.]

IRINA. [Laying out cards, thoughtfully] Balzac was married at Berdichev.

TUZENBACH. The die is cast. I've handed in my resignation, Maria Sergeyevna.

MASHA. So I heard. I don't see what good it is; I don't like civilians.

TUZENBACH. Never mind.... [Gets up] I'm not handsome; what use am I as a soldier? Well, it makes no difference... I shall work. If only just once in my life I could work so that I could come home in the evening, fall exhausted on my bed, and go to sleep at once. [Going into the dining-room] Workmen, I suppose, do sleep soundly!

FEDOTIK. [To IRINA] I bought some coloured pencils for you at Pizhikov's in the Moscow Road, just now. And here is a little knife.

IRINA. You have got into the habit of behaving to me as if I am a little girl, but I am grown up. [Takes the pencils and the knife, then, with joy] How lovely!

FEDOTIK. And I bought myself a knife... look at it... one blade, another, a third, an ear-scoop, scissors, nail-cleaners.

RODE. [Loudly] Doctor, how old are you?

CHEBUTIKIN. I? Thirty-two. [Laughter]

FEDOTIK. I'll show you another kind of patience.... [Lays out cards.]

[A samovar is brought in; ANFISA attends to it; a little later NATASHA enters and helps by the table; SOLENI arrives and, after greetings, sits by the table.]

VERSHININ. What a wind!

MASHA. Yes. I'm tired of winter. I've already forgotten what summer's like.

IRINA. It's coming out, I see. We're going to Moscow.

FEDOTIK. No, it won't come out. Look, the eight was on the two of spades. [Laughs] That means you won't go to Moscow.

CHEBUTIKIN. [Reading paper] Tsitsigar. Smallpox is raging here.

ANFISA. [Coming up to MASHA] Masha, have some tea, little mother. [To VERSHININ] Please have some, sir... excuse me, but I've forgotten your name....

MASHA. Bring some here, nurse. I shan't go over there.

IRINA. Nurse!

ANFISA. Coming, coming!

NATASHA. [To SOLENI] Children at the breast understand perfectly. I said "Good morning, Bobby; good morning, dear!" And he looked at me in quite an unusual way. You think it's only the mother in me that is speaking; I assure you that isn't so! He's a wonderful child.

SOLENI. If he was my child I'd roast him on a frying-pan and eat him. [Takes his tumbler into the drawing-room and sits in a corner.]

NATASHA. [Covers her face in her hands] Vulgar, ill-bred man!

MASHA. He's lucky who doesn't notice whether it's winter now, or summer. I think that if I were in Moscow, I shouldn't mind about the weather.

VERSHININ. A few days ago I was reading the prison diary of a French minister. He had been sentenced on account of the Panama scandal. With what joy, what delight, he speaks of the birds he saw through the prison windows, which he had never noticed while he was a minister. Now, of course, that he is at liberty, he notices birds no more than he did before. When you go to live in Moscow you'll not notice it, in just the same way. There can be no happiness for us, it only exists in our wishes.

TUZENBACH. [Takes cardboard box from the table] Where are the pastries?

IRINA. Soleni has eaten them.

TUZENBACH. All of them?

ANFISA. [Serving tea] There's a letter for you.

VERSHININ. For me? [Takes the letter] From my daughter. [Reads] Yes, of course... I will go quietly. Excuse me, Maria Sergeyevna. I shan't have any tea. [Stands up, excited] That eternal story....

MASHA. What is it? Is it a secret?

VERSHININ. [Quietly] My wife has poisoned herself again. I must go. I'll go out quietly. It's all awfully unpleasant. [Kisses MASHA'S hand] My dear, my splendid, good woman... I'll go this way, quietly. [Exit.]

ANFISA. Where has he gone? And I'd served tea.... What a man.

MASHA. [Angrily] Be quiet! You bother so one can't have a moment's peace.... [Goes to the table with her cup] I'm tired of you, old woman!

ANFISA. My dear! Why are you offended!

ANDREY'S VOICE. Anfisa!

ANFISA. [Mocking] Anfisa! He sits there and... [Exit.]

MASHA. [In the dining-room, by the table angrily] Let me sit down! [Disturbs the cards on the table] Here you are, spreading your cards out. Have some tea!

IRINA. You are cross, Masha.

MASHA. If I am cross, then don't talk to me. Don't touch me!

CHEBUTIKIN. Don't touch her, don't touch her....

MASHA. You're sixty, but you're like a boy, always up to some beastly nonsense.

NATASHA. [Sighs] Dear Masha, why use such expressions? With your beautiful exterior you would be simply fascinating in good society, I tell you so directly, if it wasn't for your words. *Je vous prie, pardonnez moi, Marie, mais vous avez des manières un peu grossières.*

TUZENBACH. [Restraining his laughter] Give me... give me... there's some cognac, I think.

NATASHA. *Il parait, que mon Bobick déjà ne dort pas*, he has awakened. He isn't well to-day. I'll go to him, excuse me... [Exit.]

IRINA. Where has Alexander Ignateyevitch gone?

MASHA. Home. Something extraordinary has happened to his wife again.

TUZENBACH. [Goes to SOLENI with a cognac-flask in his hands] You go on sitting by yourself, thinking of something—goodness knows what. Come and let's make peace. Let's have some cognac. [They drink] I expect I'll have to play the piano all night, some rubbish most likely... well, so be it!

SOLENI. Why make peace? I haven't quarrelled with you.

TUZENBACH. You always make me feel as if something has taken place between us. You've a strange character, you must admit.

SOLENI. [Declaims] "I am strange, but who is not? Don't be angry, Aleko!"

TUZENBACH. And what has Aleko to do with it? [Pause.]

SOLENI. When I'm with one other man I behave just like everybody else, but in company I'm dull and shy and... talk all manner of rubbish. But I'm more honest and more honourable than very, very many people. And I can prove it.

TUZENBACH. I often get angry with you, you always fasten on to me in company, but I like you all the same. I'm going to drink my fill to-night, whatever happens. Drink, now!

SOLENI. Let's drink. [They drink] I never had anything against you, Baron. But my character is like Lermontov's [In a low voice] I even rather resemble Lermontov, they say.... [Takes a scent-bottle from his pocket, and scents his hands.]

TUZENBACH. I've sent in my resignation. Basta! I've been thinking about it for five years, and at last made up my mind. I shall work.

SOLENI. [Declaims] "Do not be angry, Aleko... forget, forget, thy dreams of yore...."

[While he is speaking ANDREY enters quietly with a book, and sits by the table.]

TUZENBACH. I shall work.

CHEBUTIKIN. [Going with IRINA into the dining-room] And the food was also real Caucasian onion soup, and, for a roast, some chehartma.

SOLENI. Cheremsha [Note: A variety of garlic.] isn't meat at all, but a plant something like an onion.

CHEBUTIKIN. No, my angel. Chehartma isn't onion, but roast mutton.

SOLENI. And I tell you, chehartma—is a sort of onion.

CHEBUTIKIN. And I tell you, chehartma—is mutton.

SOLENI. And I tell you, cheremsha—is a sort of onion.

CHEBUTIKIN. What's the use of arguing! You've never been in the Caucasus, and never ate any chehartma.

SOLENI. I never ate it, because I hate it. It smells like garlic.

ANDREY. [Imploring] Please, please! I ask you!

TUZENBACH. When are the entertainers coming?

IRINA. They promised for about nine; that is, quite soon.

TUZENBACH. [Embraces ANDREY]

"Oh my house, my house, my new-built house."

ANDREY. [Dances and sings] "Newly-built of maple-wood."

CHEBUTIKIN. [Dances]

"Its walls are like a sieve!" [Laughter.]

TUZENBACH. [Kisses ANDREY] Hang it all, let's drink. Andrey, old boy, let's drink with you. And I'll go with you, Andrey, to the University of Moscow.

SOLENI. Which one? There are two universities in Moscow.

ANDREY. There's one university in Moscow.

SOLENI. Two, I tell you.

ANDREY. Don't care if there are three. So much the better.

SOLENI. There are two universities in Moscow! [There are murmurs and "hushes"] There are two universities in Moscow, the old one and the new one. And if you don't like to listen, if my words annoy you, then I need not speak. I can even go into another room.... [Exit.]

TUZENBACH. Bravo, bravo! [Laughs] Come on, now. I'm going to play. Funny man, Soleni.... [Goes to the piano and plays a waltz.]

MASHA. [Dancing solo] The Baron's drunk, the Baron's drunk, the Baron's drunk!

[NATASHA comes in.]

NATASHA. [To CHEBUTIKIN] Ivan Romanovitch!

[Says something to CHEBUTIKIN, then goes out quietly; CHEBUTIKIN touches TUZENBACH on the shoulder and whispers something to him.]

IRINA. What is it?

CHEBUTIKIN. Time for us to go. Good-bye.

TUZENBACH. Good-night. It's time we went.

IRINA. But, really, the entertainers?

ANDREY. [In confusion] There won't be any entertainers. You see, dear, Natasha says that Bobby isn't quite well, and so.... In a word, I don't care, and it's absolutely all one to me.

IRINA. [Shrugging her shoulders] Bobby ill!

MASHA. What is she thinking of! Well, if they are sent home, I suppose they must go. [To IRINA] Bobby's all right, it's she herself.... Here! [Taps her forehead] Little bourgeoise!

[ANDREY goes to his room through the right-hand door, CHEBUTIKIN follows him. In the dining-room they are saying good-bye.]

FEDOTIK. What a shame! I was expecting to spend the evening here, but of course, if the little baby is ill... I'll bring him some toys to-morrow.

RODE. [Loudly] I slept late after dinner to-day because I thought I was going to dance all night. It's only nine o'clock now!

MASHA. Let's go into the street, we can talk there. Then we can settle things.

(Good-byes and good nights are heard. TUZENBACH'S merry laughter is heard. [All go out] ANFISA and the maid clear the table, and put out the lights. [The nurse sings] ANDREY, wearing an overcoat and a hat, and CHEBUTIKIN enter silently.)

CHEBUTIKIN. I never managed to get married because my life flashed by like lightning, and because I was madly in love with your mother, who was married.

ANDREY. One shouldn't marry. One shouldn't, because it's dull.

CHEBUTIKIN. So there I am, in my loneliness. Say what you will, loneliness is a terrible thing, old fellow.... Though really... of course, it absolutely doesn't matter!

ANDREY. Let's be quicker.

CHEBUTIKIN. What are you in such a hurry for? We shall be in time.

ANDREY. I'm afraid my wife may stop me.

CHEBUTIKIN. Ah!

ANDREY. I shan't play to-night, I shall only sit and look on. I don't feel very well.... What am I to do for my asthma, Ivan Romanovitch?

CHEBUTIKIN. Don't ask me! I don't remember, old fellow, I don't know.

ANDREY. Let's go through the kitchen. [They go out.]

[A bell rings, then a second time; voices and laughter are heard.]

IRINA. [Enters] What's that?

ANFISA. [Whispers] The entertainers! [Bell.]

IRINA. Tell them there's nobody at home, nurse. They must excuse us.

[ANFISA goes out. IRINA walks about the room deep in thought; she is excited. SOLENI enters.]

SOLENI. [In surprise] There's nobody here.... Where are they all?

IRINA. They've gone home.

SOLENI. How strange. Are you here alone?

IRINA. Yes, alone. [A pause] Good-bye.

SOLENI. Just now I behaved tactlessly, with insufficient reserve. But you are not like all the others, you are noble and pure, you can see the truth.... You alone can understand me. I love you, deeply, beyond measure, I love you.

IRINA. Good-bye! Go away.

SOLENI. I cannot live without you. [Follows her] Oh, my happiness! [Through his tears] Oh, joy! Wonderful, marvellous, glorious eyes, such as I have never seen before....

IRINA. [Coldly] Stop it, Vassili Vassilevitch!

SOLENI. This is the first time I speak to you of love, and it is as if I am no longer on the earth, but on another planet. [Wipes his forehead] Well, never mind. I can't make you love me by force, of course... but I don't intend to have any more-favoured rivals.... No... I swear to you by all the saints, I shall kill my rival.... Oh, beautiful one!

[NATASHA enters with a candle; she looks in through one door, then through another, and goes past the door leading to her husband's room.]

NATASHA. Here's Andrey. Let him go on reading. Excuse me, Vassili Vassilevitch, I did not know you were here; I am engaged in domesticities.

SOLENI. It's all the same to me. Good-bye! [Exit.]

NATASHA. You're so tired, my poor dear girl! [Kisses IRINA] If you only went to bed earlier.

IRINA. Is Bobby asleep?

NATASHA. Yes, but restlessly. By the way, dear, I wanted to tell you, but either you weren't at home, or I was busy... I think Bobby's present nursery is cold and damp. And your room would be so nice for the child. My dear, darling girl, do change over to Olga's for a bit!

IRINA. [Not understanding] Where?

[The bells of a troika are heard as it drives up to the house.]

NATASHA. You and Olga can share a room, for the time being, and Bobby can have yours. He's such a darling; to-day I said to him, "Bobby, you're mine! Mine!" And he looked at me with his dear little eyes. [A bell rings] It must be Olga. How late she is! [The maid enters and whispers to NATASHA] Protopopov? What a queer man to do such a thing. Protopopov's come and wants me to go for a drive with him in his troika. [Laughs] How funny these men are.... [A bell rings] Somebody has come. Suppose I did go and have half an hour's drive.... [To the maid] Say I shan't be long. [Bell rings] Somebody's ringing, it must be Olga. [Exit.]

[The maid runs out; IRINA sits deep in thought; KULIGIN and OLGA enter, followed by VERSHININ.]

KULIGIN. Well, there you are. And you said there was going to be a party.

VERSHININ. It's queer; I went away not long ago, half an hour ago, and they were expecting entertainers.

IRINA. They've all gone.

KULIGIN. Has Masha gone too? Where has she gone? And what's Protopopov waiting for downstairs in his troika? Whom is he expecting?

IRINA. Don't ask questions... I'm tired.

KULIGIN. Oh, you're all whimsies....

OLGA. My committee meeting is only just over. I'm tired out. Our chairwoman is ill, so I had to take her place. My head, my head is aching.... [Sits] Andrey lost 200 roubles at cards yesterday... the whole town is talking about it....

KULIGIN. Yes, my meeting tired me too. [Sits.]

VERSHININ. My wife took it into her head to frighten me just now by nearly poisoning herself. It's all right now, and I'm glad; I can rest now.... But perhaps we ought to go away? Well, my best wishes, Feodor Ilitch, let's go somewhere together! I can't, I absolutely can't stop at home.... Come on!

KULIGIN. I'm tired. I won't go. [Gets up] I'm tired. Has my wife gone home?

IRINA. I suppose so.

KULIGIN. [Kisses IRINA'S hand] Good-bye, I'm going to rest all day to-morrow and the day after. Best wishes! [Going] I should like some tea. I was looking forward to spending the whole evening in pleasant company and—o, fallacem hominum spem!... Accusative case after an interjection....

VERSHININ. Then I'll go somewhere by myself. [Exit with KULIGIN, whistling.]

OLGA. I've such a headache... Andrey has been losing money.... The whole town is talking.... I'll go and lie down. [Going] I'm free to-morrow.... Oh, my God, what a mercy! I'm free to-morrow, I'm free the day after.... Oh my head, my head.... [Exit.]

IRINA. [alone] They've all gone. Nobody's left.

[A concertina is being played in the street. The nurse sings.]

NATASHA. [in fur coat and cap, steps across the dining-room, followed by the maid] I'll be back in half an hour. I'm only going for a little drive. [Exit.]

IRINA. [Alone in her misery] To Moscow! Moscow! Moscow!

Curtain.

ACT III

[The room shared by OLGA and IRINA. Beds, screened off, on the right and left. It is past 2 a.m. Behind the stage a fire-alarm is ringing; it has apparently been going for some time. Nobody in the house has gone to bed yet. MASHA is lying on a sofa dressed, as usual, in black. Enter OLGA and ANFISA.]

ANFISA. Now they are downstairs, sitting under the stairs. I said to them, "Won't you come up," I said, "You can't go on like this," and they simply cried, "We don't know where father is." They said, "He may be burnt up by now." What an idea! And in the yard there are some people... also undressed.

OLGA. [Takes a dress out of the cupboard] Take this grey dress.... And this... and the blouse as well.... Take the skirt, too, nurse.... My God! How awful it is! The whole of the Kirsanovsky Road seems to have burned down. Take this... and this.... [Throws clothes into her hands] The poor Vershinins are so frightened.... Their house was nearly burnt. They ought to come here for the night.... They shouldn't be allowed to go home.... Poor Fedotik is completely burnt out, there's nothing left....

ANFISA. Couldn't you call Ferapont, Olga dear. I can hardly manage....

OLGA. [Rings] They'll never answer.... [At the door] Come here, whoever there is! [Through the open door can be seen a window, red with flame: afire-engine is heard passing the house] How awful this is. And how I'm sick of it! [FERAPONT enters] Take these things down.... The Kolotilin girls are down below... and let them have them. This, too.

FERAPONT. Yes'm. In the year twelve Moscow was burning too. Oh, my God! The Frenchmen were surprised.

OLGA. Go on, go on....

FERAPONT. Yes'm. [Exit.]

OLGA. Nurse, dear, let them have everything. We don't want anything. Give it all to them, nurse.... I'm tired, I can hardly keep on my legs.... The Vershinins mustn't be allowed to go home.... The girls can sleep in the drawing-room, and Alexander Ignateyevitch can go downstairs to the Baron's flat... Fedotik can go there, too, or else into our dining-room.... The doctor is drunk, beastly drunk, as if on purpose, so nobody can go to him. Vershinin's wife, too, may go into the drawing-room.

ANFISA. [Tired] Olga, dear girl, don't dismiss me! Don't dismiss me!

OLGA. You're talking nonsense, nurse. Nobody is dismissing you.

ANFISA. [Puts OLGA'S head against her bosom] My dear, precious girl, I'm working, I'm toiling away... I'm growing weak, and they'll all say go away! And where shall I go? Where? I'm eighty. Eighty-one years old....

OLGA. You sit down, nurse dear.... You're tired, poor dear.... [Makes her sit down] Rest, dear. You're so pale!

[NATASHA comes in.]

NATASHA. They are saying that a committee to assist the sufferers from the fire must be formed at once. What do you think of that? It's a beautiful idea. Of course the poor ought to be helped, it's the duty of the rich. Bobby and little Sophy are sleeping, sleeping as if nothing at all was the matter. There's such a lot of people here, the place is full of them, wherever you go. There's influenza in the town now. I'm afraid the children may catch it.

OLGA. [Not attending] In this room we can't see the fire, it's quiet here.

NATASHA. Yes... I suppose I'm all untidy. [Before the looking-glass] They say I'm growing stout... it isn't true! Certainly it isn't! Masha's asleep; the poor thing is tired out.... [Coldly, to ANFISA] Don't dare to be seated in my presence! Get up! Out of this! [Exit ANFISA; a pause] I don't understand what makes you keep on that old woman!

OLGA. [Confusedly] Excuse me, I don't understand either...

NATASHA. She's no good here. She comes from the country, she ought to live there.... Spoiling her, I call it! I like order in the house! We don't want any unnecessary people here. [Strokes her cheek] You're tired, poor thing! Our head mistress is tired! And when my little Sophie grows up and goes to school I shall be so afraid of you.

OLGA. I shan't be head mistress.

NATASHA. They'll appoint you, Olga. It's settled.

OLGA. I'll refuse the post. I can't... I'm not strong enough.... [Drinks water] You were so rude to nurse just now... I'm sorry. I can't stand it... everything seems dark in front of me....

NATASHA. [Excited] Forgive me, Olga, forgive me... I didn't want to annoy you.

[MASHA gets up, takes a pillow and goes out angrily.]

OLGA. Remember, dear... we have been brought up, in an unusual way, perhaps, but I can't bear this. Such behaviour has a bad effect on me, I get ill... I simply lose heart!

NATASHA. Forgive me, forgive me.... [Kisses her.]

OLGA. Even the least bit of rudeness, the slightest impoliteness, upsets me.

NATASHA. I often say too much, it's true, but you must agree, dear, that she could just as well live in the country.

OLGA. She has been with us for thirty years.

NATASHA. But she can't do any work now. Either I don't understand, or you don't want to understand me. She's no good for work, she can only sleep or sit about.

OLGA. And let her sit about.

NATASHA. [Surprised] What do you mean? She's only a servant. [Crying] I don't understand you, Olga. I've got a nurse, a wet-nurse, we've a cook, a housemaid... what do we want that old woman for as well? What good is she? [Fire-alarm behind the stage.]

OLGA. I've grown ten years older to-night.

NATASHA. We must come to an agreement, Olga. Your place is the school, mine—the home. You devote yourself to teaching, I, to the household. And if I talk about servants, then I do know what I am talking about; I do know what I am talking about... And to-morrow there's to be no more of that old thief, that old hag... [Stamping] that witch! And don't you dare to annoy me! Don't you dare! [Stopping short] Really, if you don't move downstairs, we shall always be quarrelling. This is awful.

[Enter KULIGIN.]

KULIGIN. Where's Masha? It's time we went home. The fire seems to be going down. [Stretches himself] Only one block has burnt down, but there was such a wind that it seemed at first the whole town was going to burn. [Sits] I'm tired out. My dear Olga... I often think that if it hadn't been for Masha, I should have married you. You are awfully nice.... I am absolutely tired out. [Listens.]

OLGA. What is it?

KULIGIN. The doctor, of course, has been drinking hard; he's terribly drunk. He might have done it on purpose! [Gets up] He seems to be coming here.... Do you hear him? Yes, here.... [Laughs] What a man... really... I'll hide myself. [Goes to the cupboard and stands in the corner] What a rogue.

OLGA. He hadn't touched a drop for two years, and now he suddenly goes and gets drunk....

[Retires with NATASHA to the back of the room. CHEBUTIKIN enters; apparently sober, he stops, looks round, then goes to the wash-stand and begins to wash his hands.]

CHEBUTIKIN. [Angrily] Devil take them all... take them all.... They think I'm a doctor and can cure everything, and I know absolutely nothing, I've forgotten all I ever knew, I remember nothing, absolutely nothing. [OLGA and NATASHA go out, unnoticed by him] Devil take it. Last Wednesday I attended a woman in Zasip—and she died, and it's my fault that she died. Yes... I used to know a certain amount five-and-twenty years ago, but I don't remember anything now. Nothing. Perhaps I'm not really a man, and am only pretending that I've got arms and legs and a head; perhaps I don't exist at all, and only imagine that I walk, and eat, and sleep. [Cries] Oh, if only I didn't exist! [Stops crying; angrily] The devil only knows.... Day before yesterday they were talking in the club; they said, Shakespeare, Voltaire... I'd never read, never read at all, and I put on an expression as if I had read. And so did the others. Oh, how beastly! How petty! And then I remembered the woman I killed on Wednesday... and I couldn't get her out of my mind, and everything in my mind became crooked, nasty, wretched.... So I went and drank....

[IRINA, VERSHININ and TUZENBACH enter; TUZENBACH is wearing new and fashionable civilian clothes.]

IRINA. Let's sit down here. Nobody will come in here.

VERSHININ. The whole town would have been destroyed if it hadn't been for the soldiers. Good men! [Rubs his hands appreciatively] Splendid people! Oh, what a fine lot!

KULIGIN. [Coming up to him] What's the time?

TUZENBACH. It's past three now. It's dawning.

IRINA. They are all sitting in the dining-room, nobody is going. And that Soleni of yours is sitting there. [To CHEBUTIKIN] Hadn't you better be going to sleep, doctor?

CHEBUTIKIN. It's all right... thank you.... [Combs his beard.]

KULIGIN. [Laughs] Speaking's a bit difficult, eh, Ivan Romanovitch! [Pats him on the shoulder] Good man! *In vino veritas*, the ancients used to say.

TUZENBACH. They keep on asking me to get up a concert in aid of the sufferers.

IRINA. As if one could do anything....

TUZENBACH. It might be arranged, if necessary. In my opinion Maria Sergeyevna is an excellent pianist.

KULIGIN. Yes, excellent!

IRINA. She's forgotten everything. She hasn't played for three years... or four.

TUZENBACH. In this town absolutely nobody understands music, not a soul except myself, but I do understand it, and assure you on my word of honour that Maria Sergeyevna plays excellently, almost with genius.

KULIGIN. You are right, Baron, I'm awfully fond of Masha. She's very fine.

TUZENBACH. To be able to play so admirably and to realize at the same time that nobody, nobody can understand you!

KULIGIN. [Sighs] Yes.... But will it be quite all right for her to take part in a concert? [Pause] You see, I don't know anything about it. Perhaps it will even be all to the good. Although I must admit that our Director is a good man, a very good man even, a very clever man, still he has such views.... Of course it isn't his business but still, if you wish it, perhaps I'd better talk to him.

[CHEBUTIKIN takes a porcelain clock into his hands and examines it.]

VERSHININ. I got so dirty while the fire was on, I don't look like anybody on earth. [Pause] Yesterday I happened to hear, casually, that they want to transfer our brigade to some distant place. Some said to Poland, others, to Chita.

TUZENBACH. I heard so, too. Well, if it is so, the town will be quite empty.

IRINA. And we'll go away, too!

CHEBUTIKIN. [Drops the clock which breaks to pieces] To smithereens!

[A pause; everybody is pained and confused.]

KULIGIN. [Gathering up the pieces] To smash such a valuable object—oh, Ivan Romanovitch, Ivan Romanovitch! A very bad mark for your misbehaviour!

IRINA. That clock used to belong to our mother.

CHEBUTIKIN. Perhaps.... To your mother, your mother. Perhaps I didn't break it; it only looks as if I broke it. Perhaps we only think that we exist, when really we don't. I don't know anything, nobody knows anything. [At the door] What are you looking at? Natasha has a little romance with Protopopov, and you don't see it.... There you sit and see nothing, and Natasha has a little romance with Protopovov.... [Sings] Won't you please accept this date.... [Exit.]

VERSHININ. Yes. [Laughs] How strange everything really is! [Pause] When the fire broke out, I hurried off home; when I get there I see the house is whole, uninjured, and in no danger, but my two girls are standing by the door in just their underclothes, their mother isn't there, the crowd is excited, horses and dogs are running about, and the girls' faces are so agitated, terrified, beseeching, and I don't know what else. My heart was pained when I saw those faces. My God, I thought, what these girls will have to put up with if they live long! I caught them up and ran, and still kept on thinking the one thing: what they will have to live through in this world! [Fire-alarm; a pause] I come here and find their mother shouting and angry. [MASHA enters with a pillow and sits on the sofa] And when my girls were standing by the door in just their underclothes, and the street was red from the fire, there was a dreadful noise, and I thought that something of the sort used to happen many years ago when an enemy made a sudden attack, and looted, and burned.... And at the same time what a difference there really is between the present and the past! And when a little more time has gone by, in two or three hundred years perhaps, people will look at our present life with just the same fear, and the same contempt, and the whole past will seem clumsy and dull, and very uncomfortable, and strange. Oh, indeed, what a life there will be, what a life! [Laughs] Forgive me, I've dropped into philosophy again. Please let me continue. I do awfully want to philosophize, it's just how I feel at present. [Pause] As if they are all asleep. As I was saying: what a life there will be! Only just imagine.... There are only three persons like yourselves in the town just now, but in future generations there will be more and more, and still more, and the time will come when everything will change and become as you would have it, people will live as you do, and then you too will go out of date; people will be born who are better than you.... [Laughs] Yes, to-day I am quite exceptionally in the vein. I am devilishly keen on living.... [Sings.]

"The power of love all ages know,
From its assaults great good does grow." [Laughs.]

MASHA. Trum-tum-tum...

VERSHININ. Tum-tum...

MASHA. Tra-ra-ra?

VERSHININ. Tra-ta-ta. [Laughs.]

[Enter FEDOTIK.]

FEDOTIK. [Dancing] I'm burnt out, I'm burnt out! Down to the ground! [Laughter.]

IRINA. I don't see anything funny about it. Is everything burnt?

FEDOTIK. [Laughs] Absolutely. Nothing left at all. The guitar's burnt, and the photographs are burnt, and all my correspondence.... And I was going to make you a present of a note-book, and that's burnt too.

[SOLENI comes in.]

IRINA. No, you can't come here, Vassili Vassilevitch. Please go away.

SOLENI. Why can the Baron come here and I can't?

VERSHININ. We really must go. How's the fire?

SOLENI. They say it's going down. No, I absolutely don't see why the Baron can, and I can't? [Scents his hands.]

VERSHININ. Trum-tum-tum.

MASHA. Trum-tum.

VERSHININ. [Laughs to SOLENI] Let's go into the dining-room.

SOLENI. Very well, we'll make a note of it. "If I should try to make this clear, the geese would be annoyed, I fear." [Looks at TUZENBACH] There, there, there.... [Goes out with VERSHININ and FEDOTIK.]

IRINA. How Soleni smelt of tobacco.... [In surprise] The Baron's asleep! Baron! Baron!

TUZENBACH. [Waking] I am tired, I must say.... The brickworks.... No, I'm not wandering, I mean it; I'm going to start work soon at the brickworks... I've already talked it over. [Tenderly, to IRINA] You're so pale, and beautiful, and charming.... Your paleness seems to shine through the dark air as if it was a light.... You are sad, displeased with life.... Oh, come with me, let's go and work together!

MASHA. Nicolai Lvovitch, go away from here.

TUZENBACH. [Laughs] Are you here? I didn't see you. [Kisses IRINA'S hand] good-bye, I'll go... I look at you now and I remember, as if it was long ago, your name-day, when you, cheerfully and merrily, were talking about the joys of labour.... And how happy life seemed to me, then! What has happened to it now? [Kisses her hand] There are tears in your eyes. Go to bed now; it is already day... the morning begins.... If only I was allowed to give my life for you!

MASHA. Nicolai Lvovitch, go away! What business...

TUZENBACH. I'm off. [Exit.]

MASHA. [Lies down] Are you asleep, Feodor?

KULIGIN. Eh?

MASHA. Shouldn't you go home.

KULIGIN. My dear Masha, my darling Masha....

IRINA. She's tired out. You might let her rest, Fedia.

KULIGIN. I'll go at once. My wife's a good, splendid... I love you, my only one....

MASHA. [Angrily] Amo, amas, amat, amamus, amatis, amant.

KULIGIN. [Laughs] No, she really is wonderful. I've been your husband seven years, and it seems as if I was only married yesterday. On my word. No, you really are a wonderful woman. I'm satisfied, I'm satisfied, I'm satisfied!

MASHA. I'm bored, I'm bored, I'm bored.... [Sits up] But I can't get it out of my head.... It's simply disgraceful. It has been gnawing away at me... I can't keep silent. I mean about Andrey.... He has mortgaged this house with the bank, and his wife has got all the money; but the house doesn't belong to him alone, but to the four of us! He ought to know that, if he's an honourable man.

KULIGIN. What's the use, Masha? Andrey is in debt all round; well, let him do as he pleases.

MASHA. It's disgraceful, anyway. [Lies down]

KULIGIN. You and I are not poor. I work, take my classes, give private lessons... I am a plain, honest man... *Omnia mea mecum porto*, as they say.

MASHA. I don't want anything, but the unfairness of it disgusts me. [Pause] You go, Feodor.

KULIGIN. [Kisses her] You're tired, just rest for half an hour, and I'll sit and wait for you. Sleep.... [Going] I'm satisfied, I'm satisfied, I'm satisfied. [Exit.]

IRINA. Yes, really, our Andrey has grown smaller; how he's snuffed out and aged with that woman! He used to want to be a professor, and yesterday he was boasting that at last he had been made a member of the district council. He is a member, and Protopopov is chairman.... The whole town talks and laughs about it, and he alone knows and sees nothing.... And now everybody's gone to look at the fire, but he sits alone in his room and pays no attention, only just plays on his fiddle. [Nervily] Oh, it's awful, awful, awful. [Weeps] I can't, I can't bear it any longer!... I can't, I can't!... [OLGA comes in and clears up at her little table. IRINA is sobbing loudly] Throw me out, throw me out, I can't bear any more!

OLGA. [Alarmed] What is it, what is it? Dear!

IRINA. [Sobbing] Where? Where has everything gone? Where is it all? Oh my God, my God! I've forgotten everything, everything... I don't remember what is the Italian for window or, well, for ceiling... I forget everything, every day I forget it, and life passes and will never return, and we'll never go away to Moscow... I see that we'll never go....

OLGA. Dear, dear....

IRINA. [Controlling herself] Oh, I am unhappy... I can't work, I shan't work. Enough, enough! I used to be a telegraphist, now I work at the town council offices, and I have nothing but hate and contempt for all they give me to do... I am already twenty-three, I have already been at work for a long while, and my brain has dried up, and I've grown thinner, plainer, older, and there is no relief of any sort, and time goes and it seems all the while as if I am going away from the real, the beautiful life, farther and farther away, down some precipice. I'm in despair and I can't understand how it is that I am still alive, that I haven't killed myself.

OLGA. Don't cry, dear girl, don't cry... I suffer, too.

IRINA. I'm not crying, not crying.... Enough.... Look, I'm not crying any more. Enough... enough!

OLGA. Dear, I tell you as a sister and a friend if you want my advice, marry the Baron. [IRINA cries softly] You respect him, you think highly of him.... It is true that he is not handsome, but he is so honourable and clean... people don't marry from love, but in order to do one's duty. I think so, at any rate, and I'd marry without being in love. Whoever he was, I should marry him, so long as he was a decent man. Even if he was old....

IRINA. I was always waiting until we should be settled in Moscow, there I should meet my true love; I used to think about him, and love him.... But it's all turned out to be nonsense, all nonsense....

OLGA. [Embraces her sister] My dear, beautiful sister, I understand everything; when Baron Nicolai Lvovitch left the army and came to us in evening dress, [Note: I.e. in the correct dress for making a proposal of marriage.] he seemed so bad-looking to me that I even started crying.... He asked, "What are you crying for?" How could I tell him! But if God brought him to marry you, I should be happy. That would be different, quite different.

[NATASHA with a candle walks across the stage from right to left without saying anything.]

MASHA. [Sitting up] She walks as if she's set something on fire.

OLGA. Masha, you're silly, you're the silliest of the family. Please forgive me for saying so. [Pause.]

MASHA. I want to make a confession, dear sisters. My soul is in pain. I will confess to you, and never again to anybody... I'll tell you this minute. [Softly] It's my secret but you must know everything... I can't be silent.... [Pause] I love, I love... I love that man.... You saw him only just now.... Why don't I say it... in one word. I love Vershinin.

OLGA. [Goes behind her screen] Stop that, I don't hear you in any case.

MASHA. What am I to do? [Takes her head in her hands] First he seemed queer to me, then I was sorry for him... then I fell in love with him... fell in love with his voice, his words, his misfortunes, his two daughters.

OLGA. [Behind the screen] I'm not listening. You may talk any nonsense you like, it will be all the same, I shan't hear.

MASHA. Oh, Olga, you are foolish. I am in love—that means that is to be my fate. It means that is to be my lot.... And he loves me.... It is all awful. Yes; it isn't good, is it? [Takes IRINA'S hand and draws her to her] Oh, my dear.... How are we going to live through our lives, what is to become of us.... When you read a novel it all seems so old and easy, but when you fall in love yourself, then you learn that nobody knows anything, and each must decide for himself.... My dear ones, my sisters... I've confessed, now I shall keep silence.... Like the lunatics in Gogol's story, I'm going to be silent... silent...

[ANDREY enters, followed by FERAPONT.]

ANDREY. [Angrily] What do you want? I don't understand.

FERAPONT. [At the door, impatiently] I've already told you ten times, Andrey Sergeyevitch.

ANDREY. In the first place I'm not Andrey Sergeyevitch, but sir. [Note: Quite literally, "your high honour," to correspond to Andrey's rank as a civil servant.]

FERAPONT. The firemen, sir, ask if they can go across your garden to the river. Else they go right round, right round; it's a nuisance.

ANDREY. All right. Tell them it's all right. [Exit FERAPONT] I'm tired of them. Where is Olga? [OLGA comes out from behind the screen] I came to you for the key of the cupboard. I lost my own. You've got a little key. [OLGA gives him the key; IRINA goes behind her screen; pause] What a huge fire! It's going down now. Hang it all, that Ferapont made me so angry that I talked nonsense to him.... Sir, indeed.... [A pause] Why are you so silent, Olga? [Pause] It's time you stopped all that nonsense and behaved as if you were properly alive.... You are here, Masha. Irina is here, well, since we're all here, let's come to a complete understanding, once and for all. What have you against me? What is it?

OLGA. Please don't, Audrey dear. We'll talk to-morrow. [Excited] What an awful night!

ANDREY. [Much confused] Don't excite yourself. I ask you in perfect calmness; what have you against me? Tell me straight.

VERSHININ'S VOICE. Trum-tum-tum!

MASHA. [Stands; loudly] Tra-ta-ta! [To OLGA] Goodbye, Olga, God bless you. [Goes behind screen and kisses IRINA] Sleep well.... Good-bye, Andrey. Go away now, they're tired... you can explain to-morrow.... [Exit.]

ANDREY. I'll only say this and go. Just now.... In the first place, you've got something against Natasha, my wife; I've noticed it since the very day of my marriage. Natasha is a beautiful and honest creature, straight and honourable—that's my opinion. I love and respect my wife; understand it, I respect her, and I insist that others should respect her too. I repeat, she's an honest and honourable person, and all your disapproval is simply silly... [Pause] In the second place, you seem to be annoyed because I am not a professor, and am not engaged in study. But I work for the zemstvo, I am a member of the district council, and I consider my service as worthy and as high as the service of science. I am a member of the district council, and I am proud of it, if you want to know. [Pause] In the third place, I have still this to say... that I have mortgaged the house without obtaining your permission.... For that I am to blame, and ask to be forgiven. My debts led me into doing it... thirty-five thousand... I do not play at cards any more, I stopped long ago, but the chief thing I have to say in my defence is that you girls receive a pension, and I don't... my wages, so to speak.... [Pause.]

KULIGIN. [At the door] Is Masha there? [Excitedly] Where is she? It's queer.... [Exit.]

ANDREY. They don't hear. Natasha is a splendid, honest person. [Walks about in silence, then stops] When I married I thought we should be happy... all of us.... But, my God.... [Weeps] My dear, dear sisters, don't believe me, don't believe me.... [Exit.]

[Fire-alarm. The stage is clear.]

IRINA. [behind her screen] Olga, who's knocking on the floor?

OLGA. It's doctor Ivan Romanovitch. He's drunk.

IRINA. What a restless night! [Pause] Olga! [Looks out] Did you hear? They are taking the brigade away from us; it's going to be transferred to some place far away.

OLGA. It's only a rumour.

IRINA. Then we shall be left alone.... Olga!

OLGA. Well?

IRINA. My dear, darling sister, I esteem, I highly value the Baron, he's a splendid man; I'll marry him, I'll consent, only let's go to Moscow! I implore you, let's go! There's nothing better than Moscow on earth! Let's go, Olga, let's go!

Curtain

ACT IV

[The old garden at the house of the PROSOROVS. There is a long avenue of firs, at the end of which the river can be seen. There is a forest on the far side of the river. On the right is the terrace of the house: bottles and tumblers are on a table here; it is evident that champagne has just been drunk. It is midday. Every now and again passers-by walk across the garden, from the road to the river; five soldiers go past rapidly. CHEBUTIKIN, in a comfortable frame of mind which does not desert him throughout the act, sits in an armchair in the garden, waiting to be called. He wears a peaked cap and has a stick. IRINA, KULIGIN with a cross hanging from his neck and without his moustaches, and TUZENBACH are standing on the terrace seeing off FEDOTIK and RODE, who are coming down into the garden; both officers are in service uniform.]

TUZENBACH. [Exchanges kisses with FEDOTIK] You're a good sort, we got on so well together. [Exchanges kisses with RODE] Once again.... Good-bye, old man!

IRINA. Au revoir!

FEDOTIK. It isn't au revoir, it's good-bye; we'll never meet again!

KULIGIN. Who knows! [Wipes his eyes; smiles] Here I've started crying!

IRINA. We'll meet again sometime.

FEDOTIK. After ten years—or fifteen? We'll hardly know one another then; we'll say, "How do you do?" coldly.... [Takes a snapshot] Keep still.... Once more, for the last time.

RODE. [Embracing TUZENBACH] We shan't meet again.... [Kisses IRINA'S hand] Thank you for everything, for everything!

FEDOTIK. [Grieved] Don't be in such a hurry!

TUZENBACH. We shall meet again, if God wills it. Write to us. Be sure to write.

RODE. [Looking round the garden] Good-bye, trees! [Shouts] Yo-ho! [Pause] Good-bye, echo!

KULIGIN. Best wishes. Go and get yourselves wives there in Poland.... Your Polish wife will clasp you and call you "kochanku!" [Note: Darling.] [Laughs.]

FEDOTIK. [Looking at the time] There's less than an hour left. Soleni is the only one of our battery who is going on the barge; the rest of us are going with the main body. Three batteries are leaving to-day, another three to-morrow and then the town will be quiet and peaceful.

TUZENBACH. And terribly dull.

RODE. And where is Maria Sergeyevna?

KULIGIN. Masha is in the garden.

FEDOTIK. We'd like to say good-bye to her.

RODE. Good-bye, I must go, or else I'll start weeping.... [Quickly embraces KULIGIN and TUZENBACH, and kisses IRINA'S hand] We've been so happy here....

FEDOTIK. [To KULIGIN] Here's a keepsake for you... a note-book with a pencil.... We'll go to the river from here.... [They go aside and both look round.]

RODE. [Shouts] Yo-ho!

KULIGIN. [Shouts] Good-bye!

[At the back of the stage FEDOTIK and RODE meet MASHA; they say good-bye and go out with her.]

IRINA. They've gone.... [Sits on the bottom step of the terrace.]

CHEBUTIKIN. And they forgot to say good-bye to me.

IRINA. But why is that?

CHEBUTIKIN. I just forgot, somehow. Though I'll soon see them again, I'm going to-morrow. Yes... just one day left. I shall be retired in a year, then I'll come here again, and finish my life near you. I've only one year before I get my pension.... [Puts one newspaper into his pocket and takes another out] I'll come here to you and change my life radically... I'll be so quiet... so agree... agreeable, respectable....

IRINA. Yes, you ought to change your life, dear man, somehow or other.

CHEBUTIKIN. Yes, I feel it. [Sings softly.] "Tarara-boom-deay...."

KULIGIN. We won't reform Ivan Romanovitch! We won't reform him!

CHEBUTIKIN. If only I was apprenticed to you! Then I'd reform.

IRINA. Feodor has shaved his moustache! I can't bear to look at him.

KULIGIN. Well, what about it?

CHEBUTIKIN. I could tell you what your face looks like now, but it wouldn't be polite.

KULIGIN. Well! It's the custom, it's modus vivendi. Our Director is clean-shaven, and so I too, when I received my inspectorship, had my moustaches removed. Nobody likes it, but it's all one to me. I'm satisfied. Whether I've got moustaches or not, I'm satisfied.... [Sits.]

[At the back of the stage ANDREY is wheeling a perambulator containing a sleeping infant.]

IRINA. Ivan Romanovitch, be a darling. I'm awfully worried. You were out on the boulevard last night; tell me, what happened?

CHEBUTIKIN. What happened? Nothing. Quite a trifling matter. [Reads paper] Of no importance!

KULIGIN. They say that Soleni and the Baron met yesterday on the boulevard near the theatre....

TUZENBACH. Stop! What right... [Waves his hand and goes into the house.]

KULIGIN. Near the theatre... Soleni started behaving offensively to the Baron, who lost his temper and said something nasty....

CHEBUTIKIN. I don't know. It's all bunkum.

KULIGIN. At some seminary or other a master wrote "bunkum" on an essay, and the student couldn't make the letters out—thought it was a Latin word "luckum." [Laughs] Awfully funny, that. They say that Soleni is in love with Irina and hates the Baron.... That's quite natural. Irina is a very nice girl. She's even like Masha, she's so thoughtful.... Only, Irina your character is gentler. Though Masha's character, too, is a very good one. I'm very fond of Masha. [Shouts of "Yo-ho!" are heard behind the stage.]

IRINA. [Shudders] Everything seems to frighten me today. [Pause] I've got everything ready, and I send my things off after dinner. The Baron and I will be married to-morrow, and to-morrow we go away to the brickworks, and the next day I go to the school, and the new life begins. God will help me! When I took my examination for the teacher's post, I actually wept for joy and gratitude.... [Pause] The cart will be here in a minute for my things....

KULIGIN. Somehow or other, all this doesn't seem at all serious. As if it was all ideas, and nothing really serious. Still, with all my soul I wish you happiness.

CHEBUTIKIN. [With deep feeling] My splendid... my dear, precious girl.... You've gone on far ahead, I won't catch up with you. I'm left behind like a migrant bird grown old, and unable to fly. Fly, my dear, fly, and God be with you! [Pause] It's a pity you shaved your moustaches, Feodor Ilitch.

KULIGIN. Oh, drop it! [Sighs] To-day the soldiers will be gone, and everything will go on as in the old days. Say what you will, Masha is a good, honest woman. I love her very much, and thank my fate for her. People have such different fates. There's a Kosirev who works in the excise department here. He was at school with me; he was expelled from the fifth class of the High School for being entirely unable to understand *ut consecutivum*. He's awfully hard up now and in very poor health, and when I meet him I say to him, "How do you do, *ut consecutivum*." "Yes," he says, "precisely *consecutivum*..." and coughs. But I've been successful all my life, I'm happy, and I even have a Stanislaus Cross, of the second class, and now I myself teach others that *ut consecutivum*. Of course, I'm a clever man, much cleverer than many, but happiness doesn't only lie in that....

["The Maiden's Prayer" is being played on the piano in the house.]

IRINA. To-morrow night I shan't hear that "Maiden's Prayer" any more, and I shan't be meeting Protopopov.... [Pause] Protopopov is sitting there in the drawing-room; and he came to-day...

KULIGIN. Hasn't the head-mistress come yet?

IRINA. No. She has been sent for. If you only knew how difficult it is for me to live alone, without Olga.... She lives at the High School; she, a head-mistress, busy all day with her affairs and I'm alone, bored, with nothing to do, and hate the room I live in.... I've made up my mind: if I can't live in Moscow, then it must come to this. It's fate. It can't be helped. It's all the will of God, that's the truth. Nicolai Lvovitch made me a proposal.... Well? I thought it over and made up my mind. He's a good man... it's quite remarkable how good he is.... And suddenly my soul put out wings, I became happy, and light-hearted, and once again the desire for work, work, came over me.... Only something happened yesterday, some secret dread has been hanging over me....

CHEBUTIKIN. Luckum. Rubbish.

NATASHA. [At the window] The head-mistress.

KULIGIN. The head-mistress has come. Let's go. [Exit with IRINA into the house.]

CHEBUTIKIN. "It is my washing day.... Tara-ra... boom-deay."

[MASHA approaches, ANDREY is wheeling a perambulator at the back.]

MASHA. Here you are, sitting here, doing nothing.

CHEBUTIKIN. What then?

MASHA. [Sits] Nothing.... [Pause] Did you love my mother?

CHEBUTIKIN. Very much.

MASHA. And did she love you?

CHEBUTIKIN. [After a pause] I don't remember that.

MASHA. Is my man here? When our cook Martha used to ask about her gendarme, she used to say my man. Is he here?

CHEBUTIKIN. Not yet.

MASHA. When you take your happiness in little bits, in snatches, and then lose it, as I have done, you gradually get coarser, more bitter. [Points to her bosom] I'm boiling in here.... [Looks at ANDREY with the perambulator] There's our brother Andrey.... All our hopes in him have gone. There was once a great bell, a thousand persons were hoisting it, much money and labour had been spent on it, when it suddenly fell and was broken. Suddenly, for no particular reason.... Andrey is like that....

ANDREY. When are they going to stop making such a noise in the house? It's awful.

CHEBUTIKIN. They won't be much longer. [Looks at his watch] My watch is very old-fashioned, it strikes the hours.... [Winds the watch and makes it strike] The first, second, and fifth batteries are to leave at one o'clock precisely. [Pause] And I go to-morrow.

ANDREY. For good?

CHEBUTIKIN. I don't know. Perhaps I'll return in a year. The devil only knows... it's all one.... [Somewhere a harp and violin are being played.]

ANDREY. The town will grow empty. It will be as if they put a cover over it. [Pause] Something happened yesterday by the theatre. The whole town knows of it, but I don't.

CHEBUTIKIN. Nothing. A silly little affair. Soleni started irritating the Baron, who lost his temper and insulted him, and so at last Soleni had to challenge him. [Looks at his watch] It's about time, I think.... At half-past twelve, in the public wood, that one you can see from here across the river.... Piff-paff. [Laughs] Soleni thinks he's Lermontov, and even writes verses. That's all very well, but this is his third duel.

MASHA. Whose?

CHEBUTIKIN. Soleni's.

MASHA. And the Baron?

CHEBUTIKIN. What about the Baron? [Pause.]

MASHA. Everything's all muddled up in my head.... But I say it ought not to be allowed. He might wound the Baron or even kill him.

CHEBUTIKIN. The Baron is a good man, but one Baron more or less—what difference does it make? It's all the same! [Beyond the garden somebody shouts "Co-ee! Hallo! "] You wait. That's Skvortsov shouting; one of the seconds. He's in a boat. [Pause.]

ANDREY. In my opinion it's simply immoral to fight in a duel, or to be present, even in the quality of a doctor.

CHEBUTIKIN. It only seems so.... We don't exist, there's nothing on earth, we don't really live, it only seems that we live. Does it matter, anyway!

MASHA. You talk and talk the whole day long. [Going] You live in a climate like this, where it might snow any moment, and there you talk.... [Stops] I won't go into the house, I can't go there.... Tell me when Vershinin comes.... [Goes along the avenue] The migrant birds are already on the wing.... [Looks up] Swans or geese.... My dear, happy things.... [Exit.]

ANDREY. Our house will be empty. The officers will go away, you are going, my sister is getting married, and I alone will remain in the house.

CHEBUTIKIN. And your wife?

[FERAPONT enters with some documents.]

ANDREY. A wife's a wife. She's honest, well-bred, yes; and kind, but with all that there is still something about her that degenerates her into a petty, blind, even in some respects misshapen animal. In any case, she isn't a man. I tell you as a friend, as the only man to whom I can lay bare my soul. I love Natasha, it's true, but sometimes she seems extraordinarily vulgar, and then I lose myself and can't understand why I love her so much, or, at any rate, used to love her....

CHEBUTIKIN. [Rises] I'm going away to-morrow, old chap, and perhaps we'll never meet again, so here's my advice. Put on your cap, take a stick in your hand, go... go on and on, without looking round. And the farther you go, the better.

[SOLENI goes across the back of the stage with two officers; he catches sight of CHEBUTIKIN, and turns to him, the officers go on.]

SOLENI. Doctor, it's time. It's half-past twelve already. [Shakes hands with ANDREY.]

CHEBUTIKIN. Half a minute. I'm tired of the lot of you. [To ANDREY] If anybody asks for me, say I'll be back soon.... [Sighs] Oh, oh, oh!

SOLENI. "He didn't have the time to sigh. The bear sat on him heavily." [Goes up to him] What are you groaning about, old man?

CHEBUTIKIN. Stop it!

SOLENI. How's your health?

CHEBUTIKIN. [Angry] Mind your own business.

SOLENI. The old man is unnecessarily excited. I won't go far, I'll only just bring him down like a snipe. [Takes out his scent-bottle and scents his hands] I've poured out a whole bottle of scent to-day and they still smell... of a dead body. [Pause] Yes.... You remember the poem

> *"But he, the rebel seeks the storm,*
> *As if the storm will bring him rest..."?*

CHEBUTIKIN. Yes.

> *"He didn't have the time to sigh,*
> *The bear sat on him heavily."*

[Exit with SOLENI.]

[Shouts are heard. ANDREY and FERAPONT come in.]

FERAPONT. Documents to sign....

ANDREY. [Irritated]. Go away! Leave me! Please! [Goes away with the perambulator.]

FERAPONT. That's what documents are for, to be signed. [Retires to back of stage.]

[Enter IRINA, with TUZENBACH in a straw hat; KULIGIN walks across the stage, shouting "Co-ee, Masha, co-ee!"]

TUZENBACH. He seems to be the only man in the town who is glad that the soldiers are going.

IRINA. One can understand that. [Pause] The town will be empty.

TUZENBACH. My dear, I shall return soon.

IRINA. Where are you going?

TUZENBACH. I must go into the town and then... see the others off.

IRINA. It's not true... Nicolai, why are you so absentminded to-day? [Pause] What took place by the theatre yesterday?

TUZENBACH. [Making a movement of impatience] In an hour's time I shall return and be with you again. [Kisses her hands] My darling... [Looking her closely in the face] it's five years now since I fell in love with you, and still I can't get used to it, and you seem to me to grow more and more beautiful. What lovely, wonderful hair! What eyes! I'm going to take you away to-morrow. We shall work, we shall be rich, my dreams will come true. You will be happy. There's only one thing, one thing only: you don't love me!

IRINA. It isn't in my power! I shall be your wife, I shall be true to you, and obedient to you, but I can't love you. What can I do! [Cries] I have never been in love in my life. Oh, I used to think so much of love, I have been thinking about it for so long by day and by night, but my soul is like an expensive piano which is locked and the key lost. [Pause] You seem so unhappy.

TUZENBACH. I didn't sleep at night. There is nothing in my life so awful as to be able to frighten me, only that lost key torments my soul and does not let me sleep. Say something to me [Pause] say something to me....

IRINA. What can I say, what?

TUZENBACH. Anything.

IRINA. Don't! don't! [Pause.]

TUZENBACH. It is curious how silly trivial little things, sometimes for no apparent reason, become significant. At first you laugh at these things, you think they are of no importance, you go on and you feel that you haven't got the strength to stop yourself. Oh don't let's talk about it! I am happy. It is as if for the first time in my life I see these firs, maples, beeches, and they all look at me inquisitively and wait. What beautiful trees and how beautiful, when one comes to think of it, life must be near them! [A shout of Co-ee! in the distance] It's time I went.... There's a tree which has dried up but it still sways in the breeze with the others. And so it seems to me that if I die, I shall still take part in life in one way or another. Good-bye, dear.... [Kisses her hands] The papers which you gave me are on my table under the calendar.

IRINA. I am coming with you.

TUZENBACH. [Nervously] No, no! [He goes quickly and stops in the avenue] Irina!

IRINA. What is it?

TUZENBACH. [Not knowing what to say] I haven't had any coffee to-day. Tell them to make me some.... [He goes out quickly.]

[IRINA stands deep in thought. Then she goes to the back of the stage and sits on a swing. ANDREY comes in with the perambulator and FERAPONT also appears.]

FERAPONT. Andrey Sergeyevitch, it isn't as if the documents were mine, they are the government's. I didn't make them.

ANDREY. Oh, what has become of my past and where is it? I used to be young, happy, clever, I used to be able to think and frame clever ideas, the present and the future seemed to me full of hope. Why do we, almost before we have begun to live, become dull, grey, uninteresting, lazy, apathetic, useless, unhappy.... This town has already been in existence for two hundred years and it has a hundred thousand inhabitants, not one of whom is in any way different from the others. There has never been, now or at any other time, a single leader of men, a single scholar, an artist, a man of even the slightest eminence who might arouse envy or a passionate desire to be imitated. They only eat, drink, sleep, and then they die... more people are born and also eat, drink, sleep, and so as not to go silly from boredom, they try to make life many-sided with their beastly backbiting, vodka, cards, and litigation. The wives deceive their husbands, and the husbands lie, and pretend they see nothing and hear nothing, and the evil influence irresistibly oppresses the children and the divine spark in them is extinguished, and they become just as pitiful corpses and just as much like one another as their fathers and mothers.... [Angrily to FERAPONT] What do you want?

FERAPONT. What? Documents want signing.

ANDREY. I'm tired of you.

FERAPONT. [Handing him papers] The hall-porter from the law courts was saying just now that in the winter there were two hundred degrees of frost in Petersburg.

ANDREY. The present is beastly, but when I think of the future, how good it is! I feel so light, so free; there is a light in the distance, I see freedom. I see myself and my children freeing ourselves from vanities, from kvass, from goose baked with cabbage, from after-dinner naps, from base idleness....

FERAPONT. He was saying that two thousand people were frozen to death. The people were frightened, he said. In Petersburg or Moscow, I don't remember which.

ANDREY. [Overcome by a tender emotion] My dear sisters, my beautiful sisters! [Crying] Masha, my sister....

NATASHA. [At the window] Who's talking so loudly out here? Is that you, Andrey? You'll wake little Sophie. *Il ne faut pas faire du bruit, la Sophie est dormée deja. Vous êtes un ours.* [Angrily] If you want to talk, then give the perambulator and the baby to somebody else. Ferapont, take the perambulator!

FERAPONT. Yes'm. [Takes the perambulator.]

ANDREY. [Confused] I'm speaking quietly.

NATASHA. [At the window, nursing her boy] Bobby! Naughty Bobby! Bad little Bobby!

ANDREY. [Looking through the papers] All right, I'll look them over and sign if necessary, and you can take them back to the offices....

[Goes into house reading papers; FERAPONT takes the perambulator to the back of the garden.]

NATASHA. [At the window] Bobby, what's your mother's name? Dear, dear! And who's this? That's Aunt Olga. Say to your aunt, "How do you do, Olga!"

[Two wandering musicians, a man and a girl, are playing on a violin and a harp. VERSHININ, OLGA, and ANFISA come out of the house and listen for a minute in silence; IRINA comes up to them.]

OLGA. Our garden might be a public thoroughfare, from the way people walk and ride across it. Nurse, give those musicians something!

ANFISA. [Gives money to the musicians] Go away with God's blessing on you. [The musicians bow and go away] A bitter sort of people. You don't play on a full stomach. [To IRINA] How do you do, Arisha! [Kisses her] Well, little girl, here I am, still alive! Still alive! In the High School, together with little Olga, in her official apartments... so the Lord has appointed for my old age. Sinful woman that I am, I've never lived like that in my life before.... A large flat, government property, and I've a whole room and bed to myself. All government property. I wake up at nights and, oh God, and Holy Mother, there isn't a happier person than I!

VERSHININ. [Looks at his watch] We are going soon, Olga Sergeyevna. It's time for me to go. [Pause] I wish you every... every.... Where's Maria Sergeyevna?

IRINA. She's somewhere in the garden. I'll go and look for her.

VERSHININ. If you'll be so kind. I haven't time.

ANFISA. I'll go and look, too. [Shouts] Little Masha, co-ee! [Goes out with IRINA down into the garden] Co-ee, co-ee!

VERSHININ. Everything comes to an end. And so we, too, must part. [Looks at his watch] The town gave us a sort of farewell breakfast, we had champagne to drink and the mayor made a speech, and I ate and listened, but my soul was here all the time.... [Looks round the garden] I'm so used to you now.

OLGA. Shall we ever meet again?

VERSHININ. Probably not. [Pause] My wife and both my daughters will stay here another two months. If anything happens, or if anything has to be done...

OLGA. Yes, yes, of course. You need not worry. [Pause] To-morrow there won't be a single soldier left in the town, it will all be a memory, and, of course, for us a new life will begin.... [Pause] None of our plans are coming right. I didn't want to be a headmistress, but they made me one, all the same. It means there's no chance of Moscow....

VERSHININ. Well... thank you for everything. Forgive me if I've... I've said such an awful lot—forgive me for that too, don't think badly of me.

OLGA. [Wipes her eyes] Why isn't Masha coming...

VERSHININ. What else can I say in parting? Can I philosophize about anything? [Laughs] Life is heavy. To many of us it seems dull and hopeless, but still, it must be acknowledged that it is getting lighter and clearer, and it seems that the time is not far off when it will be quite clear. [Looks at his watch] It's time I went! Mankind used to be absorbed in wars, and all its existence was filled with campaigns, attacks, defeats, now we've outlived all that, leaving after us a great waste place, which there is nothing to fill with at present; but mankind is looking for something, and will certainly find it. Oh, if it only happened more quickly. [Pause] If only education could be added to industry, and industry to education. [Looks at his watch] It's time I went....

OLGA. Here she comes.

[Enter MASHA.]

VERSHININ. I came to say good-bye....

[OLGA steps aside a little, so as not to be in their way.]

MASHA. [Looking him in the face] Good-bye. [Prolonged kiss.]

OLGA. Don't, don't. [MASHA is crying bitterly]

VERSHININ. Write to me.... Don't forget! Let me go.... It's time. Take her, Olga Sergeyevna... it's time... I'm late...

[He kisses OLGA'S hand in evident emotion, then embraces MASHA once more and goes out quickly.]

OLGA. Don't, Masha! Stop, dear.... [KULIGIN enters.]

KULIGIN. [Confused] Never mind, let her cry, let her.... My dear Masha, my good Masha.... You're my wife, and I'm happy, whatever happens... I'm not complaining, I don't reproach you at all.... Olga is a witness to it. Let's begin to live again as we used to, and not by a single word, or hint...

> MASHA. [Restraining her sobs] "There stands a green oak by the sea,
> And a chain of bright gold is around it....
> And a chain of bright gold is around it...."

I'm going off my head... "There stands... a green oak... by the sea."...

OLGA. Don't, Masha, don't... give her some water....

MASHA. I'm not crying any more....

KULIGIN. She's not crying any more... she's a good... [A shot is heard from a distance.]

> MASHA. "There stands a green oak by the sea,
> And a chain of bright gold is around it...
> An oak of green gold...."

I'm mixing it up.... [Drinks some water] Life is dull... I don't want anything more now... I'll be all right in a moment.... It doesn't matter.... What do those lines mean? Why do they run in my head? My thoughts are all tangled.

[IRINA enters.]

OLGA. Be quiet, Masha. There's a good girl.... Let's go in.

MASHA. [Angrily] I shan't go in there. [Sobs, but controls herself at once] I'm not going to go into the house, I won't go....

IRINA. Let's sit here together and say nothing. I'm going away to-morrow.... [Pause.]

KULIGIN. Yesterday I took away these whiskers and this beard from a boy in the third class.... [He puts on the whiskers and beard] Don't I look like the German master.... [Laughs] Don't I? The boys are amusing.

MASHA. You really do look like that German of yours.

OLGA. [Laughs] Yes. [MASHA weeps.]

IRINA. Don't, Masha!

KULIGIN. It's a very good likeness....

[Enter NATASHA.]

NATASHA. [To the maid] What? Mihail Ivanitch Protopopov will sit with little Sophie, and Andrey Sergeyevitch can take little Bobby out. Children are such a bother.... [To IRINA] Irina, it's such a pity you're going away to-morrow. Do stop just another week. [Sees KULIGIN and screams; he laughs and takes off his beard and whiskers] How you frightened me! [To IRINA] I've grown used to you and do you think it will be easy for me to part from you? I'm going to have Andrey and his violin put into your room—let him fiddle away in there!—and we'll put little Sophie into his room. The beautiful, lovely child! What a little girlie! To-day she looked at me with such pretty eyes and said "Mamma!"

KULIGIN. A beautiful child, it's quite true.

NATASHA. That means I shall have the place to myself to-morrow. [Sighs] In the first place I shall have that avenue of fir-trees cut down, then that maple. It's so ugly at nights.... [To IRINA] That belt doesn't suit you at all, dear.... It's an error of taste. And I'll give orders to have lots and lots of little flowers planted here, and they'll smell.... [Severely] Why is there a fork lying about here on the seat? [Going towards the house, to the maid] Why is there a fork lying about here on the seat, I say? [Shouts] Don't you dare to answer me!

KULIGIN. Temper! temper! [A march is played off; they all listen.]

OLGA. They're going.

[CHEBUTIKIN comes in.]

MASHA. They're going. Well, well.... Bon voyage! [To her husband] We must be going home.... Where's my coat and hat?

KULIGIN. I took them in... I'll bring them, in a moment.

OLGA. Yes, now we can all go home. It's time.

CHEBUTIKIN. Olga Sergeyevna!

OLGA. What is it? [Pause] What is it?

CHEBUTIKIN. Nothing... I don't know how to tell you.... [Whispers to her.]

OLGA. [Frightened] It can't be true!

CHEBUTIKIN. Yes... such a story... I'm tired out, exhausted, I won't say any more.... [Sadly] Still, it's all the same!

MASHA. What's happened?

OLGA. [Embraces IRINA] This is a terrible day... I don't know how to tell you, dear....

IRINA. What is it? Tell me quickly, what is it? For God's sake! [Cries.]

CHEBUTIKIN. The Baron was killed in the duel just now.

IRINA. [Cries softly] I knew it, I knew it....

CHEBUTIKIN. [Sits on a bench at the back of the stage] I'm tired.... [Takes a paper from his pocket] Let 'em cry.... [Sings softly] "Tarara-boom-deay, it is my washing day...." Isn't it all the same!

[The three sisters are standing, pressing against one another.]

MASHA. Oh, how the music plays! They are leaving us, one has quite left us, quite and for ever. We remain alone, to begin our life over again. We must live... we must live....

IRINA. [Puts her head on OLGA's bosom] There will come a time when everybody will know why, for what purpose, there is all this suffering, and there will be no more mysteries. But now we must live... we must work, just work! To-morrow, I'll go away alone, and I'll teach and give my whole life to those who, perhaps, need it. It's autumn now, soon it will be winter, the snow will cover everything, and I shall be working, working....

OLGA. [Embraces both her sisters] The bands are playing so gaily, so bravely, and one does so want to live! Oh, my God! Time will pass on, and we shall depart for ever, we shall be forgotten; they will forget our faces, voices, and even how many there were of us, but our sufferings will turn into joy for those who will live after us, happiness and peace will reign on earth, and people will remember with kindly words, and bless those who are living now. Oh dear sisters, our life is not yet at an end. Let us live. The music is so gay, so joyful, and, it seems that in a little while we shall know why we are living, why we are suffering.... If we could only know, if we could only know!

[The music has been growing softer and softer; KULIGIN, smiling happily, brings out the hat and coat; ANDREY wheels out the perambulator in which BOBBY is sitting.]

CHEBUTIKIN. [Sings softly] "Tara... ra-boom-deay.... It is my washing-day."... [Reads a paper] It's all the same! It's all the same!

OLGA. If only we could know, if only we could know!

Curtain.

THE CHERRY ORCHARD

A COMEDY IN FOUR ACTS

CHARACTERS

LUBOV ANDREYEVNA RANEVSKY (Mme. RANEVSKY), a landowner
ANYA, her daughter, aged seventeen
VARYA (BARBARA), her adopted daughter, aged twenty-seven
LEONID ANDREYEVITCH GAEV, Mme. Ranevsky's brother
ERMOLAI ALEXEYEVITCH LOPAKHIN, a merchant
PETER SERGEYEVITCH TROFIMOV, a student
BORIS BORISOVITCH SIMEONOV-PISCHIN, a landowner
CHARLOTTA IVANOVNA, a governess
SIMEON PANTELEYEVITCH EPIKHODOV, a clerk
DUNYASHA (AVDOTYA FEDOROVNA), a maidservant
FIERS, an old footman, aged eighty-seven
YASHA, a young footman
A TRAMP
A STATION-MASTER
POST-OFFICE CLERK
GUESTS
A SERVANT

The action takes place on Mme. RANEVSKY'S estate

ACT ONE

[A room which is still called the nursery. One of the doors leads into ANYA'S room. It is close on sunrise. It is May. The cherry-trees are in flower but it is chilly in the garden. There is an early frost. The windows of the room are shut. DUNYASHA comes in with a candle, and LOPAKHIN with a book in his hand.]

LOPAKHIN. The train's arrived, thank God. What's the time?

DUNYASHA. It will soon be two. [Blows out candle] It is light already.

LOPAKHIN. How much was the train late? Two hours at least. [Yawns and stretches himself] I have made a rotten mess of it! I came here on purpose to meet them at the station, and then overslept myself... in my chair. It's a pity. I wish you'd wakened me.

DUNYASHA. I thought you'd gone away. [Listening] I think I hear them coming.

LOPAKHIN. [Listens] No.... They've got to collect their luggage and so on.... [Pause] Lubov Andreyevna has been living abroad for five years; I don't know what she'll be like now.... She's a good sort—an easy, simple person. I remember when I was a boy of fifteen, my father, who is dead—he used to keep a shop in the village here—hit me on the face with his fist, and my nose bled.... We had gone into the yard together for something or other, and he was a little drunk. Lubov Andreyevna, as I remember her now, was still young, and very thin, and she took me to the washstand here in this very room, the nursery. She said, "Don't cry, little man, it'll be all right in time for your wedding." [Pause] "Little man".... My father was a peasant, it's true, but here I am in a white waistcoat and yellow shoes... a pearl out of an oyster. I'm rich now, with lots of money, but just think about it and examine me, and you'll find I'm still a peasant down to the marrow of my bones. [Turns over the pages of his book] Here I've been reading this book, but I understood nothing. I read and fell asleep. [Pause.]

DUNYASHA. The dogs didn't sleep all night; they know that they're coming.

LOPAKHIN. What's up with you, Dunyasha...?

DUNYASHA. My hands are shaking. I shall faint.

LOPAKHIN. You're too sensitive, Dunyasha. You dress just like a lady, and you do your hair like one too. You oughtn't. You should know your place.

EPIKHODOV. [Enters with a bouquet. He wears a short jacket and brilliantly polished boots which squeak audibly. He drops the bouquet as he enters, then picks it up] The gardener sent these; says they're to go into the dining-room. [Gives the bouquet to DUNYASHA.]

LOPAKHIN. And you'll bring me some kvass.

DUNYASHA. Very well. [Exit.]

EPIKHODOV. There's a frost this morning—three degrees, and the cherry-trees are all in flower. I can't approve of our climate. [Sighs] I can't. Our climate is indisposed to favour us even this once. And, Ermolai Alexeyevitch, allow me to say to you, in addition, that I bought myself some boots two days ago, and I beg to assure you that they squeak in a perfectly unbearable manner. What shall I put on them?

LOPAKHIN. Go away. You bore me.

EPIKHODOV. Some misfortune happens to me every day. But I don't complain; I'm used to it, and I can smile. [DUNYASHA comes in and brings LOPAKHIN some kvass] I shall go. [Knocks over a chair] There.... [Triumphantly] There, you see, if I may use the word, what circumstances I am in, so to speak. It is even simply marvellous. [Exit.]

DUNYASHA. I may confess to you, Ermolai Alexeyevitch, that Epikhodov has proposed to me.

LOPAKHIN. Ah!

DUNYASHA. I don't know what to do about it. He's a nice young man, but every now and again, when he begins talking, you can't understand a word he's saying. I think I like him. He's madly in love with me. He's an unlucky man; every day something happens. We tease him about it. They call him "Two-and-twenty troubles."

LOPAKHIN. [Listens] There they come, I think.

DUNYASHA. They're coming! What's the matter with me? I'm cold all over.

LOPAKHIN. There they are, right enough. Let's go and meet them. Will she know me? We haven't seen each other for five years.

DUNYASHA. [Excited] I shall faint in a minute.... Oh, I'm fainting!

[Two carriages are heard driving up to the house. LOPAKHIN and DUNYASHA quickly go out. The stage is empty. A noise begins in the next room. FIERS, leaning on a stick, walks quickly across the stage; he has just been to meet LUBOV ANDREYEVNA. He wears an old-fashioned livery and a tall hat. He is saying something to himself, but not a word of it can be made out. The noise behind the stage gets louder and louder. A voice is heard: "Let's go in there." Enter LUBOV ANDREYEVNA, ANYA, and CHARLOTTA IVANOVNA with a little dog on a chain, and all dressed in travelling clothes, VARYA in a long coat and with a kerchief on her head. GAEV, SIMEONOV-PISCHIN, LOPAKHIN, DUNYASHA with a parcel and an umbrella, and a servant with luggage—all cross the room.]

ANYA. Let's come through here. Do you remember what this room is, mother?

LUBOV. [Joyfully, through her tears] The nursery!

VARYA. How cold it is! My hands are quite numb. [To LUBOV ANDREYEVNA] Your rooms, the white one and the violet one, are just as they used to be, mother.

LUBOV. My dear nursery, oh, you beautiful room.... I used to sleep here when I was a baby. [Weeps] And here I am like a little girl again. [Kisses her brother, VARYA, then her brother again] And Varya is just as she used to be, just like a nun. And I knew Dunyasha. [Kisses her.]

GAEV. The train was two hours late. There now; how's that for punctuality?

CHARLOTTA. [To PISCHIN] My dog eats nuts too.

PISCHIN. [Astonished] To think of that, now!

[All go out except ANYA and DUNYASHA.]

DUNYASHA. We did have to wait for you!

[Takes off ANYA'S cloak and hat.]

ANYA. I didn't get any sleep for four nights on the journey.... I'm awfully cold.

DUNYASHA. You went away during Lent, when it was snowing and frosty, but now? Darling! [Laughs and kisses her] We did have to wait for you, my joy, my pet.... I must tell you at once, I can't bear to wait a minute.

ANYA. [Tired] Something else now...?

DUNYASHA. The clerk, Epikhodov, proposed to me after Easter.

ANYA. Always the same.... [Puts her hair straight] I've lost all my hairpins.... [She is very tired, and even staggers as she walks.]

DUNYASHA. I don't know what to think about it. He loves me, he loves me so much!

ANYA. [Looks into her room; in a gentle voice] My room, my windows, as if I'd never gone away. I'm at home! To-morrow morning I'll get up and have a run in the garden....Oh, if I could only get to sleep! I didn't sleep the whole journey, I was so bothered.

DUNYASHA. Peter Sergeyevitch came two days ago.

ANYA. [Joyfully] Peter!

DUNYASHA. He sleeps in the bath-house, he lives there. He said he was afraid he'd be in the way. [Looks at her pocket-watch] I ought to wake him, but Barbara Mihailovna told me not to. "Don't wake him," she said.

[Enter VARYA, a bunch of keys on her belt.]

VARYA. Dunyasha, some coffee, quick. Mother wants some.

DUNYASHA. This minute. [Exit.]

VARYA. Well, you've come, glory be to God. Home again. [Caressing her] My darling is back again! My pretty one is back again!

ANYA. I did have an awful time, I tell you.

VARYA. I can just imagine it!

ANYA. I went away in Holy Week; it was very cold then. Charlotta talked the whole way and would go on performing her tricks. Why did you tie Charlotta on to me?

VARYA. You couldn't go alone, darling, at seventeen!

ANYA. We went to Paris; it's cold there and snowing. I talk French perfectly horribly. My mother lives on the fifth floor. I go to her, and find her there with various Frenchmen, women, an old abbé with a book, and everything in tobacco smoke and with no comfort at all. I suddenly became very sorry for mother—so sorry that I took her head in my arms and hugged her and wouldn't let her go. Then mother started hugging me and crying....

VARYA. [Weeping] Don't say any more, don't say any more....

ANYA. She's already sold her villa near Mentone; she's nothing left, nothing. And I haven't a copeck left either; we only just managed to get here. And mother won't understand! We had dinner at a station; she asked for all the expensive things, and tipped the waiters one rouble each. And Charlotta too. Yasha wants his share too—it's too bad. Mother's got a footman now, Yasha; we've brought him here.

VARYA. I saw the wretch.

ANYA. How's business? Has the interest been paid?

VARYA. Not much chance of that.

ANYA. Oh God, oh God...

VARYA. The place will be sold in August.

ANYA. O God....

LOPAKHIN. [Looks in at the door and moos] Moo!... [Exit.]

VARYA. [Through her tears] I'd like to.... [Shakes her fist.]

ANYA. [Embraces VARYA, softly] Varya, has he proposed to you? [VARYA shakes head] But he loves you.... Why don't you make up your minds? Why do you keep on waiting?

VARYA. I think that it will all come to nothing. He's a busy man. I'm not his affair... he pays no attention to me. Bless the man, I don't want to see him.... But everybody talks about our marriage, everybody congratulates me, and there's nothing in it at all, it's all like a dream. [In another tone] You've got a brooch like a bee.

ANYA. [Sadly] Mother bought it. [Goes into her room, and talks lightly, like a child] In Paris I went up in a balloon!

VARYA. My darling's come back, my pretty one's come back! [DUNYASHA has already returned with the coffee-pot and is making the coffee, VARYA stands near the door] I go about all day, looking after the house, and I think all the time, if only you could marry a rich man, then I'd be happy and would go away somewhere by myself, then to Kiev... to Moscow, and so on, from one holy place to another. I'd tramp and tramp. That would be splendid!

ANYA. The birds are singing in the garden. What time is it now?

VARYA. It must be getting on for three. Time you went to sleep, darling. [Goes into ANYA'S room] Splendid!

[Enter YASHA with a plaid shawl and a travelling bag.]

YASHA. [Crossing the stage: Politely] May I go this way?

DUNYASHA. I hardly knew you, Yasha. You have changed abroad.

YASHA. Hm... and who are you?

DUNYASHA. When you went away I was only so high. [Showing with her hand] I'm Dunyasha, the daughter of Theodore Kozoyedov. You don't remember!

YASHA. Oh, you little cucumber!

[Looks round and embraces her. She screams and drops a saucer. YASHA goes out quickly.]

VARYA. [In the doorway: In an angry voice] What's that?

DUNYASHA. [Through her tears] I've broken a saucer.

VARYA. It may bring luck.

ANYA. [Coming out of her room] We must tell mother that Peter's here.

VARYA. I told them not to wake him.

ANYA. [Thoughtfully] Father died six years ago, and a month later my brother Grisha was drowned in the river—such a dear little boy of seven! Mother couldn't bear it; she went away, away, without looking round.... [Shudders] How I understand her; if only she knew! [Pause] And Peter Trofimov was Grisha's tutor, he might tell her....

[Enter FIERS in a short jacket and white waistcoat.]

FIERS. [Goes to the coffee-pot, nervously] The mistress is going to have some food here.... [Puts on white gloves] Is the coffee ready? [To DUNYASHA, severely] You! Where's the cream?

DUNYASHA. Oh, dear me...! [Rapid exit.]

FIERS. [Fussing round the coffee-pot] Oh, you bungler.... [Murmurs to himself] Back from Paris... the master went to Paris once... in a carriage.... [Laughs.]

VARYA. What are you talking about, Fiers?

FIERS. I beg your pardon? [Joyfully] The mistress is home again. I've lived to see her! Don't care if I die now.... [Weeps with joy.]

[Enter LUBOV ANDREYEVNA, GAEV, LOPAKHIN, and SIMEONOV-PISCHIN, the latter in a long jacket of thin cloth and loose trousers. GAEV, coming in, moves his arms and body about as if he is playing billiards.]

LUBOV. Let me remember now. Red into the corner! Twice into the centre!

GAEV. Right into the pocket! Once upon a time you and I used both to sleep in this room, and now I'm fifty-one; it does seem strange.

LOPAKHIN. Yes, time does go.

GAEV. Who does?

LOPAKHIN. I said that time does go.

GAEV. It smells of patchouli here.

ANYA. I'm going to bed. Good-night, mother. [Kisses her.]

LUBOV. My lovely little one. [Kisses her hand] Glad to be at home? I can't get over it.

ANYA. Good-night, uncle.

GAEV. [Kisses her face and hands] God be with you. How you do resemble your mother! [To his sister] You were just like her at her age, Luba.

[ANYA gives her hand to LOPAKHIN and PISCHIN and goes out, shutting the door behind her.]

LUBOV. She's awfully tired.

PISCHIN. It's a very long journey.

VARYA. [To LOPAKHIN and PISCHIN] Well, sirs, it's getting on for three, quite time you went.

LUBOV. [Laughs] You're just the same as ever, Varya. [Draws her close and kisses her] I'll have some coffee now, then we'll all go. [FIERS lays a cushion under her feet] Thank you, dear. I'm used to coffee. I drink it day and night. Thank you, dear old man. [Kisses FIERS.]

VARYA. I'll go and see if they've brought in all the luggage. [Exit.]

LUBOV. Is it really I who am sitting here? [Laughs] I want to jump about and wave my arms. [Covers her face with her hands] But suppose I'm dreaming! God knows I love my own country, I love it deeply; I couldn't look out of the railway carriage, I cried so much. [Through her tears] Still, I must have my coffee. Thank you, Fiers. Thank you, dear old man. I'm so glad you're still with us.

FIERS. The day before yesterday.

GAEV. He doesn't hear well.

LOPAKHIN. I've got to go off to Kharkov by the five o'clock train. I'm awfully sorry! I should like to have a look at you, to gossip a little. You're as fine-looking as ever.

PISCHIN. [Breathes heavily] Even finer-looking... dressed in Paris fashions... confound it all.

LOPAKHIN. Your brother, Leonid Andreyevitch, says I'm a snob, a usurer, but that is absolutely nothing to me. Let him talk. Only I do wish you would believe in me as you once did, that your wonderful, touching eyes would look at me as they did before. Merciful God! My father was the serf of your grandfather and your own father, but you—you more than anybody else—did so much for me once upon a time that I've forgotten everything and love you as if you belonged to my family... and even more.

LUBOV. I can't sit still, I'm not in a state to do it. [Jumps up and walks about in great excitement] I'll never survive this happiness.... You can laugh at me; I'm a silly woman.... My dear little cupboard. [Kisses cupboard] My little table.

GAEV. Nurse has died in your absence.

LUBOV. [Sits and drinks coffee] Yes, bless her soul. I heard by letter.

GAEV. And Anastasius has died too. Peter Kosoy has left me and now lives in town with the Commissioner of Police. [Takes a box of sugar-candy out of his pocket and sucks a piece.]

PISCHIN. My daughter, Dashenka, sends her love.

LOPAKHIN. I want to say something very pleasant, very delightful, to you. [Looks at his watch] I'm going away at once, I haven't much time... but I'll tell you all about it in two or three words. As you already know, your cherry orchard is to be sold to pay your debts, and the sale is fixed for August 22; but you needn't be alarmed, dear madam, you may sleep in peace; there's a way out. Here's my plan. Please attend carefully! Your estate is only thirteen miles from the town, the railway runs by, and if the cherry orchard and the land by the river are broken up into building lots and are then leased off for villas you'll get at least twenty-five thousand roubles a year profit out of it.

GAEV. How utterly absurd!

LUBOV. I don't understand you at all, Ermolai Alexeyevitch.

LOPAKHIN. You will get twenty-five roubles a year for each dessiatin from the leaseholders at the very least, and if you advertise now I'm willing to bet that you won't have a vacant plot left by the autumn; they'll all go. In a word, you're saved. I congratulate you. Only, of course, you'll have to put things straight, and clean up.... For instance, you'll have to pull down all the old buildings, this house, which isn't any use to anybody now, and cut down the old cherry orchard....

LUBOV. Cut it down? My dear man, you must excuse me, but you don't understand anything at all. If there's anything interesting or remarkable in the whole province, it's this cherry orchard of ours.

LOPAKHIN. The only remarkable thing about the orchard is that it's very large. It only bears fruit every other year, and even then you don't know what to do with them; nobody buys any.

GAEV. This orchard is mentioned in the "Encyclopaedic Dictionary."

LOPAKHIN. [Looks at his watch] If we can't think of anything and don't make up our minds to anything, then on August 22, both the cherry orchard and the whole estate will be up for auction. Make up your mind! I swear there's no other way out, I'll swear it again.

FIERS. In the old days, forty or fifty years back, they dried the cherries, soaked them and pickled them, and made jam of them, and it used to happen that...

GAEV. Be quiet, Fiers.

FIERS. And then we'd send the dried cherries off in carts to Moscow and Kharkov. And money! And the dried cherries were soft, juicy, sweet, and nicely scented.... They knew the way....

LUBOV. What was the way?

FIERS. They've forgotten. Nobody remembers.

PISCHIN. [To LUBOV ANDREYEVNA] What about Paris? Eh? Did you eat frogs?

LUBOV. I ate crocodiles.

PISCHIN. To think of that, now.

LOPAKHIN. Up to now in the villages there were only the gentry and the labourers, and now the people who live in villas have arrived. All towns now, even small ones, are surrounded by villas. And it's safe to say that in twenty years' time the villa resident will be all over the place. At present he sits on his balcony and drinks tea, but it may well come to pass that he'll begin to cultivate his patch of land, and then your cherry orchard will be happy, rich, splendid....

GAEV. [Angry] What rot!

[Enter VARYA and YASHA.]

VARYA. There are two telegrams for you, little mother. [Picks out a key and noisily unlocks an antique cupboard] Here they are.

LUBOV. They're from Paris.... [Tears them up without reading them] I've done with Paris.

GAEV. And do you know, Luba, how old this case is? A week ago I took out the bottom drawer; I looked and saw figures burnt out in it. That case was made exactly a hundred years ago. What do you think of that? What? We could celebrate its jubilee. It hasn't a soul of its own, but still, say what you will, it's a fine bookcase.

PISCHIN. [Astonished] A hundred years.... Think of that!

GAEV. Yes... it's a real thing. [Handling it] My dear and honoured case! I congratulate you on your existence, which has already for more than a hundred years been directed towards the bright ideals of good and justice; your silent call to productive labour has not grown less in the hundred years [Weeping] during which you have upheld virtue and faith in a better future to the generations of our race, educating us up to ideals of goodness and to the knowledge of a common consciousness. [Pause.]

LOPAKHIN. Yes....

LUBOV. You're just the same as ever, Leon.

GAEV. [A little confused] Off the white on the right, into the corner pocket. Red ball goes into the middle pocket!

LOPAKHIN. [Looks at his watch] It's time I went.

YASHA. [Giving LUBOV ANDREYEVNA her medicine] Will you take your pills now?

PISCHIN. You oughtn't to take medicines, dear madam; they do you neither harm nor good.... Give them here, dear madam. [Takes the pills, turns them out into the palm of his hand, blows on them, puts them into his mouth, and drinks some kvass] There!

LUBOV. [Frightened] You're off your head!

PISCHIN. I've taken all the pills.

LOPAKHIN. Gormandizer! [All laugh.]

FIERS. They were here in Easter week and ate half a pailful of cucumbers.... [Mumbles.]

LUBOV. What's he driving at?

VARYA. He's been mumbling away for three years. We're used to that.

YASHA. Senile decay.

[CHARLOTTA IVANOVNA crosses the stage, dressed in white: she is very thin and tightly laced; has a lorgnette at her waist.]

LOPAKHIN. Excuse me, Charlotta Ivanovna, I haven't said "How do you do" to you yet. [Tries to kiss her hand.]

CHARLOTTA. [Takes her hand away] If you let people kiss your hand, then they'll want your elbow, then your shoulder, and then...

LOPAKHIN. My luck's out to-day! [All laugh] Show us a trick, Charlotta Ivanovna!

LUBOV ANDREYEVNA. Charlotta, do us a trick.

CHARLOTTA. It's not necessary. I want to go to bed. [Exit.]

LOPAKHIN. We shall see each other in three weeks. [Kisses LUBOV ANDREYEVNA'S hand] Now, good-bye. It's time to go. [To GAEV] See you again. [Kisses PISCHIN] Au revoir. [Gives his hand to VARYA, then to FIERS and to YASHA] I don't want to go away. [To LUBOV ANDREYEVNA]. If you think about the villas and make up your mind, then just let me know, and I'll raise a loan of 50,000 roubles at once. Think about it seriously.

VARYA. [Angrily] Do go, now!

LOPAKHIN. I'm going, I'm going.... [Exit.]

GAEV. Snob. Still, I beg pardon.... Varya's going to marry him, he's Varya's young man.

VARYA. Don't talk too much, uncle.

LUBOV. Why not, Varya? I should be very glad. He's a good man.

PISCHIN. To speak the honest truth... he's a worthy man.... And my Dashenka... also says that... she says lots of things. [Snores, but wakes up again at once] But still, dear madam, if you could lend me... 240 roubles... to pay the interest on my mortgage to-morrow...

VARYA. [Frightened] We haven't got it, we haven't got it!

LUBOV. It's quite true. I've nothing at all.

PISCHIN. I'll find it all right [Laughs] I never lose hope. I used to think, "Everything's lost now. I'm a dead man," when, lo and behold, a railway was built over my land... and they paid me for it. And something else will happen to-day or to-morrow. Dashenka may win 20,000 roubles... she's got a lottery ticket.

LUBOV. The coffee's all gone, we can go to bed.

FIERS. [Brushing GAEV'S trousers; in an insistent tone] You've put on the wrong trousers again. What am I to do with you?

VARYA. [Quietly] Anya's asleep. [Opens window quietly] The sun has risen already; it isn't cold. Look, little mother: what lovely trees! And the air! The starlings are singing!

GAEV. [Opens the other window] The whole garden's white. You haven't forgotten, Luba? There's that long avenue going straight, straight, like a stretched strap; it shines on moonlight nights. Do you remember? You haven't forgotten?

LUBOV. [Looks out into the garden] Oh, my childhood, days of my innocence! In this nursery I used to sleep; I used to look out from here into the orchard. Happiness used to wake with me every morning, and then it was just as it is now; nothing has changed. [Laughs from joy] It's all, all white! Oh, my orchard! After the dark autumns and the cold winters, you're young again, full of happiness, the angels of heaven haven't left you.... If only I could take my heavy burden off my breast and shoulders, if I could forget my past!

GAEV. Yes, and they'll sell this orchard to pay off debts. How strange it seems!

LUBOV. Look, there's my dead mother going in the orchard... dressed in white! [Laughs from joy] That's she.

GAEV. Where?

VARYA. God bless you, little mother.

LUBOV. There's nobody there; I thought I saw somebody. On the right, at the turning by the summer-house, a white little tree bent down, looking just like a woman. [Enter TROFIMOV in a worn student uniform and spectacles] What a marvellous garden! White masses of flowers, the blue sky....

TROFIMOV. Lubov Andreyevna! [She looks round at him] I only want to show myself, and I'll go away. [Kisses her hand warmly] I was told to wait till the morning, but I didn't have the patience.

[LUBOV ANDREYEVNA looks surprised.]

VARYA. [Crying] It's Peter Trofimov.

TROFIMOV. Peter Trofimov, once the tutor of your Grisha.... Have I changed so much?

[LUBOV ANDREYEVNA embraces him and cries softly.]

GAEV. [Confused] That's enough, that's enough, Luba.

VARYA. [Weeps] But I told you, Peter, to wait till to-morrow.

LUBOV. My Grisha... my boy... Grisha... my son.

VARYA. What are we to do, little mother? It's the will of God.

TROFIMOV. [Softly, through his tears] It's all right, it's all right.

LUBOV. [Still weeping] My boy's dead; he was drowned. Why? Why, my friend? [Softly] Anya's asleep in there. I am speaking so loudly, making such a noise.... Well, Peter? What's made you look so bad? Why have you grown so old?

TROFIMOV. In the train an old woman called me a decayed gentleman.

LUBOV. You were quite a boy then, a nice little student, and now your hair is not at all thick and you wear spectacles. Are you really still a student? [Goes to the door.]

TROFIMOV. I suppose I shall always be a student.

LUBOV. [Kisses her brother, then VARYA] Well, let's go to bed.... And you've grown older, Leonid.

PISCHIN. [Follows her] Yes, we've got to go to bed.... Oh, my gout! I'll stay the night here. If only, Lubov Andreyevna, my dear, you could get me 240 roubles to-morrow morning—

GAEV. Still the same story.

PISCHIN. Two hundred and forty roubles... to pay the interest on the mortgage.

LUBOV. I haven't any money, dear man.

PISCHIN. I'll give it back... it's a small sum....

LUBOV. Well, then, Leonid will give it to you.... Let him have it, Leonid.

GAEV. By all means; hold out your hand.

LUBOV. Why not? He wants it; he'll give it back.

[LUBOV ANDREYEVNA, TROFIMOV, PISCHIN, and FIERS go out. GAEV, VARYA, and YASHA remain.]

GAEV. My sister hasn't lost the habit of throwing money about. [To YASHA] Stand off, do; you smell of poultry.

YASHA. [Grins] You are just the same as ever, Leonid Andreyevitch.

GAEV. Really? [To VARYA] What's he saying?

VARYA. [To YASHA] Your mother's come from the village; she's been sitting in the servants' room since yesterday, and wants to see you....

YASHA. Bless the woman!

VARYA. Shameless man.

YASHA. A lot of use there is in her coming. She might have come tomorrow just as well. [Exit.]

VARYA. Mother hasn't altered a scrap, she's just as she always was. She'd give away everything, if the idea only entered her head.

GAEV. Yes.... [Pause] If there's any illness for which people offer many remedies, you may be sure that particular illness is incurable, I think. I work my brains to their hardest. I've several remedies, very many, and that really means I've none at all. It would be nice to inherit a fortune from somebody, it would be nice to marry our Anya to a rich man, it would be nice to go to Yaroslav and try my luck with my aunt the Countess. My aunt is very, very rich.

VARYA. [Weeps] If only God helped us.

GAEV. Don't cry. My aunt's very rich, but she doesn't like us. My sister, in the first place, married an advocate, not a noble.... [ANYA appears in the doorway] She not only married a man who was not a noble, but she behaved herself in a way which cannot be described as proper. She's nice and kind and charming, and I'm very fond of her, but say what you will in her favour and you still have to admit that she's wicked; you can feel it in her slightest movements.

VARYA. [Whispers] Anya's in the doorway.

GAEV. Really? [Pause] It's curious, something's got into my right eye... I can't see properly out of it. And on Thursday, when I was at the District Court...

[Enter ANYA.]

VARYA. Why aren't you in bed, Anya?

ANYA. Can't sleep. It's no good.

GAEV. My darling! [Kisses ANYA'S face and hands] My child.... [Crying] You're not my niece, you're my angel, you're my all.... Believe in me, believe...

ANYA. I do believe in you, uncle. Everybody loves you and respects you... but, uncle dear, you ought to say nothing, no more than that. What were you saying just now about my mother, your own sister? Why did you say those things?

GAEV. Yes, yes. [Covers his face with her hand] Yes, really, it was awful. Save me, my God! And only just now I made a speech before a bookcase... it's so silly! And only when I'd finished I knew how silly it was.

VARYA. Yes, uncle dear, you really ought to say less. Keep quiet, that's all.

ANYA. You'd be so much happier in yourself if you only kept quiet.

GAEV. All right, I'll be quiet. [Kisses their hands] I'll be quiet. But let's talk business. On Thursday I was in the District Court, and a lot of us met there together, and we began to talk of this, that, and the other, and now I think I can arrange a loan to pay the interest into the bank.

VARYA. If only God would help us!

GAEV. I'll go on Tuesday. I'll talk with them about it again. [To VARYA] Don't howl. [To ANYA] Your mother will have a talk to Lopakhin; he, of course, won't refuse... And when you've rested you'll go to Yaroslav to the Countess, your grandmother. So you see, we'll have three irons in the fire, and we'll be safe. We'll pay up the interest. I'm certain. [Puts some sugar-candy into his mouth] I swear on my honour, on anything you will, that the estate will not be sold! [Excitedly] I swear on my happiness! Here's my hand. You may call me a dishonourable wretch if I let it go to auction! I swear by all I am!

ANYA. [She is calm again and happy] How good and clever you are, uncle. [Embraces him] I'm happy now! I'm happy! All's well!

[Enter FIERS.]

FIERS. [Reproachfully] Leonid Andreyevitch, don't you fear God? When are you going to bed?

GAEV. Soon, soon. You go away, Fiers. I'll undress myself. Well, children, bye-bye...! I'll give you the details to-morrow, but let's go to bed now. [Kisses ANYA and VARYA] I'm a man of the eighties.... People don't praise those years much, but I can still say that I've suffered for my beliefs. The peasants don't love me for nothing, I assure you. We've got to learn to know the peasants! We ought to learn how....

ANYA. You're doing it again, uncle!

VARYA. Be quiet, uncle!

FIERS. [Angrily] Leonid Andreyevitch!

GAEV. I'm coming, I'm coming.... Go to bed now. Off two cushions into the middle! I turn over a new leaf.... [Exit. FIERS goes out after him.]

ANYA. I'm quieter now. I don't want to go to Yaroslav, I don't like grandmother; but I'm calm now; thanks to uncle. [Sits down.]

VARYA. It's time to go to sleep. I'll go. There's been an unpleasantness here while you were away. In the old servants' part of the house, as you know, only the old people live—little old Efim and Polya and Evstigney, and Karp as well. They started letting some tramps or other spend the night there—I said nothing. Then I heard that they were saying that I had ordered them to be fed on peas and nothing else; from meanness, you see.... And it was all Evstigney's doing.... Very well, I thought, if that's what the matter is, just you wait. So I call Evstigney.... [Yawns] He comes. "What's this," I say, "Evstigney, you old fool."... [Looks at ANYA] Anya dear! [Pause] She's dropped off.... [Takes ANYA'S arm] Let's go to bye-bye.... Come along!... [Leads her] My darling's gone to sleep! Come on.... [They go. In the distance, the other side of the orchard, a shepherd plays his pipe. TROFIMOV crosses the stage and stops on seeing VARYA and ANYA] Sh! She's asleep, asleep. Come on, dear.

ANYA. [Quietly, half-asleep] I'm so tired... all the bells... uncle, dear! Mother and uncle!

VARYA. Come on, dear, come on! [They go into ANYA'S room.]

TROFIMOV. [Moved] My sun! My spring!

Curtain.

ACT TWO

[In a field. An old, crooked shrine, which has been long abandoned; near it a well and large stones, which apparently are old tombstones, and an old garden seat. The road is seen to GAEV'S estate. On one side rise dark poplars, behind them begins the cherry orchard. In the distance is a row of telegraph poles, and far, far away on the horizon are the indistinct signs of a large town, which can only be seen on the finest and clearest days. It is close on sunset. CHARLOTTA, YASHA, and DUNYASHA are sitting on the seat; EPIKHODOV stands by and plays on a guitar; all seem thoughtful. CHARLOTTA wears a man's old peaked cap; she has unslung a rifle from her shoulders and is putting to rights the buckle on the strap.]

CHARLOTTA. [Thoughtfully] I haven't a real passport. I don't know how old I am, and I think I'm young. When I was a little girl my father and mother used to go round fairs and give very good performances and I used to do the *salto mortale* and various little things. And when papa and mamma died a German lady took me to her and began to teach me. I liked it. I grew up and became a governess. And where I came from and who I am, I don't know.... Who my parents were—perhaps they weren't married—I don't know. [Takes a cucumber out of her pocket and eats] I don't know anything. [Pause] I do want to talk, but I haven't anybody to talk to... I haven't anybody at all.

EPIKHODOV. [Plays on the guitar and sings]

> *"What is this noisy earth to me,*
> *What matter friends and foes?"*
> *I do like playing on the mandoline!*

DUNYASHA. That's a guitar, not a mandoline. [Looks at herself in a little mirror and powders herself.]

EPIKHODOV. For the enamoured madman, this is a mandoline. [Sings]

> *"Oh that the heart was warmed,*

By all the flames of love returned!"

[YASHA sings too.]

CHARLOTTA. These people sing terribly.... Foo! Like jackals.

DUNYASHA. [To YASHA] Still, it must be nice to live abroad.

YASHA. Yes, certainly. I cannot differ from you there. [Yawns and lights a cigar.]

EPIKHODOV. That is perfectly natural. Abroad everything is in full complexity.

YASHA. That goes without saying.

EPIKHODOV. I'm an educated man, I read various remarkable books, but I cannot understand the direction I myself want to go—whether to live or to shoot myself, as it were. So, in case, I always carry a revolver about with me. Here it is. [Shows a revolver.]

CHARLOTTA. I've done. Now I'll go. [Slings the rifle] You, Epikhodov, are a very clever man and very terrible; women must be madly in love with you. Brrr! [Going] These wise ones are all so stupid. I've nobody to talk to. I'm always alone, alone; I've nobody at all... and I don't know who I am or why I live. [Exit slowly.]

EPIKHODOV. As a matter of fact, independently of everything else, I must express my feeling, among other things, that fate has been as pitiless in her dealings with me as a storm is to a small ship. Suppose, let us grant, I am wrong; then why did I wake up this morning, to give an example, and behold an enormous spider on my chest, like that. [Shows with both hands] And if I do drink some kvass, why is it that there is bound to be something of the most indelicate nature in it, such as a beetle? [Pause] Have you read Buckle? [Pause] I should like to trouble you, Avdotya Fedorovna, for two words.

DUNYASHA. Say on.

EPIKHODOV. I should prefer to be alone with you. [Sighs.]

DUNYASHA. [Shy] Very well, only first bring me my little cloak.... It's by the cupboard. It's a little damp here.

EPIKHODOV. Very well... I'll bring it.... Now I know what to do with my revolver. [Takes guitar and exits, strumming.]

YASHA. Two-and-twenty troubles! A silly man, between you and me and the gatepost. [Yawns.]

DUNYASHA. I hope to goodness he won't shoot himself. [Pause] I'm so nervous, I'm worried. I went into service when I was quite a little girl, and now I'm not used to common life, and my hands are white, white as a lady's. I'm so tender and so delicate now; respectable and afraid of everything.... I'm so frightened. And I don't know what will happen to my nerves if you deceive me, Yasha.

YASHA. [Kisses her] Little cucumber! Of course, every girl must respect herself; there's nothing I dislike more than a badly behaved girl.

DUNYASHA. I'm awfully in love with you; you're educated, you can talk about everything. [Pause.]

YASHA. [Yawns] Yes. I think this: if a girl loves anybody, then that means she's immoral. [Pause] It's nice to smoke a cigar out in the open air.... [Listens] Somebody's coming. It's the mistress, and people with her. [DUNYASHA embraces him suddenly] Go to the house, as if you'd been bathing in the river; go by this path, or they'll meet you and will think I've been meeting you. I can't stand that sort of thing.

DUNYASHA. [Coughs quietly] My head's aching because of your cigar.

[Exit. YASHA remains, sitting by the shrine. Enter LUBOV ANDREYEVNA, GAEV, and LOPAKHIN.]

LOPAKHIN. You must make up your mind definitely—there's no time to waste. The question is perfectly plain. Are you willing to let the land for villas or no? Just one word, yes or no? Just one word!

LUBOV. Who's smoking horrible cigars here? [Sits.]

GAEV. They built that railway; that's made this place very handy. [Sits] Went to town and had lunch... red in the middle! I'd like to go in now and have just one game.

LUBOV. You'll have time.

LOPAKHIN. Just one word! [Imploringly] Give me an answer!

GAEV. [Yawns] Really!

LUBOV. [Looks in her purse] I had a lot of money yesterday, but there's very little to-day. My poor Varya feeds everybody on milk soup to save money, in the kitchen the old people only get peas, and I spend recklessly. [Drops the purse, scattering gold coins] There, they are all over the place.

YASHA. Permit me to pick them up. [Collects the coins.]

LUBOV. Please do, Yasha. And why did I go and have lunch there?... A horrid restaurant with band and tablecloths smelling of soap.... Why do you drink so much, Leon? Why do you eat so much? Why do you talk so much? You talked again too much to-day in the restaurant, and it wasn't at all to the point—about the seventies and about decadents. And to whom? Talking to the waiters about decadents!

LOPAKHIN. Yes.

GAEV. [Waves his hand] I can't be cured, that's obvious.... [Irritably to YASHA] What's the matter? Why do you keep twisting about in front of me?

YASHA. [Laughs] I can't listen to your voice without laughing.

GAEV. [To his sister] Either he or I...

LUBOV. Go away, Yasha; get out of this....

YASHA. [Gives purse to LUBOV ANDREYEVNA] I'll go at once. [Hardly able to keep from laughing] This minute.... [Exit.]

LOPAKHIN. That rich man Deriganov is preparing to buy your estate. They say he'll come to the sale himself.

LUBOV. Where did you hear that?

LOPAKHIN. They say so in town.

GAEV. Our Yaroslav aunt has promised to send something, but I don't know when or how much.

LOPAKHIN. How much will she send? A hundred thousand roubles? Or two, perhaps?

LUBOV. I'd be glad of ten or fifteen thousand.

LOPAKHIN. You must excuse my saying so, but I've never met such frivolous people as you before, or anybody so unbusinesslike and peculiar. Here I am telling you in plain language that your estate will be sold, and you don't seem to understand.

LUBOV. What are we to do? Tell us, what?

LOPAKHIN. I tell you every day. I say the same thing every day. Both the cherry orchard and the land must be leased off for villas and at once, immediately—the auction is staring you in the face: Understand! Once you do definitely make up your minds to the villas, then you'll have as much money as you want and you'll be saved.

LUBOV. Villas and villa residents—it's so vulgar, excuse me.

GAEV. I entirely agree with you.

LOPAKHIN. I must cry or yell or faint. I can't stand it! You're too much for me! [To GAEV] You old woman!

GAEV. Really!

LOPAKHIN. Old woman! [Going out.]

LUBOV. [Frightened] No, don't go away, do stop; be a dear. Please. Perhaps we'll find some way out!

LOPAKHIN. What's the good of trying to think!

LUBOV. Please don't go away. It's nicer when you're here.... [Pause] I keep on waiting for something to happen, as if the house is going to collapse over our heads.

GAEV. [Thinking deeply] Double in the corner... across the middle....

LUBOV. We have been too sinful....

LOPAKHIN. What sins have you committed?

GAEV. [Puts candy into his mouth] They say that I've eaten all my substance in sugar-candies. [Laughs.]

LUBOV. Oh, my sins.... I've always scattered money about without holding myself in, like a madwoman, and I married a man who made nothing but debts. My husband died of champagne—he drank terribly—and to my misfortune, I fell in love with another man and went off with him, and just at that time—it was my first punishment, a blow that hit me right on the head—here, in the river... my boy was drowned, and I went away, quite away, never to return, never to see this river again...I shut my eyes and ran without thinking, but *he* ran after me... without pity, without respect. I bought a villa near Mentone because *he* fell ill there, and for three years I knew no rest either by day or night; the sick man wore me out, and my soul dried up. And last year, when they had sold the villa to pay my debts, I went away to Paris, and there he robbed me of all I had and threw me over and went off with another woman. I tried to poison myself.... It was so silly, so shameful.... And suddenly I longed to be back in Russia, my own land, with my little girl.... [Wipes her tears] Lord, Lord be merciful to me, forgive me my sins! Punish me no more! [Takes a telegram out of her pocket] I had this to-day from Paris.... He begs my forgiveness, he implores me to return.... [Tears it up] Don't I hear music? [Listens.]

GAEV. That is our celebrated Jewish band. You remember—four violins, a flute, and a double-bass.

LUBOV So it still exists? It would be nice if they came along some evening.

LOPAKHIN. [Listens] I can't hear.... [Sings quietly] "For money will the Germans make a Frenchman of a Russian." [Laughs] I saw such an awfully funny thing at the theatre last night.

LUBOV. I'm quite sure there wasn't anything at all funny. You oughtn't to go and see plays, you ought to go and look at yourself. What a grey life you lead, what a lot you talk unnecessarily.

LOPAKHIN. It's true. To speak the straight truth, we live a silly life. [Pause] My father was a peasant, an idiot, he understood nothing, he didn't teach me, he was always drunk, and always used a stick on me. In point of fact, I'm a fool and an idiot too. I've never learned anything, my handwriting is bad, I write so that I'm quite ashamed before people, like a pig!

LUBOV. You ought to get married, my friend.

LOPAKHIN. Yes... that's true.

LUBOV. Why not to our Varya? She's a nice girl.

LOPAKHIN. Yes.

LUBOV. She's quite homely in her ways, works all day, and, what matters most, she's in love with you. And you've liked her for a long time.

LOPAKHIN. Well? I don't mind... she's a nice girl. [Pause.]

GAEV. I'm offered a place in a bank. Six thousand roubles a year.... Did you hear?

LUBOV. What's the matter with you! Stay where you are....

[Enter FIERS with an overcoat.]

FIERS. [To GAEV] Please, sir, put this on, it's damp.

GAEV. [Putting it on] You're a nuisance, old man.

FIERS It's all very well.... You went away this morning without telling me. [Examining GAEV.]

LUBOV. How old you've grown, Fiers!

FIERS. I beg your pardon?

LOPAKHIN. She says you've grown very old!

FIERS. I've been alive a long time. They were already getting ready to marry me before your father was born.... [Laughs] And when the Emancipation came I was already first valet. Only I didn't agree with the Emancipation and remained with my people.... [Pause] I remember everybody was happy, but they didn't know why.

LOPAKHIN. It was very good for them in the old days. At any rate, they used to beat them.

FIERS. [Not hearing] Rather. The peasants kept their distance from the masters and the masters kept their distance from the peasants, but now everything's all anyhow and you can't understand anything.

GAEV. Be quiet, Fiers. I've got to go to town tomorrow. I've been promised an introduction to a General who may lend me money on a bill.

LOPAKHIN. Nothing will come of it. And you won't pay your interest, don't you worry.

LUBOV. He's talking rubbish. There's no General at all.

[Enter TROFIMOV, ANYA, and VARYA.]

GAEV. Here they are.

ANYA. Mother's sitting down here.

LUBOV. [Tenderly] Come, come, my dears.... [Embracing ANYA and VARYA] If you two only knew how much I love you. Sit down next to me, like that. [All sit down.]

LOPAKHIN. Our eternal student is always with the ladies.

TROFIMOV. That's not your business.

LOPAKHIN. He'll soon be fifty, and he's still a student.

TROFIMOV. Leave off your silly jokes!

LOPAKHIN. Getting angry, eh, silly?

TROFIMOV. Shut up, can't you.

LOPAKHIN. [Laughs] I wonder what you think of me?

TROFIMOV. I think, Ermolai Alexeyevitch, that you're a rich man, and you'll soon be a millionaire. Just as the wild beast which eats everything it finds is needed for changes to take place in matter, so you are needed too.

[All laugh.]

VARYA. Better tell us something about the planets, Peter.

LUBOV ANDREYEVNA. No, let's go on with yesterday's talk!

TROFIMOV. About what?

GAEV. About the proud man.

TROFIMOV. Yesterday we talked for a long time but we didn't come to anything in the end. There's something mystical about the proud man, in your sense. Perhaps you are right from your point of view, but if you take the matter simply, without complicating it, then what pride can there be, what sense can there be in it, if a man is imperfectly made, physiologically speaking, if in the vast majority of cases he is coarse and stupid and deeply unhappy? We must stop admiring one another. We must work, nothing more.

GAEV. You'll die, all the same.

TROFIMOV. Who knows? And what does it mean—you'll die? Perhaps a man has a hundred senses, and when he dies only the five known to us are destroyed and the remaining ninety-five are left alive.

LUBOV. How clever of you, Peter!

LOPAKHIN. [Ironically] Oh, awfully!

TROFIMOV. The human race progresses, perfecting its powers. Everything that is unattainable now will some day be near at hand and comprehensible, but we must work, we must help with all our strength those who seek to know what fate will bring. Meanwhile in Russia only a very few of us work. The vast majority of those intellectuals whom I know seek for nothing, do nothing, and are at present incapable of hard work. They call themselves intellectuals, but they use "thou" and "thee" to their servants, they treat the peasants like animals, they learn badly, they read nothing seriously, they do absolutely nothing, about science they only talk, about art they understand little. They are all serious, they all have severe faces, they all talk about important things. They philosophize, and at the same time, the vast majority of us, ninety-nine out of a hundred, live like savages, fighting and cursing at the slightest opportunity, eating filthily, sleeping in the dirt, in stuffiness, with fleas, stinks, smells, moral filth, and so on... And it's obvious that all our nice talk is only carried on to distract ourselves and others. Tell me, where are those crèches we hear so much of? and where are those reading-rooms? People only write novels about them; they don't really exist. Only dirt, vulgarity, and Asiatic plagues really exist.... I'm afraid, and I don't at all like serious faces; I don't like serious conversations. Let's be quiet sooner.

LOPAKHIN. You know, I get up at five every morning, I work from morning till evening, I am always dealing with money—my own and other people's—and I see what people are like. You've only got to begin to do anything to find out how few honest, honourable people there are. Sometimes, when I can't sleep, I think: "Oh Lord, you've given us huge forests, infinite fields, and endless horizons, and we, living here, ought really to be giants."

LUBOV. You want giants, do you?... They're only good in stories, and even there they frighten one. [EPIKHODOV enters at the back of the stage playing his guitar. Thoughtfully:] Epikhodov's there.

ANYA. [Thoughtfully] Epikhodov's there.

GAEV. The sun's set, ladies and gentlemen.

TROFIMOV. Yes.

GAEV [Not loudly, as if declaiming] O Nature, thou art wonderful, thou shinest with eternal radiance! Oh, beautiful and indifferent one, thou whom we call mother, thou containest in thyself existence and death, thou livest and destroyest....

VARYA. [Entreatingly] Uncle, dear!

ANYA. Uncle, you're doing it again!

TROFIMOV. You'd better double the red into the middle.

GAEV. I'll be quiet, I'll be quiet.

[They all sit thoughtfully. It is quiet. Only the mumbling of FIERS is heard. Suddenly a distant sound is heard as if from the sky, the sound of a breaking string, which dies away sadly.]

LUBOV. What's that?

LOPAKHIN. I don't know. It may be a bucket fallen down a well somewhere. But it's some way off.

GAEV. Or perhaps it's some bird... like a heron.

TROFIMOV. Or an owl.

LUBOV. [Shudders] It's unpleasant, somehow. [A pause.]

FIERS. Before the misfortune the same thing happened. An owl screamed and the samovar hummed without stopping.

GAEV. Before what misfortune?

FIERS. Before the Emancipation. [A pause.]

LUBOV. You know, my friends, let's go in; it's evening now. [To ANYA] You've tears in your eyes.... What is it, little girl? [Embraces her.]

ANYA. It's nothing, mother.

TROFIMOV. Some one's coming.

[Enter a TRAMP in an old white peaked cap and overcoat. He is a little drunk.]

TRAMP. Excuse me, may I go this way straight through to the station?

GAEV. You may. Go along this path.

TRAMP. I thank you from the bottom of my heart. [Hiccups] Lovely weather.... [Declaims] My brother, my suffering brother.... Come out on the Volga, you whose groans... [To VARYA] Mademoiselle, please give a hungry Russian thirty copecks....

[VARYA screams, frightened.]

LOPAKHIN. [Angrily] There's manners everybody's got to keep!

LUBOV. [With a start] Take this... here you are.... [Feels in her purse] There's no silver.... It doesn't matter, here's gold.

TRAMP. I am deeply grateful to you! [Exit. Laughter.]

VARYA. [Frightened] I'm going, I'm going.... Oh, little mother, at home there's nothing for the servants to eat, and you gave him gold.

LUBOV. What is to be done with such a fool as I am! At home I'll give you everything I've got. Ermolai Alexeyevitch, lend me some more!...

LOPAKHIN. Very well.

LUBOV. Let's go, it's time. And Varya, we've settled your affair; I congratulate you.

VARYA. [Crying] You shouldn't joke about this, mother.

LOPAKHIN. Oh, feel me, get thee to a nunnery.

GAEV. My hands are all trembling; I haven't played billiards for a long time.

LOPAKHIN. Oh, feel me, nymph, remember me in thine orisons.

LUBOV. Come along; it'll soon be supper-time.

VARYA. He did frighten me. My heart is beating hard.

LOPAKHIN. Let me remind you, ladies and gentlemen, on August 22 the cherry orchard will be sold. Think of that!... Think of that!...

[All go out except TROFIMOV and ANYA.]

ANYA. [Laughs] Thanks to the tramp who frightened Barbara, we're alone now.

TROFIMOV. Varya's afraid we may fall in love with each other and won't get away from us for days on end. Her narrow mind won't allow her to understand that we are above love. To escape all the petty and deceptive things which prevent our being happy and free, that is the aim and meaning of our lives. Forward! We go irresistibly on to that bright star which burns there, in the distance! Don't lag behind, friends!

ANYA. [Clapping her hands] How beautifully you talk! [Pause] It is glorious here to-day!

TROFIMOV. Yes, the weather is wonderful.

ANYA. What have you done to me, Peter? I don't love the cherry orchard as I used to. I loved it so tenderly, I thought there was no better place in the world than our orchard.

TROFIMOV. All Russia is our orchard. The land is great and beautiful, there are many marvellous places in it. [Pause] Think, Anya, your grandfather, your great-grandfather, and all your ancestors were serf-owners, they owned living souls; and now, doesn't something human look at you from every cherry in the orchard, every leaf and every stalk? Don't you hear voices...? Oh, it's awful, your orchard is terrible; and when in the evening or at night you walk through the orchard, then the old bark on the trees sheds a dim light and the old cherry-trees seem to be dreaming of all that was a hundred, two hundred years ago, and are oppressed by their heavy visions. Still, at any rate, we've left those two hundred years behind us. So far we've gained nothing at all—we don't yet know what the past is to be to us—we only philosophize, we complain that we are dull, or we drink vodka. For it's so clear that in order to begin to live in the present we must first redeem the past, and that can only be done by suffering, by strenuous, uninterrupted labour. Understand that, Anya.

ANYA. The house in which we live has long ceased to be our house; I shall go away. I give you my word.

TROFIMOV. If you have the housekeeping keys, throw them down the well and go away. Be as free as the wind.

ANYA. [Enthusiastically] How nicely you said that!

TROFIMOV. Believe me, Anya, believe me! I'm not thirty yet, I'm young, I'm still a student, but I have undergone a great deal! I'm as hungry as the winter, I'm ill, I'm shaken. I'm as poor as a beggar, and where haven't I been—fate has tossed me everywhere! But my soul is always my own; every minute of the day and the night it is filled with unspeakable presentiments. I know that happiness is coming, Anya, I see it already....

ANYA. [Thoughtful] The moon is rising.

[EPIKHODOV is heard playing the same sad song on his guitar. The moon rises. Somewhere by the poplars VARYA is looking for ANYA and calling, "Anya, where are you?"]

TROFIMOV. Yes, the moon has risen. [Pause] There is happiness, there it comes; it comes nearer and nearer; I hear its steps already. And if we do not see it we shall not know it, but what does that matter? Others will see it!

THE VOICE OF VARYA. Anya! Where are you?

TROFIMOV. That's Varya again! [Angry] Disgraceful!

ANYA. Never mind. Let's go to the river. It's nice there.

TROFIMOV Let's go. [They go out.]

THE VOICE OF VARYA. Anya! Anya!

Curtain.

ACT THREE

[A reception-room cut off from a drawing-room by an arch. Chandelier lighted. A Jewish band, the one mentioned in Act II, is heard playing in another room. Evening. In the drawing-room the grand rond is being danced. Voice of SIMEONOV PISCHIN "Promenade a une paire!" Dancers come into the reception-room; the first pair are PISCHIN and CHARLOTTA IVANOVNA; the second, TROFIMOV and LUBOV ANDREYEVNA; the third, ANYA and the POST OFFICE CLERK; the fourth, VARYA and the STATION-MASTER, and so on. VARYA is crying gently and wipes away her tears as she dances. DUNYASHA is in the last pair. They go off into the drawing-room, PISCHIN shouting, "Grand rond, balancez:" and "Les cavaliers à genou et remerciez vos dames!" FIERS, in a dress-coat, carries a tray with seltzer-water across. Enter PISCHIN and TROFIMOV from the drawing-room.]

PISCHIN. I'm full-blooded and have already had two strokes; it's hard for me to dance, but, as they say, if you're in Rome, you must do as Rome does. I've got the strength of a horse. My dead father, who liked a joke, peace to his bones, used to say, talking of our ancestors, that the ancient stock of the Simeonov-Pischins was descended from that identical horse that Caligula made a senator.... [Sits] But the trouble is, I've no money! A hungry dog only believes in meat. [Snores and wakes up again immediately] So I... only believe in money....

TROFIMOV. Yes. There is something equine about your figure.

PISCHIN. Well... a horse is a fine animal... you can sell a horse.

[Billiard playing can be heard in the next room. VARYA appears under the arch.]

TROFIMOV. [Teasing] Madame Lopakhin! Madame Lopakhin!

VARYA. [Angry] Decayed gentleman!

TROFIMOV. Yes, I am a decayed gentleman, and I'm proud of it!

VARYA. [Bitterly] We've hired the musicians, but how are they to be paid? [Exit.]

TROFIMOV. [To PISCHIN] If the energy which you, in the course of your life, have spent in looking for money to pay interest had been used for something else, then, I believe, after all, you'd be able to turn everything upside down.

PISCHIN. Nietzsche... a philosopher... a very great, a most celebrated man... a man of enormous brain, says in his books that you can forge bank-notes.

TROFIMOV. And have you read Nietzsche?

PISCHIN. Well... Dashenka told me. Now I'm in such a position, I wouldn't mind forging them... I've got to pay 310 roubles the day after to-morrow... I've got 130 already.... [Feels his pockets, nervously] I've lost the money! The money's gone! [Crying] Where's the money? [Joyfully] Here it is behind the lining... I even began to perspire.

[Enter LUBOV ANDREYEVNA and CHARLOTTA IVANOVNA.]

LUBOV. [Humming a Caucasian dance] Why is Leonid away so long? What's he doing in town? [To DUNYASHA] Dunyasha, give the musicians some tea.

TROFIMOV. Business is off, I suppose.

LUBOV. And the musicians needn't have come, and we needn't have got up this ball.... Well, never mind.... [Sits and sings softly.]

CHARLOTTA. [Gives a pack of cards to PISCHIN] Here's a pack of cards, think of any one card you like.

PISCHIN. I've thought of one.

CHARLOTTA. Now shuffle. All right, now. Give them here, oh my dear Mr. Pischin. *Ein, zwei, drei*! Now look and you'll find it in your coat-tail pocket.

PISCHIN. [Takes a card out of his coat-tail pocket] Eight of spades, quite right! [Surprised] Think of that now!

CHARLOTTA. [Holds the pack of cards on the palm of her hand. To TROFIMOV] Now tell me quickly. What's the top card?

TROFIMOV. Well, the queen of spades.

CHARLOTTA. Right! [To PISCHIN] Well now? What card's on top?

PISCHIN. Ace of hearts.

CHARLOTTA. Right! [Claps her hands, the pack of cards vanishes] How lovely the weather is to-day. [A mysterious woman's voice answers her, as if from under the floor, "Oh yes, it's lovely weather, madam."] You are so beautiful, you are my ideal. [Voice, "You, madam, please me very much too."]

STATION-MASTER. [Applauds] Madame ventriloquist, bravo!

PISCHIN. [Surprised] Think of that, now! Delightful, Charlotte Ivanovna... I'm simply in love....

CHARLOTTA. In love? [Shrugging her shoulders] Can you love? *Guter Mensch aber schlechter Musikant.*

TROFIMOV. [Slaps PISCHIN on the shoulder] Oh, you horse!

CHARLOTTA. Attention please, here's another trick. [Takes a shawl from a chair] Here's a very nice plaid shawl, I'm going to sell it.... [Shakes it] Won't anybody buy it?

PISCHIN. [Astonished] Think of that now!

CHARLOTTA. *Ein, zwei, drei.*

[She quickly lifts up the shawl, which is hanging down. ANYA is standing behind it; she bows and runs to her mother, hugs her and runs back to the drawing-room amid general applause.]

LUBOV. [Applauds] Bravo, bravo!

CHARLOTTA. Once again! *Ein, zwei, drei*!

[Lifts the shawl. VARYA stands behind it and bows.]

PISCHIN. [Astonished] Think of that, now.

CHARLOTTA. The end!

[Throws the shawl at PISCHIN, curtseys and runs into the drawing-room.]

PISCHIN. [Runs after her] Little wretch.... What? Would you? [Exit.]

LUBOV. Leonid hasn't come yet. I don't understand what he's doing so long in town! Everything must be over by now. The estate must be sold; or, if the sale never came off, then why does he stay so long?

VARYA. [Tries to soothe her] Uncle has bought it. I'm certain of it.

TROFIMOV. [Sarcastically] Oh, yes!

VARYA. Grandmother sent him her authority for him to buy it in her name and transfer the debt to her. She's doing it for Anya. And I'm certain that God will help us and uncle will buy it.

LUBOV. Grandmother sent fifteen thousand roubles from Yaroslav to buy the property in her name—she won't trust us—and that wasn't even enough to pay the interest. [Covers her face with her hands] My fate will be settled to-day, my fate....

TROFIMOV. [Teasing VARYA] Madame Lopakhin!

VARYA. [Angry] Eternal student! He's already been expelled twice from the university.

LUBOV. Why are you getting angry, Varya? He's teasing you about Lopakhin, well what of it? You can marry Lopakhin if you want to, he's a good, interesting man.... You needn't if you don't want to; nobody wants to force you against your will, my darling.

VARYA. I do look at the matter seriously, little mother, to be quite frank. He's a good man, and I like him.

LUBOV. Then marry him. I don't understand what you're waiting for.

VARYA. I can't propose to him myself, little mother. People have been talking about him to me for two years now, but he either says nothing, or jokes about it. I understand. He's getting rich, he's busy, he can't bother about me. If I had some money, even a little, even only a hundred roubles, I'd throw up everything and go away. I'd go into a convent.

TROFIMOV. How nice!

VARYA. [To TROFIMOV] A student ought to have sense! [Gently, in tears] How ugly you are now, Peter, how old you've grown! [To LUBOV ANDREYEVNA, no longer crying] But I can't go on without working, little mother. I want to be doing something every minute.

[Enter YASHA.]

YASHA. [Nearly laughing] Epikhodov's broken a billiard cue! [Exit.]

VARYA. Why is Epikhodov here? Who said he could play billiards? I don't understand these people. [Exit.]

LUBOV. Don't tease her, Peter, you see that she's quite unhappy without that.

TROFIMOV. She takes too much on herself, she keeps on interfering in other people's business. The whole summer she's given no peace to me or to Anya, she's afraid we'll have a romance all to ourselves. What has it to do with her? As if I'd ever given her grounds to believe I'd stoop to such vulgarity! We are above love.

LUBOV. Then I suppose I must be beneath love. [In agitation] Why isn't Leonid here? If I only knew whether the estate is sold or not! The disaster seems to me so improbable that I don't know what to think, I'm all at sea... I may scream... or do something silly. Save me, Peter. Say something, say something.

TROFIMOV. Isn't it all the same whether the estate is sold to-day or isn't? It's been all up with it for a long time; there's no turning back, the path's grown over. Be calm, dear, you shouldn't deceive yourself, for once in your life at any rate you must look the truth straight in the face.

LUBOV. What truth? You see where truth is, and where untruth is, but I seem to have lost my sight and see nothing. You boldly settle all important questions, but tell me, dear, isn't it because you're young, because you haven't had time to suffer till you settled a single one of your questions? You boldly look forward, isn't it because you cannot foresee or expect anything terrible, because so far life has been hidden from your young eyes? You are bolder, more honest, deeper than we are, but think only, be just a little magnanimous, and have mercy on me. I was born here, my father and mother lived here, my grandfather too, I love this house. I couldn't understand my life without that cherry orchard, and if it really must be sold, sell me with it! [Embraces TROFIMOV, kisses his forehead]. My son was drowned here.... [Weeps] Have pity on me, good, kind man.

TROFIMOV. You know I sympathize with all my soul.

LUBOV. Yes, but it ought to be said differently, differently.... [Takes another handkerchief, a telegram falls on the floor] I'm so sick at heart to-day, you can't imagine. Here it's so noisy, my soul shakes at every sound. I shake all over, and I can't go away by myself, I'm afraid of the silence. Don't judge me harshly, Peter... I loved you, as if you belonged to my family. I'd gladly let Anya marry you, I swear it, only dear, you ought to work, finish your studies. You don't do anything, only fate throws you about from place to place, it's so odd.... Isn't it true? Yes? And you ought to do something to your beard to make it grow better [Laughs] You are funny!

TROFIMOV. [Picking up telegram] I don't want to be a Beau Brummel.

LUBOV. This telegram's from Paris. I get one every day. Yesterday and to-day. That wild man is ill again, he's bad again.... He begs for forgiveness, and implores me to come, and I really ought to go to Paris to be near him. You look severe, Peter, but what can I do, my dear, what can I do; he's ill, he's alone, unhappy, and who's to look after him, who's to keep him away from his errors, to give him his medicine punctually? And why should I conceal it and say nothing about it; I love him, that's plain, I love him, I love him.... That love is a stone round my neck; I'm going with it to the bottom, but I love that stone and can't live without it. [Squeezes TROFIMOV'S hand] Don't think badly of me, Peter, don't say anything to me, don't say...

TROFIMOV. [Weeping] For God's sake forgive my speaking candidly, but that man has robbed you!

LUBOV. No, no, no, you oughtn't to say that! [Stops her ears.]

TROFIMOV. But he's a wretch, you alone don't know it! He's a petty thief, a nobody....

LUBOV. [Angry, but restrained] You're twenty-six or twenty-seven, and still a schoolboy of the second class!

TROFIMOV. Why not!

LUBOV. You ought to be a man, at your age you ought to be able to understand those who love. And you ought to be in love yourself, you must fall in love! [Angry] Yes, yes! You aren't pure, you're just a freak, a queer fellow, a funny growth...

TROFIMOV. [In horror] What is she saying!

LUBOV. "I'm above love!" You're not above love, you're just what our Fiers calls a bungler. Not to have a mistress at your age!

TROFIMOV. [In horror] This is awful! What is she saying? [Goes quickly up into the drawing-room, clutching his head] It's awful... I can't stand it, I'll go away. [Exit, but returns at once] All is over between us! [Exit.]

LUBOV. [Shouts after him] Peter, wait! Silly man, I was joking! Peter! [Somebody is heard going out and falling downstairs noisily. ANYA and VARYA scream; laughter is heard immediately] What's that?

[ANYA comes running in, laughing.]

ANYA. Peter's fallen downstairs! [Runs out again.]

LUBOV. This Peter's a marvel.

[The STATION-MASTER stands in the middle of the drawing-room and recites "The Magdalen" by Tolstoy. He is listened to, but he has only delivered a few lines when a waltz is heard from the front room, and the recitation is stopped. Everybody dances. TROFIMOV, ANYA, VARYA, and LUBOV ANDREYEVNA come in from the front room.]

LUBOV. Well, Peter... you pure soul... I beg your pardon... let's dance.

[She dances with PETER. ANYA and VARYA dance. FIERS enters and stands his stick by a side door. YASHA has also come in and looks on at the dance.]

YASHA. Well, grandfather?

FIERS. I'm not well. At our balls some time back, generals and barons and admirals used to dance, and now we send for post-office clerks and the Station-master, and even they come as a favour. I'm very weak. The dead master, the grandfather, used to give everybody sealing-wax when anything was wrong. I've taken sealing-wax every day for twenty years, and more; perhaps that's why I still live.

YASHA. I'm tired of you, grandfather. [Yawns] If you'd only hurry up and kick the bucket.

FIERS. Oh you... bungler! [Mutters.]

[TROFIMOV and LUBOV ANDREYEVNA dance in the reception-room, then into the sitting-room.]

LUBOV. *Merci.* I'll sit down. [Sits] I'm tired.

[Enter ANYA.]

ANYA. [Excited] Somebody in the kitchen was saying just now that the cherry orchard was sold to-day.

LUBOV. Sold to whom?

ANYA. He didn't say to whom. He's gone now. [Dances out into the reception-room with TROFIMOV.]

YASHA. Some old man was chattering about it a long time ago. A stranger!

FIERS. And Leonid Andreyevitch isn't here yet, he hasn't come. He's wearing a light, *demi-saison* overcoat. He'll catch cold. Oh these young fellows.

LUBOV. I'll die of this. Go and find out, Yasha, to whom it's sold.

YASHA. Oh, but he's been gone a long time, the old man. [Laughs.]

LUBOV. [Slightly vexed] Why do you laugh? What are you glad about?

YASHA. Epikhodov's too funny. He's a silly man. Two-and-twenty troubles.

LUBOV. Fiers, if the estate is sold, where will you go?

FIERS. I'll go wherever you order me to go.

LUBOV. Why do you look like that? Are you ill? I think you ought to go to bed....

FIERS. Yes... [With a smile] I'll go to bed, and who'll hand things round and give orders without me? I've the whole house on my shoulders.

YASHA. [To LUBOV ANDREYEVNA] Lubov Andreyevna! I want to ask a favour of you, if you'll be so kind! If you go to Paris again, then please take me with you. It's absolutely impossible for me to stop here. [Looking round; in an undertone] What's the good of talking about it, you see for yourself that this is an uneducated country, with an immoral population, and it's so dull. The food in the kitchen is beastly, and here's this Fiers walking about mumbling various inappropriate things. Take me with you, be so kind!

[Enter PISCHIN.]

PISCHIN. I come to ask for the pleasure of a little waltz, dear lady.... [LUBOV ANDREYEVNA goes to him] But all the same, you wonderful woman, I must have 180 little roubles from you... I must.... [They dance] 180 little roubles.... [They go through into the drawing-room.]

> YASHA. [Sings softly] "Oh, will you understand
> My soul's deep restlessness?"

[In the drawing-room a figure in a grey top-hat and in baggy check trousers is waving its hands and jumping about; there are cries of "Bravo, Charlotta Ivanovna!"]

DUNYASHA. [Stops to powder her face] The young mistress tells me to dance—there are a lot of gentlemen, but few ladies—and my head goes round when I dance, and my heart beats, Fiers Nicolaevitch; the Post-office clerk told me something just now which made me catch my breath. [The music grows faint.]

FIERS. What did he say to you?

DUNYASHA. He says, "You're like a little flower."

YASHA. [Yawns] Impolite.... [Exit.]

DUNYASHA. Like a little flower. I'm such a delicate girl; I simply love words of tenderness.

FIERS. You'll lose your head.

[Enter EPIKHODOV.]

EPIKHODOV. You, Avdotya Fedorovna, want to see me no more than if I was some insect. [Sighs] Oh, life!

DUNYASHA. What do you want?

EPIKHODOV. Undoubtedly, perhaps, you may be right. [Sighs] But, certainly, if you regard the matter from the aspect, then you, if I may say so, and you must excuse my candidness, have absolutely reduced me to a state of mind. I know my fate, every day something unfortunate happens to me, and I've grown used to it a long time ago, I even look at my fate with a smile. You gave me your word, and though I...

DUNYASHA. Please, we'll talk later on, but leave me alone now. I'm meditating now. [Plays with her fan.]

EPIKHODOV. Every day something unfortunate happens to me, and I, if I may so express myself, only smile, and even laugh.

[VARYA enters from the drawing-room.]

VARYA. Haven't you gone yet, Simeon? You really have no respect for anybody. [To DUNYASHA] You go away, Dunyasha. [To EPIKHODOV] You play billiards and break a cue, and walk about the drawing-room as if you were a visitor!

EPIKHODOV. You cannot, if I may say so, call me to order.

VARYA. I'm not calling you to order, I'm only telling you. You just walk about from place to place and never do your work. Goodness only knows why we keep a clerk.

EPIKHODOV. [Offended] Whether I work, or walk about, or eat, or play billiards, is only a matter to be settled by people of understanding and my elders.

VARYA. You dare to talk to me like that! [Furious] You dare? You mean that I know nothing? Get out of here! This minute!

EPIKHODOV. [Nervous] I must ask you to express yourself more delicately.

VARYA. [Beside herself] Get out this minute. Get out! [He goes to the door, she follows] Two-and-twenty troubles! I don't want any sign of you here! I don't want to see anything of you! [EPIKHODOV has gone out; his voice can be heard outside: "I'll make a complaint against you."] What, coming back? [Snatches up the stick left by FIERS by the door] Go... go... go, I'll show you.... Are you going? Are you going? Well, then take that. [She hits out as LOPAKHIN enters.]

LOPAKHIN. Much obliged.

VARYA. [Angry but amused] I'm sorry.

LOPAKHIN. Never mind. I thank you for my pleasant reception.

VARYA. It isn't worth any thanks. [Walks away, then looks back and asks gently] I didn't hurt you, did I?

LOPAKHIN. No, not at all. There'll be an enormous bump, that's all.

VOICES FROM THE DRAWING-ROOM. Lopakhin's returned! Ermolai Alexeyevitch!

PISCHIN. Now we'll see what there is to see and hear what there is to hear... [Kisses LOPAKHIN] You smell of cognac, my dear, my soul. And we're all having a good time.

[Enter LUBOV ANDREYEVNA.]

LUBOV. Is that you, Ermolai Alexeyevitch? Why were you so long? Where's Leonid?

LOPAKHIN. Leonid Andreyevitch came back with me, he's coming....

LUBOV. [Excited] Well, what? Is it sold? Tell me?

LOPAKHIN. [Confused, afraid to show his pleasure] The sale ended up at four o'clock.... We missed the train, and had to wait till half-past nine. [Sighs heavily] Ooh! My head's going round a little.

[Enter GAEV; in his right hand he carries things he has bought, with his left he wipes away his tears.]

LUBOV. Leon, what's happened? Leon, well? [Impatiently, in tears] Quick, for the love of God....

GAEV. [Says nothing to her, only waves his hand; to FIERS, weeping] Here, take this.... Here are anchovies, herrings from Kertch.... I've had no food to-day.... I have had a time! [The door from the billiard-room is open; the clicking of the balls is heard, and YASHA'S voice, "Seven, eighteen!" GAEV'S expression changes, he cries no more] I'm awfully tired. Help me change my clothes, Fiers.

[Goes out through the drawing-room; FIERS after him.]

PISCHIN. What happened? Come on, tell us!

LUBOV. Is the cherry orchard sold?

LOPAKHIN. It is sold.

LUBOV. Who bought it?

LOPAKHIN. I bought it.

[LUBOV ANDREYEVNA is overwhelmed; she would fall if she were not standing by an armchair and a table. VARYA takes her keys off her belt, throws them on the floor, into the middle of the room and goes out.]

LOPAKHIN. I bought it! Wait, ladies and gentlemen, please, my head's going round, I can't talk.... [Laughs] When we got to the sale, Deriganov was there already. Leonid Andreyevitch had only fifteen thousand roubles, and Deriganov offered thirty thousand on top of the mortgage to begin with. I saw how matters were, so I grabbed hold of him and bid forty. He went up to forty-five, I offered fifty-five. That means he went up by fives and I went up by tens.... Well, it came to an end. I bid ninety more than the mortgage; and it stayed with me. The cherry orchard is mine now, mine! [Roars with laughter] My God, my God, the cherry orchard's mine! Tell me I'm drunk, or mad, or dreaming.... [Stamps his feet] Don't laugh at me! If my father and grandfather rose from their graves and looked at the whole affair, and saw how their Ermolai, their beaten and uneducated Ermolai, who used to run barefoot in the winter, how that very Ermolai has bought an estate, which is the most beautiful thing in the world! I've bought the estate where my grandfather and my father were slaves, where they weren't even allowed into the kitchen. I'm asleep, it's only a dream, an illusion.... It's the fruit of imagination, wrapped in the fog of the unknown.... [Picks up the keys, nicely smiling] She threw down the keys, she wanted to show she was no longer mistress here.... [Jingles keys] Well, it's all one! [Hears the band tuning up] Eh, musicians, play, I want to hear you! Come and look at Ermolai Lopakhin laying his axe to the cherry orchard, come and look at the trees falling! We'll build villas here, and our grandsons and great-grandsons will see a new life here.... Play on, music! [The band plays. LUBOV ANDREYEVNA sinks into a chair and weeps bitterly. LOPAKHIN continues reproachfully] Why then, why didn't you take my advice? My poor, dear woman, you can't go back now. [Weeps] Oh, if only the whole thing was done with, if only our uneven, unhappy life were changed!

PISCHIN. [Takes his arm; in an undertone] She's crying. Let's go into the drawing-room and leave her by herself... come on.... [Takes his arm and leads him out.]

LOPAKHIN. What's that? Bandsmen, play nicely! Go on, do just as I want you to! [Ironically] The new owner, the owner of the cherry orchard is coming! [He accidentally knocks up against a little table and nearly upsets the candelabra] I can pay for everything! [Exit with PISCHIN]

[In the reception-room and the drawing-room nobody remains except LUBOV ANDREYEVNA, who sits huddled up and weeping bitterly. The band plays softly. ANYA and TROFIMOV come in quickly. ANYA goes up to her mother and goes on her knees in front of her. TROFIMOV stands at the drawing-room entrance.]

ANYA. Mother! mother, are you crying? My dear, kind, good mother, my beautiful mother, I love you! Bless you! The cherry orchard is sold, we've got it no longer, it's true, true, but don't cry mother, you've still got your life before you, you've still your beautiful pure soul... Come with me, come, dear, away from here, come! We'll plant a new garden, finer than this, and you'll see it, and you'll understand, and deep joy, gentle joy will sink into your soul, like the evening sun, and you'll smile, mother! Come, dear, let's go!

Curtain.

ACT FOUR

[The stage is set as for Act I. There are no curtains on the windows, no pictures; only a few pieces of furniture are left; they are piled up in a corner as if for sale. The emptiness is felt. By the door that leads out of the house and at the back of the stage, portmanteaux and travelling paraphernalia are piled up. The door on the left is open; the voices of VARYA and ANYA can be heard through it. LOPAKHIN stands and waits. YASHA holds a tray with little tumblers of champagne. Outside, EPIKHODOV is tying up a box. Voices are heard behind the stage. The peasants have come to say good-bye. The voice of GAEV is heard: "Thank you, brothers, thank you."]

YASHA. The common people have come to say good-bye. I am of the opinion, Ermolai Alexeyevitch, that they're good people, but they don't understand very much.

[The voices die away. LUBOV ANDREYEVNA and GAEV enter. She is not crying but is pale, and her face trembles; she can hardly speak.]

GAEV. You gave them your purse, Luba. You can't go on like that, you can't!

LUBOV. I couldn't help myself, I couldn't! [They go out.]

LOPAKHIN. [In the doorway, calling after them] Please, I ask you most humbly! Just a little glass to say good-bye. I didn't remember to bring any from town and I only found one bottle at the station. Please, do! [Pause] Won't you really have any? [Goes away from the door] If I only knew—I wouldn't have bought any. Well, I shan't drink any either. [YASHA carefully puts the tray on a chair] You have a drink, Yasha, at any rate.

YASHA. To those departing! And good luck to those who stay behind! [Drinks] I can assure you that this isn't real champagne.

LOPAKHIN. Eight roubles a bottle. [Pause] It's devilish cold here.

YASHA. There are no fires to-day, we're going away. [Laughs]

LOPAKHIN. What's the matter with you?

YASHA. I'm just pleased.

LOPAKHIN. It's October outside, but it's as sunny and as quiet as if it were summer. Good for building. [Looking at his watch and speaking through the door] Ladies and gentlemen, please remember that it's only forty-seven minutes till the train goes! You must go off to the station in twenty minutes. Hurry up.

[TROFIMOV, in an overcoat, comes in from the grounds.]

TROFIMOV. I think it's time we went. The carriages are waiting. Where the devil are my goloshes? They're lost. [Through the door] Anya, I can't find my goloshes! I can't!

LOPAKHIN. I've got to go to Kharkov. I'm going in the same train as you. I'm going to spend the whole winter in Kharkov. I've been hanging about with you people, going rusty without work. I can't live without working. I must have something to do with my hands; they hang about as if they weren't mine at all.

TROFIMOV. We'll go away now and then you'll start again on your useful labours.

LOPAKHIN. Have a glass.

TROFIMOV. I won't.

LOPAKHIN. So you're off to Moscow now?

TROFIMOV Yes. I'll see them into town and to-morrow I'm off to Moscow.

LOPAKHIN. Yes.... I expect the professors don't lecture nowadays; they're waiting till you turn up!

TROFIMOV. That's not your business.

LOPAKHIN. How many years have you been going to the university?

TROFIMOV. Think of something fresh. This is old and flat. [Looking for his goloshes] You know, we may not meet each other again, so just let me give you a word of advice on parting: "Don't wave your hands about! Get rid of that habit of waving them about. And then, building villas and reckoning on their residents becoming freeholders in time—that's the same thing; it's all a matter of waving your hands about.... Whether I want to or not, you know, I like you. You've thin, delicate fingers, like those of an artist, and you've a thin, delicate soul...."

LOPAKHIN. [Embraces him] Good-bye, dear fellow. Thanks for all you've said. If you want any, take some money from me for the journey.

TROFIMOV. Why should I? I don't want it.

LOPAKHIN. But you've nothing!

TROFIMOV. Yes, I have, thank you; I've got some for a translation. Here it is in my pocket. [Nervously] But I can't find my goloshes!

VARYA. [From the other room] Take your rubbish away! [Throws a pair of rubber goloshes on to the stage.]

TROFIMOV. Why are you angry, Varya? Hm! These aren't my goloshes!

LOPAKHIN. In the spring I sowed three thousand acres of poppies, and now I've made forty thousand roubles net profit. And when my poppies were in flower, what a picture it was! So I, as I was saying, made forty thousand roubles, and I mean I'd like to lend you some, because I can afford it. Why turn up your nose at it? I'm just a simple peasant....

TROFIMOV. Your father was a peasant, mine was a chemist, and that means absolutely nothing. [LOPAKHIN takes out his pocket-book] No, no.... Even if you gave me twenty thousand I should refuse. I'm a free man. And everything that all you people, rich and poor, value so highly and so dearly hasn't the least influence over me; it's like a flock of down in the wind. I can do without you, I can pass you by. I'm strong and proud. Mankind goes on to the highest truths and to the highest happiness such as is only possible on earth, and I go in the front ranks!

LOPAKHIN. Will you get there?

TROFIMOV. I will. [Pause] I'll get there and show others the way. [Axes cutting the trees are heard in the distance.]

LOPAKHIN. Well, good-bye, old man. It's time to go. Here we stand pulling one another's noses, but life goes its own way all the time. When I work for a long time, and I don't get tired, then I think more easily, and I think I get to understand why I exist. And there are so many people in Russia, brother, who live for nothing at all. Still, work goes on without that. Leonid Andreyevitch, they say, has accepted a post in a bank; he will get sixty thousand roubles a year.... But he won't stand it; he's very lazy.

ANYA. [At the door] Mother asks if you will stop them cutting down the orchard until she has gone away.

TROFIMOV. Yes, really, you ought to have enough tact not to do that. [Exit.]

LOPAKHIN, All right, all right... yes, he's right. [Exit.]

ANYA. Has Fiers been sent to the hospital?

YASHA. I gave the order this morning. I suppose they've sent him.

ANYA. [To EPIKHODOV, who crosses the room] Simeon Panteleyevitch, please make inquiries if Fiers has been sent to the hospital.

YASHA. [Offended] I told Egor this morning. What's the use of asking ten times!

EPIKHODOV. The aged Fiers, in my conclusive opinion, isn't worth mending; his forefathers had better have him. I only envy him. [Puts a trunk on a hat-box and squashes it] Well, of course. I thought so! [Exit.]

YASHA. [Grinning] Two-and-twenty troubles.

VARYA. [Behind the door] Has Fiers been taken away to the hospital?

ANYA. Yes.

VARYA. Why didn't they take the letter to the doctor?

ANYA. It'll have to be sent after him. [Exit.]

VARYA. [In the next room] Where's Yasha? Tell him his mother's come and wants to say good-bye to him.

YASHA. [Waving his hand] She'll make me lose all patience!

[DUNYASHA has meanwhile been bustling round the luggage; now that YASHA is left alone, she goes up to him.]

DUNYASHA. If you only looked at me once, Yasha. You're going away, leaving me behind.

[Weeps and hugs him round the neck.]

YASHA. What's the use of crying? [Drinks champagne] In six days I'll be again in Paris. To-morrow we get into the express and off we go. I can hardly believe it. Vive la France! It doesn't suit me here, I can't live here... it's no good. Well, I've seen the uncivilized world; I have had enough of it. [Drinks champagne] What do you want to cry for? You behave yourself properly, and then you won't cry.

DUNYASHA. [Looks in a small mirror and powders her face] Send me a letter from Paris. You know I loved you, Yasha, so much! I'm a sensitive creature, Yasha.

YASHA. Somebody's coming.

[He bustles around the luggage, singing softly. Enter LUBOV ANDREYEVNA, GAEV, ANYA, and CHARLOTTA IVANOVNA.]

GAEV. We'd better be off. There's no time left. [Looks at YASHA] Somebody smells of herring!

LUBOV. We needn't get into our carriages for ten minutes.... [Looks round the room] Good-bye, dear house, old grandfather. The winter will go, the spring will come, and then you'll exist no more, you'll be pulled down. How much these walls have seen! [Passionately kisses her daughter] My treasure, you're radiant, your eyes flash like two jewels! Are you happy? Very?

ANYA. Very! A new life is beginning, mother!

GAEV. [Gaily] Yes, really, everything's all right now. Before the cherry orchard was sold we all were excited and we suffered, and then, when the question was solved once and for all, we all calmed down, and even became cheerful. I'm a bank official now, and a financier... red in the middle; and you, Luba, for some reason or other, look better, there's no doubt about it.

LUBOV Yes. My nerves are better, it's true. [She puts on her coat and hat] I sleep well. Take my luggage out, Yasha. It's time. [To ANYA] My little girl, we'll soon see each other again.... I'm off to Paris. I'll live there on the money your grandmother from Yaroslav sent along to buy the estate—bless her!—though it won't last long.

ANYA. You'll come back soon, soon, mother, won't you? I'll get ready, and pass the exam at the Higher School, and then I'll work and help you. We'll read all sorts of books to one another, won't we? [Kisses her mother's hands] We'll read in the autumn evenings; we'll read many books, and a beautiful new world will open up before us.... [Thoughtfully] You'll come, mother....

LUBOV. I'll come, my darling. [Embraces her.]

[Enter LOPAKHIN. CHARLOTTA is singing to herself.]

GAEV. Charlotta is happy; she sings!

CHARLOTTA. [Takes a bundle, looking like a wrapped-up baby] My little baby, bye-bye. [The baby seems to answer, "Oua! Oua!"] Hush, my nice little boy. ["Oua! Oua!"] I'm so sorry for you! [Throws the bundle back] So please find me a new place. I can't go on like this.

LOPAKHIN. We'll find one, Charlotta Ivanovna, don't you be afraid.

GAEV. Everybody's leaving us. Varya's going away... we've suddenly become unnecessary.

CHARLOTTA. I've nowhere to live in town. I must go away. [Hums] Never mind.

[Enter PISCHIN.]

LOPAKHIN. Nature's marvel!

PISCHIN. [Puffing] Oh, let me get my breath back.... I'm fagged out... My most honoured, give me some water....

GAEV. Come for money, what? I'm your humble servant, and I'm going out of the way of temptation. [Exit.]

PISCHIN. I haven't been here for ever so long... dear madam. [To LOPAKHIN] You here? Glad to see you... man of immense brain... take this... take it.... [Gives LOPAKHIN money] Four hundred roubles.... That leaves 840....

LOPAKHIN. [Shrugs his shoulders in surprise] As if I were dreaming. Where did you get this from?

PISCHIN. Stop... it's hot.... A most unexpected thing happened. Some Englishmen came along and found some white clay on my land.... [To LUBOV ANDREYEVNA] And here's four hundred for you... beautiful lady.... [Gives her money] Give you the rest later.... [Drinks water] Just now a young man in the train was saying that some great philosopher advises us all to jump off roofs. "Jump!" he says, and that's all. [Astonished] To think of that, now! More water!

LOPAKHIN. Who were these Englishmen?

PISCHIN. I've leased off the land with the clay to them for twenty-four years.... Now, excuse me, I've no time.... I must run off.... I must go to Znoikov and to Kardamonov... I owe them all money.... [Drinks] Good-bye. I'll come in on Thursday.

LUBOV. We're just off to town, and to-morrow I go abroad.

PISCHIN. [Agitated] What? Why to town? I see furniture... trunks.... Well, never mind. [Crying] Never mind. These Englishmen are men of immense intellect.... Never mind.... Be happy.... God will help you.... Never mind.... Everything in this world comes to an end.... [Kisses LUBOV ANDREYEVNA'S hand] And if you should happen to hear that my end has come, just remember this old... horse and say: "There was one such and such a Simeonov-Pischin, God bless his soul...." Wonderful weather... yes.... [Exit deeply moved, but returns at once and says in the door] Dashenka sent her love! [Exit.]

LUBOV. Now we can go. I've two anxieties, though. The first is poor Fiers [Looks at her watch] We've still five minutes....

ANYA. Mother, Fiers has already been sent to the hospital. Yasha sent him off this morning.

LUBOV. The second is Varya. She's used to getting up early and to work, and now she's no work to do she's like a fish out of water. She's grown thin and pale, and she cries, poor thing.... [Pause] You know very well, Ermolai Alexeyevitch, that I used to hope to marry her to you, and I suppose you are going to marry somebody? [Whispers to ANYA, who nods to CHARLOTTA, and they both go out] She loves you, she's your sort, and I don't understand, I really don't, why you seem to be keeping away from each other. I don't understand!

LOPAKHIN. To tell the truth, I don't understand it myself. It's all so strange.... If there's still time, I'll be ready at once... Let's get it over, once and for all; I don't feel as if I could ever propose to her without you.

LUBOV. Excellent. It'll only take a minute. I'll call her.

LOPAKHIN. The champagne's very appropriate. [Looking at the tumblers] They're empty, somebody's already drunk them. [YASHA coughs] I call that licking it up....

LUBOV. [Animated] Excellent. We'll go out. Yasha, allez. I'll call her in.... [At the door] Varya, leave that and come here. Come! [Exit with YASHA.]

LOPAKHIN. [Looks at his watch] Yes.... [Pause.]

[There is a restrained laugh behind the door, a whisper, then VARYA comes in.]

VARYA. [Looking at the luggage in silence] I can't seem to find it....

LOPAKHIN. What are you looking for?

VARYA. I packed it myself and I don't remember. [Pause.]

LOPAKHIN. Where are you going to now, Barbara Mihailovna?

VARYA. I? To the Ragulins.... I've got an agreement to go and look after their house... as housekeeper or something.

LOPAKHIN. Is that at Yashnevo? It's about fifty miles. [Pause] So life in this house is finished now....

VARYA. [Looking at the luggage] Where is it?... perhaps I've put it away in the trunk.... Yes, there'll be no more life in this house....

LOPAKHIN. And I'm off to Kharkov at once... by this train. I've a lot of business on hand. I'm leaving Epikhodov here... I've taken him on.

VARYA. Well, well!

LOPAKHIN. Last year at this time the snow was already falling, if you remember, and now it's nice and sunny. Only it's rather cold.... There's three degrees of frost.

VARYA. I didn't look. [Pause] And our thermometer's broken.... [Pause.]

VOICE AT THE DOOR. Ermolai Alexeyevitch!

LOPAKHIN. [As if he has long been waiting to be called] This minute. [Exit quickly.]

[VARYA, sitting on the floor, puts her face on a bundle of clothes and weeps gently. The door opens. LUBOV ANDREYEVNA enters carefully.]

LUBOV. Well? [Pause] We must go.

VARYA. [Not crying now, wipes her eyes] Yes, it's quite time, little mother. I'll get to the Ragulins to-day, if I don't miss the train....

LUBOV. [At the door] Anya, put on your things. [Enter ANYA, then GAEV, CHARLOTTA IVANOVNA. GAEV wears a warm overcoat with a cape. A servant and drivers come in. EPIKHODOV bustles around the luggage] Now we can go away.

ANYA. [Joyfully] Away!

GAEV. My friends, my dear friends! Can I be silent, in leaving this house for evermore?—can I restrain myself, in saying farewell, from expressing those feelings which now fill my whole being...?

ANYA. [Imploringly] Uncle!

VARYA. Uncle, you shouldn't!

GAEV. [Stupidly] Double the red into the middle.... I'll be quiet.

[Enter TROFIMOV, then LOPAKHIN.]

TROFIMOV. Well, it's time to be off.

LOPAKHIN. Epikhodov, my coat!

LUBOV. I'll sit here one more minute. It's as if I'd never really noticed what the walls and ceilings of this house were like, and now I look at them greedily, with such tender love....

GAEV. I remember, when I was six years old, on Trinity Sunday, I sat at this window and looked and saw my father going to church....

LUBOV. Have all the things been taken away?

LOPAKHIN. Yes, all, I think. [To EPIKHODOV, putting on his coat] You see that everything's quite straight, Epikhodov.

EPIKHODOV. [Hoarsely] You may depend upon me, Ermolai Alexeyevitch!

LOPAKHIN. What's the matter with your voice?

EPIKHODOV. I swallowed something just now; I was having a drink of water.

YASHA. [Suspiciously] What manners....

LUBOV. We go away, and not a soul remains behind.

LOPAKHIN. Till the spring.

VARYA. [Drags an umbrella out of a bundle, and seems to be waving it about. LOPAKHIN appears to be frightened] What are you doing?... I never thought...

TROFIMOV. Come along, let's take our seats... it's time! The train will be in directly.

VARYA. Peter, here they are, your goloshes, by that trunk. [In tears] And how old and dirty they are....

TROFIMOV. [Putting them on] Come on!

GAEV. [Deeply moved, nearly crying] The train... the station.... Cross in the middle, a white double in the corner....

LUBOV. Let's go!

LOPAKHIN. Are you all here? There's nobody else? [Locks the side-door on the left] There's a lot of things in there. I must lock them up. Come!

ANYA. Good-bye, home! Good-bye, old life!

TROFIMOV. Welcome, new life! [Exit with ANYA.]

[VARYA looks round the room and goes out slowly. YASHA and CHARLOTTA, with her little dog, go out.]

LOPAKHIN. Till the spring, then! Come on... till we meet again! [Exit.]

[LUBOV ANDREYEVNA and GAEV are left alone. They might almost have been waiting for that. They fall into each other's arms and sob restrainedly and quietly, fearing that somebody might hear them.]

GAEV. [In despair] My sister, my sister....

LUBOV. My dear, my gentle, beautiful orchard! My life, my youth, my happiness, good-bye! Good-bye!

ANYA'S VOICE. [Gaily] Mother!

TROFIMOV'S VOICE. [Gaily, excited] Coo-ee!

LUBOV. To look at the walls and the windows for the last time.... My dead mother used to like to walk about this room....

GAEV. My sister, my sister!

ANYA'S VOICE. Mother!

TROFIMOV'S VOICE. Coo-ee!

LUBOV. We're coming! [They go out.]

[The stage is empty. The sound of keys being turned in the locks is heard, and then the noise of the carriages going away. It is quiet. Then the sound of an axe against the trees is heard in the silence sadly and by itself. Steps are heard. FIERS comes in from the door on the right. He is dressed as usual, in a short jacket and white waistcoat; slippers on his feet. He is ill. He goes to the door and tries the handle.]

FIERS. It's locked. They've gone away. [Sits on a sofa] They've forgotten about me.... Never mind, I'll sit here.... And Leonid Andreyevitch will have gone in a light overcoat instead of putting on his fur coat.... [Sighs anxiously] I didn't see.... Oh, these young people! [Mumbles something that cannot be understood] Life's gone on as if I'd never lived. [Lying down] I'll lie down.... You've no strength left in you, nothing left at all.... Oh, you... bungler!

[He lies without moving. The distant sound is heard, as if from the sky, of a breaking string, dying away sadly. Silence follows it, and only the sound is heard, some way away in the orchard, of the axe falling on the trees.]

Curtain.

Made in United States
North Haven, CT
08 September 2022